For Doug

Best wishes,

Kay Uutert

Seasons of Change

Reflections on an England Spiritual Journey

Kay Quinn Mutert

ISBN 978-0-9647083-6-5

Cover design by Scott McGrew
Cover photo by Kay Mutert
Text design by Annie Long with Kay Mutert
Journal sketches by Stephen Smith
Produced by Keen Custom Media

TABLE of CONTENTS

Map of Derbyshire stitched by Mr. William Sterland, member of Crich Wesley Chapel.

RELUDE

*A*ll of us face transition times in our lives, critical points when we can choose to risk a new direction or continue as we are. On those occasions we face questions: What do we build our life around? When we find ourselves at a threshold, what do we do? How do we risk the new? In the midst of it all, what is our spirit, our heart, our body telling us? At the end of the day, what really matters?

In the midtime of my life—my fiftieth year—I was at a threshold. Having spent my adult life in music, school, and church work, I decided to take a major step: return to school in a theology graduate program, consider a move into pastoral ministry, and begin a new focus of life and calling. At the halfway point through a Master of Divinity program at Emory University's Candler School of Theology, I entered the ordination candidacy program in my church's conference and applied for an internship with the British Methodist Conference. The British church and American theology schools worked together to offer this opportunity for people moving into ordained ministry, as there was a shortage of British Methodist ministers. Following the application process, I was selected to participate in the program, to spend a year as a minister in England.

This book is the story of my year's experience as minister to five small churches in the East Midlands of England. Drawn from both my journal and later reflections, it is a window into the church work, but more so, it is a story of people, places, and experiences; of relationships that held deep and endearing meaning; of a land that caught my heart; and work that brought fulfillment and richness. It is the story of my own journey of growth and discovery.

These people whose lives I entered as minister offered friendship and care to me, to my family, and to my friends. They shared their life with me. The beautiful English landscapes awakened in me a sense of my Irish/Celtic roots. This ministry setting provided my own Vicar of Dibley village memories as it began the pastoral work I would be undertaking for the next decades of my life.

I entered the year with an easy settling in, but then unexpected tragedies occurred that reshaped the whole experience. Illness, death, and crisis impacted the community dramatically. Together we faced crisis, found strength in each other, and looked to the new seasons of life that lay ahead. Only years later did I realize how much the events of this year prefigured critical events in my own life.

Scriptures speak of the need for sabbath time, for jubilee years. At the end of this jubilee year I returned to America mindful of the fragility of life: no day is a given, yet each day is holy, holding the chance for us to discover beauty and love around us. I returned aware that there are quiet places, loving people, a slower pace to be discovered here at home, even in the midst of a hectic world.

Vernon Cracknell, the minister who welcomed me to England and began me on my new road of ministry and life there, often used the phrase *"at the end of the day…."* For me, it became a descriptor of the deeper meaning of the year's experience, with all its many facets. At the end of many days during this year, I sat at the computer and reflected on what life had been like, what this experience had meant.

I believe this is a story both unique to a particular time and place and universal for all who choose to follow the calling of their heart. I share my story in hope that it offers something for you in your journey. May we live our lives remembering that:

> *At the end of the day,*
>> *there is only the preciousness of each day,*
> *At the end of the day,*
>> *there is the unique gift of life and relationship,*
> *At the end of the day,*
>> *there is the unending presence of Eternal Love.*

Praise for Kay Mutert's *Seasons of Change*

"Kay Mutert shares with us an extraordinary year of her life—a year of challenge, change, and unexpected circumstances of loss. Through it comes clarity of calling, grounding in wisdom, and a deepening of her spiritual maturity. Kay's clear, articulate voice allows her experiences to become a mirror for our own."

—The Reverend Dr. Lauren Artress,
Honorary Canon of Grace Cathedral, San Francisco
and author of *Walking a Sacred Path:
Rediscovering the Labyrinth as a Spiritual Practice*

"Many of our Theology students at Emory University have participated in the British Internship Program sponsored by the Methodist Church in Great Britain. No one has provided so many insights into how the arrangement works until this account by Kay Mutert.

She takes us through her year month by month, and even day by day, until we feel as if we were there with her relating to her parishioners with their joys and sorrows, their illnesses and strengths, and their celebrations to which they invited her as she quickly became a part of their communities.

Music has always been important to Kay, and you can sense the satisfaction she felt in their lusty singing of hymns and their response to any special music she was able to arrange. We also experience with her the importance of the Lord's Supper, not only in joyful regular celebrations with her congregations but in the Communion shared with the sick and those at the end of life.

This immersion in the full life of the church proves how important the British Internship has been not only in broadening horizons for the student pastors but also for the congregations they serve, building ties across the Atlantic. Kay will never again be able to think of the church just in terms of her home state of Alabama but as the body of Christ reaching around the world to every land."

—Theodore Runyon, Professor Emeritus of Theology
Candler School of Theology, Emory University

SUMMER
into WINTER

$\mathscr{A}$ Crazy Possibility

For everything there is a season . . .

from Ecclesiastes 3

"$\mathscr{A}$ year in England? As a minister?"

Why not?

Here I was, at fifty, my jubilee year. I had already made changes in my life, undertaken new risks, new directions. As I traveled the interstate back and forth each week between Alabama and Georgia, moving from work to studies, I was not sure where this new road would lead, sometimes questioning the stress of it all, but I knew that there were new stirrings and needs in my heart. Like many other women and men at the midpoint of life, I was considering the future. Now I had a chance to spend this significant year in England.

I had always seen my work as living out a *vocatio*, a calling: helping people see and expand their creative gifts and expression, trust their abilities, live life in the fullest. Now I found myself looking at my own new possibilities, a turn in my own journey.

Most recently, as director of music at a large congregation in Mountain Brook, Alabama, I had worked with an outstanding choir, performing some of my favorite major works with orchestra. We revitalized and expanded a drama and arts ministry and shaped worship in a beautiful setting. I was aware, however, that new thoughts were stirring. My love for sacramental life, a desire to support people in their faith journeys, a quest for learning more, had led me onto this new road.

Circumstances in my family life were also changing. Davis, our youngest son, had now moved from high school to his first year at university, not quite sure where he wanted to focus. Our middle son, Dan, was completing his undergraduate study in finance while playing on the university golf team. Our oldest son, Doug, had married Becky, completed his undergraduate work, and was now in law school. My husband Carl worked in golf sales, a job that had him on the road every week, while through the years I often went away to various study/work settings. We recognized the differences of our interests and have respected that for each other. But we were also in a transitional period. Our boys had always been a central focus of our family life. Now they were grown, no longer at home, no longer bringing their activities into our lives. As I recognized that my sons were moving on, I realized what friends they had been for me over the years, a feeling surely felt by many parents as children move into adulthood. I could use an extended time to reflect upon this move into the second half-century of my life.

There was another factor floating in my head. I had always lived life in high gear, filling each minute and hour with activity, moving at a workaholic pace of energy. Is it possible to change such patterns? I said I wanted to do so. Could I, at fifty? Such a year beyond the known patterns of life in the home state might help me clarify these questions. Finally, spending my first year of pastoral ministry in a place far beyond where they knew me as a musician might not be a bad thing.

Only possibilities emerged in my mind. No fears or doubts crept into my thoughts then—just possibilities and the whys to do it. We had traveled to England on several occasions, sometimes taking one of the boys with us, and had fallen in love with the country and people. We drove down countryside lanes, listening to classical BBC radio selections and enjoying the beautiful green countryside, staying in bed-and-breakfast homes and quaint inns, learning what it meant to "queue up," to navigate a roundabout, and to survive the narrow, crowded, and tangled one-way streets of the large British cities. We explored London and York, the Lake District, and university towns.

We appreciated the great golf traditions of St. Andrews and Gleneagles as Carl played the beautiful historic courses and I walked alongside. I had also experienced some exclusive British golf traditions, where as a woman I was turned away from the clubhouse. In spite of an occasional cultural challenge, we loved the English ways as we knew them.

In the 1984 American Methodist bicentennial year, I co-led a group from our local church on a Methodist heritage tour/choir tour that included visits to various historical John Wesley sites, with excursions to Wesley's home village of Epworth and Bristol's New Room Chapel. We even had an overnight stay with English families in Louth.

Now I had an opportunity to live there and to do so in pastoral ministry. It would mean extending my schoolwork for a year after returning, but wouldn't it be worth it? Why not just apply and see what happens. I barely remember suggesting the idea to my family:

"Everybody loves to travel—it would be a wonderful opportunity!" I joyfully declared.

Was there even much conversation about it? Was it a crazy idea? Did I even hear what they might have said? Did I actually think through what it might mean for each of us? I just knew it felt like a step toward something I needed, a follow-my-heart move.

A great encourager during the application process, Dr. Ted Runyan, head of the internship program at Candler, shared letters from a couple who were serving the current year there. "It's a chance to be a part of Methodism in its home roots," he suggested. "A life-changing experience." After filing the necessary papers and going through the interview process, two persons were recommended from Candler: a young white male ministerial student from the Atlanta area and myself. Now we waited to see if we were to be chosen and appointed by the British Methodist Church.

In December I saw Dr. Runyan in the hallway of Butler Hall. "You've been selected," he greeted me. Unbelievably, the British Methodist Church chose both of us to be appointed within its Conference for September 1995 through July 1996. Now I had to practice patience until I heard of the appointed location. We began the guessing game: Would it be in a quaint Cotswold or Kent village? In London or the Lake District? "St. Andrews?" the golfers threw in. Ireland might even be a possibility.

The wait began.

$\mathcal{A}$N INTRODUCTION

Grace to you and peace . . .

from Paul's letters

$\mathcal{T}$he official letter arrived: "I am happy to confirm that I am able to offer you an appointment in the Ripley Circuit, Nottingham and Derby District of the British Methodist Church. During your stay we shall provide you with accommodation in a manse currently not occupied and we shall provide a maintenance allowance at the same level as would be paid to a probationer minister. It is expected that the stipend will be round about £12,000."

Another letter arrived with that official letter confirming my appointment. The second one gave me the name of the minister I would be working with, "The Revd. Vernon F. Cracknell," saying that soon I would hear from him.

After what seemed an eternity but was actually only a few days, I heard from Vernon himself. A thick brown envelope arrived in my mailbox postmarked "Derbyshire, England" and addressed to "Revd. Kay M. Mutert."

This was now the second time I had seen in print the new title that was reshaping my entire life. Although it was winter, I felt a warm glow like that of an early summer sunrise; I knew that an emerging world was about to open. In the quiet of the living room, the sun streaming in over my shoulder, I settled down onto our old tan corduroy couch which had known so many family stories: first years of marriage, the bounces of young boys during home-made New Year celebrations, teenage energies and gatherings, grandparents sitting and supporting. It had held us in move after move, from first apartments in Florida to our home in Tuscaloosa and now the home we occupied at this stage of life—Carl, Davis, and I. I eagerly opened the large brown envelope, a new life chapter in my hands. The heading stretched across the page:

THE METHODIST CHURCH:
RIPLEY CIRCUIT

As I read the typed words, I had the first glimpse of my new colleague and my new world.

Dear Kay,

I have a letter from the Division of Ministries of the British Methodist Church, telling me that you have been allocated to our circuit for a period of one year. I am writing to bid you welcome, and to say that we are delighted that you have committed yourself to coming to UK.

Briefly, you may like to know that in your section there is a group of five churches, three of them in or around Ripley, and two more distant villages. The biggest had 69 members last year, and the smallest just 9.

This area was once heavily dependent on coal mining, but almost all the mines have closed. There has been some new industry in more recent years, which has helped the unemployment situation. It is not as bad as some other parts of the country, but there is still room for improvement.

Ripley is a small town, with a good range of local shops for day-to-day needs. Nottingham and Derby are both within easy reach and provide a selection of larger shops, including departmental stores.

We are on the edge of the Derbyshire Peak District, which is a beautiful area, with lots of opportunity for walking and sightseeing. As we only arrived here last September, we have not had much opportunity yet to explore, but, with the better weather, hope to do so ourselves.

The manse is situated in a cul-de-sac, and is a modern house, with central heating. It has four bedrooms, plus a bathroom. One of the bedrooms is currently being used as a study. The main bedroom has ensuite facilities. Downstairs is a lounge, dining room, kitchen, and toilet. Ministers here have their own furniture, so we are having to furnish it for your arrival. We will aim to provide a fridge, washing machine, and television. We will also take into account that you will need to be able to accommodate your husband when he is in UK and Doug, Dan, and Davis, when they wish to visit. We do hope that it will be possible for you all to be together for some part of your time here.

We also need to find a car for you to use while you are here. I presume that you drive? When we have found a suitable vehicle, we may need details of your driving experience, to pass on to the insurance company. More about this later!

One thing another visiting American intern noticed about UK was that in winter it was colder than they were used to. We get quite a lot of night frosts in the winter months. So far this winter, we have escaped much snow—just one fall last week that only lasted a few hours. In summer, temperatures are often 60–75°F but can get up into the 80s when we have the occasional heatwave! Houses in this country are not normally air-conditioned, as there doesn't seem to be any great need for it.

I look forward to working with you while you are here. This is just a two-minister circuit, and so we have no other colleagues. There are no retired ministers either, which is a disadvantage when an extra pair of hands is required.

The university has provided us with a copy of your application, which tells us something about you. In return, you may like to know something about us. I have a wife, Anne, and two daughters, Alison (21 years) and Elizabeth (almost 19 years). Both girls are studying at Nottingham Trent University and live at home. We are all interested in music, photography, and gentle walking. We have a rather noisy dog called Tessa, who makes sure that we get out regularly for exercise!

Please do not hesitate to contact us with any questions and queries. We pray that you will enjoy the work of the next few months, and that God will bless your preparations for your year in UK.

With all good wishes, Yours sincerely,

Vernon Cracknell

THIS LETTER INTRODUCING MY FUTURE surroundings stirred many thoughts. As I was unfamiliar with the Peak District or Midlands area, I immediately went to my maps of England gathered from visits there, spread them on the floor, and searched. There was no Ripley on any map I owned, but at least I located Derby and Nottingham. Of the places I had considered, a recovering coal-mining area had not been in my mind, though it did sound like parts of Alabama.

Little did I know how much I would grow to love the open sparse peaks, greystone walls, narrow winding roads, picturesque villages and hillsides, grazing sheep, gentle streams, and fiercely proud folk. All I knew in the moment was that it was not exactly what I had pictured. As to weather, for a southerner with thin blood, the letter raised some serious questions of cold survival.

Regarding the manse, to have an ensuite facility as a bonus reminded me of all I take for granted, such things as extra bathrooms, clothes dryers, and dishwashers. I realized the burden my coming put on this circuit to provide the needed living necessities, much less to find added comforts for my year with them. Vernon's concern for my family's visits reflected his insightfulness into what the year meant for them.

As to the car and my driving, I remembered my almost three speeding tickets in the past two years, driving that Alabama–Georgia interstate on the way to a divinity degree. My life needed to slow down in more ways than one as I looked forward to this new old-world experience. Is it really possible to slow one's life down, to change? I hoped that it could be done.

In a later letter, Vernon asked if I could drive *a manual gearbox car.* "Oh, yes, I can do that," I wrote back. Never once did I consider that I would have to combine left-side road driving with right-side driver-seat cars, shifting gears with the left hand. We had always rented an automatic transmission when traveling in England. The driving in those first few weeks almost became my stress overload downfall. But for that moment, living on powerwoman adrenaline flow, there was no obstacle I could not handle.

The future began to take a clearer form, with deepening understanding of what lay ahead. This letter had provided my first insight into a person who would soon affect my life and influence my way of ministry. I immediately appreciated what I read, as Vernon's warm words helped relieve questions and concerns. He revealed a view of not only his own heart but also the heart of a close-knit family interested in learning and education, with a penchant for the arts, aesthetics, and "gentle walking." He even introduced me to his dog Tessa in the very first letter. And his closing benediction was that "God would bless your preparations for your year in the UK."

What an introduction. In something so simple as a welcome letter, Vernon had offered me a way of living life, honoring the simple and daily, blessing each moment of our journeys. Though I could not know it at the time, this was surely the place, the setting for me to be.

OVER THE NEXT MONTHS, I continued to share correspondence with Vernon and representatives of the British Methodist Conference as I also began to hear from individuals in the Ripley circuit where I would serve. Images began to take shape on the canvas of my mind.

First a letter of greeting came from Patrick Dawson, senior circuit steward, the volunteer lay leader for the circuit. Then one day as I stood at the kitchen sink my telephone rang. "Hello!" a rich, melodic baritone British voice at the other end of the line greeted me. "Is this the new American lady minister coming to Ripley, England?" As we talked, Patrick told me of his work in Gilbert and Sullivan musical theatre. Already, a musical figure in my future, I gratefully thought.

A picture postcard with a postmark from the US soon arrived. A second steward, Glenis Quible, and her husband Geoff were on holiday along the John Wayne trail in our great American West. "You might even beat us back to England," she wrote. Another U.S. post arrived at the house from a chap named Barrie Blount, who was visiting his friends in Kansas, where "I have been made honorary sheriff," he shared. From England, church steward Mark Ratcliffe and others wrote to welcome me and give information about first services. One afternoon my mail brought a pale blue folded-and-glued aerogram from a woman named Constance, with a cat named Topsy. Her handwriting a little shaky and blurred, Constance welcomed me with words warm and inviting. "Know that you are always welcome at my home as a place to get away and relax," she wrote. In these letters I was already on my way to a lovely new community family.

"Sure, Mom, I'd love to go with you," Davis responded when I suggested the idea. After one year of college, he had no clear idea of what he wanted his major to be. The time away plus an experience living abroad might help him get a focus on his future. He could take the semester off from university, and we'd see what we could arrange related to any study while in England. It would give me a family member over there and would be a wonderful experience for him. "I really can't leave my work for the year," Carl reflected, "but I can come over for short visits when the selling season is not so busy." We began to envision the family trips.

Deciding for Davis to go, we turned to Vernon for information:

"Is there a college where he might attend?" Out of sight, expense-wise.

"What kind of entry visa does he need?" He could not work while he was in England, so a tourist visa would do.

"He played soccer in high school; is there a team he could play with?" That idea was quickly abandoned; England takes its football seriously.

"Can he be considered a church worker, too?" It is probably a good thing for Davis's sake that this proposal did not work out.

Vernon wisely guided us through most of the questions we had. As it turned out, Davis was unable to stay beyond the six-month limit, and the cost of attempting to do any schoolwork was prohibitive, so he lucked into a long fall vacation in England. We attended to our passport matters and began to plan the packing and the trip.

> *In the name of all new beginnings, may the blessing of daily life, of simple living, touch us each, on both sides of the ocean, as we prepare to journey together. I give thanks for those who have offered me such an invitation to living.*

$\mathcal{E}$NDINGS AND BEGINNINGS

Go from your country and your kindred . . .
to the land that I will show you.

Genesis 12.1

$\mathcal{A}$ugust was a dizzy spin. So many endings came in such a short period of time: closure on this work I had done for a lifetime, on this place I had worked for six years, packing and moving, goodbyes to friends, last visits with my parents in Mississippi, with my sisters, so many loose ends, and then final goodbyes to family. The last two weeks of life before our flight seemed unreal.

I worked at church until August 13. I remember the care with which I chose the last anthems my choir would sing in the last time I would lead them as director of music, three of my favorites, Durufle, Brahms, and Rutter. In those weeks, I packed an office of six years into a mountain range of boxes, most not clearly marked. Friend and work assistant Mark Lawrence, whom I had hired at the church early on as bass soloist and drama director, helped place my office treasures into the sea of boxes, carefully wrapping each breakable in newsprint, then trying to help sort a lifetime of music books and scores and octavos.

"What do you want me to do with this?" he would ask.

"What do you think?" I often replied. I was of little help in helping him help me. I was not ready to let go of my life of thirty years, all my music and the library of music education/church music texts I had gathered to use in helping others in my field. The teacher in me always saw the value of good resources, but now, when it came to a new direction, a new life, "What to keep, what to let go of?" my mind fretted. Too many emotions at work—now was not the time to make those decisions. "Pack it up and put it all in storage."

At the same time I was cleaning out an office and storing a life's work, I was also trying to pack my home. For his residence while I was gone, Carl had decided to purchase a furnished two-bedroom condominium villa with a good view of the fifth fairway on the North River golf course in Tuscaloosa, the town where we had lived for eleven years before moving to Birmingham. So I was putting a family lifetime into storage also. We rented two storage rooms in Birmingham and did a combination of self-moving and hiring professional movers. My ebony baby grand piano went to Tuscaloosa; the rest of the furniture made it into storage except for some items, including the tan couch, spontaneously left at a junk pile along the way as Carl, Dan, and Davis tired of being the moving crew. My stress level started an upward climb that did not end until some point far along the next trek of the journey across the ocean. I gave my plants to friends: the African violets to Em, a rose bush to Cam, a few pots to Joe. Many collectors' items I simply gave away, with little thought about letting go of them. "Just get the job done!" my mind throbbed. Reality began to sink in as to what this year abroad was meaning to our lives and belongings.

In the midst of this crazy summer, my first grandchild was born. Doug and Becky were living in Crozet, Virginia, while Doug attended law school at the University of Virginia. Their first child was due midsummer, and they invited me to come up and be present the week the baby was due. What a very special gift, to be present at the birth of my grandchild. I loved the visit in their home there, waking every morning to walk outside and greet the hazy Blue Ridge mountains, discovering the bookstores and cafes of downtown Charlottesville, but most of all being a part of the preparation for their precious new child, little Douglas Collier, born on July 19. I will be forever grateful for that experience.

Only a few weeks later, they traveled down to Alabama for my final Sunday at church. I am still amazed and grateful that they as new parents were willing and eager to make that journey. "We love you and want to be there," they simply said. Following the farewell Sunday and all the wonderful goodbye events, our family drove down to Sandestin, Florida, for a traditional Mutert annual golf tournament.

Then it was back to Tuscaloosa for final preparations. I was unpacking from the home in Birmingham, packing into a new home I hardly knew in another town, preparing to go across the ocean to a new home of which I certainly knew nothing. No wonder I was anxious.

After calling the airline international number many times about exactly what would be allowed onto the plane, I found three large navy blue denim duffle bags that met airline specifications. These bags and Davis's golf bag, plus our carry-on bags would push us to the luggage limit. Denim bags weighed less than pull-cart bags, making more available for our precious items. Never mind how to pick the duffle bags up when full.

Davis and I stuffed every available inch with clothes, books, shoes, coats, clubs and cassocks, under- and over-wear.

"Do you have room for just one more thing in any of your bags?" we called from bedroom to bedroom.

"Yeah, I think so, if you can fit this into your bag."

Who knew what to pack? I had received suggestions and lists, but how can you possibly know what you need for such a long time in such a different setting? Living as active participants in a world of ever-expanding space and tantalizing consumerism coercion, we had much to choose from. And I, the eternal book monger, painstakingly narrowed the booklist down to a few minimum resources, as I planned to take advantage of Vernon's offer for me to use his library. What a challenge, to decide what to take with you for one year, yet the more interesting observation is to see how much can be left behind as unneeded for simple living.

We packed, weighed and measured, packed and weighed, packed and repacked.

"Use every available ounce of space and weight," an evil inner voice kept saying. Where was that inner voice's help when we arrived in England and had to carry the luggage?

Our send-off at the Atlanta airport included lots of love, hugs, and kisses. Carl and Dan were there, then Doug, Becky, and little Collier dashed through the airport and arrived at the departure gate in the brink of time to see us off. After a few more quick camera flashes, "Smile!" "Look this way!" "Hold Collier up!" "Everybody in this one!" and one last long goodbye hug for each person, Davis and I were at the moment of departure, walking through the door and embarking the plane.

No turning back.

AS IN ANY NEW ADVENTURE, my mind and heart began the games:

"What am I doing? Did I even think about this carefully? Am I crazy, or what!"

Then oblivion set in. Davis remembers the flight and the movie; I remember little, if anything, until we arrived. I stirred as we flew into the sight range of land where the green patchwork fields became visible beneath the thick blanket of clouds with blue sky above and grey haze below. The plane cut through the landmass of clouds, descended onto earth and set down on English soil, alighting at Manchester, our port of entry.

"We made it," I declared. "Of course we did, mom," Davis in his wisdom of youth responded. Disembarking the plane, we moved with the crowd down the long grey receiving hallway. At the direction of agents, we processed into the non-British customs aisle and waited at the front do-not-cross line until the next available agent glanced up from behind the tall desk and nodded to us. Davis and I then eagerly stepped forward with passports in hand.

In a crisp British clip, he spoke:

"Good day, madam. And why are you here?"

Work, brain, wake up! Help with this, Davis! Oh, good, he's speaking again.

"I see you are a Methodist minister from America. Your son is with you? ... And where and how long will you be staying? ... Oh, Derbyshire is a lovely county."

After a few more inquiries, he dismissed us with "Have a good stay," and looked to the next in line.

That was it. We were through the entry. All the worry about arrival seemed to melt away. Like a looped tape, the voice over the airport loudspeaker was mechanically reminding us to mind our luggage. If that voice only knew what a task that was. I certainly did mind having to claim and cart it in an unfamiliar place—did they know how much it weighed? Fortunately, we found that carry carts were easily and freely available. Why don't American airlines make it so easy and free? Grabbing two carts, we staked out our spot by the luggage claim mover and watched the rotating belt like two hungry tigers ready to pounce.

"There's one, that's ours!" "You grab it, quick." "Uh, there it goes—get the next one!" Finally reclaiming all four pieces of our baggage, we tried loading our overstuffed cigar-shaped bags frontways, then succeeded with sideways onto the carts and strolled our way through the last customs check without a hitch, and then through the arrival door.

I later learned that the other minister from Candler arrived at a London airport to be strip searched and questioned about drugs. That would have been the immediate end of my venture, back to America with no second thought, do not pass go, do not collect anything. Fortunately, I had no such welcome, and so the year in England began.

"MUTERT." The sign was held high. We spotted it as we rounded the corner; our personal transportation was waiting for us just outside the gate. Now back from America, Glenis had made arrangements for her friend Alan Small to meet us in his Land Rover, which would provide "plenty of space" for our luggage. Little did they know the packing power of the Muterts, the fullness of the stuffing into the bags in the chaos of the last days at home.

"Greetings! Welcome to England and to Derbyshire," the words came, but the look on Alan's face indicated our luggage was much more than he expected. Our combined luggage would barely fit into the back of the vehicle. It obviously was not the way the locals packed when they traveled.

Tired, stressed, and overflowing with emotions, I settled into the crowded back seat next to the golf bag and entered rolling-eyes-falling-head sleep mode on the cross-countryside ride to our new home, while Davis sat up front on the left passenger's seat. As we headed across the Derbyshire Peaks and Dales, I could hear the lull of voices as Davis and Alan discussed the flight and the beautiful landscape and scenery while I moved in and out of consciousness.

Somehow I can still recall as if unconsciously marked in my memory the winding route we took up the stone-layered mountainside, the feel of the back-seat ride, and my first glimpses of the marvelous barren open expanses of the Peak District. The views were magnificent as we traveled up and down and around through the narrow twisting hairpin-curve back roads, past picturesque old farm ruins and sheep-filled pastures. For a couple of hours we meandered through quaint greystone villages and rolling green dales. But the vehicle's gentle movement lured me back into the hazy fog of sleep and emotion. Any sense of riding on the left side of the road blurred in the tiredness of my mind and body. And through the exhaustion, my apprehension at this whole venture played its tune.

Finally, at the end of the countryside ride, we entered a large roundabout, which encircled a huge green grass tree-iced cupcake mound. Alan took the third road off the roundabout toward the town sign: RIPLEY. Up a hill, bending left round a curve, past rows of two-storied red-brick houses, and there it was: the town of Ripley. We were here, destination and new hometown. Adrenaline restirred as sleep left and the dream began.

A pub stood on the left side of the road, then up farther we passed another pub named "The Red Lion," this one closed and deserted. On our left and right were various small shops, red-brick buildings, closed storefronts, red-brick walls, modern-but-not-modern designs. Moving through the little maze of one-way streets lined by a few graffitied walls, we came to a T-stop, turned left onto Derby Road, and passed the open square of the town marketplace, with a red-brick council building at one end and a red-brick pub at the other. The town was only a few blocks wide, yet with pubs on every corner. Alan guided the Rover past the co-op grocery and a gas station (known in England as a petrol station), where we turned left off Derby Road onto Heath Road into the estate where the manse was located. A short block down the narrow street with cars parked on both sides, then we turned right and immediately turned left again, passing a few charming cottage houses with lovely low brick walls protecting blooming front flower gardens, then right around the corner to another narrow street, where all the houses ahead suddenly looked nice and new and very similar: red brick, detached, two-story, close together. Straight down the street, at the end we rode up into the cul-de-sac to "9 Clumber Close," looking just like the picture. Alan stopped the Rover, turned off the engine, and declared,

"Right! Now here we are."

Davis and I unfolded from the ride, stepped out, walked up the short walk past the palm tree to the brown front door, and we began the year's life.

Kay's House - 3 Chumber Close, Ripley

ℱIRST IMPRESSIONS

All shall be well, and all shall be well,
and all manner of thing shall be well.
                                    Julian of Norwich

Arrival . . .

"Wel-come, wel-come!"

A cheery voice floated out to greet us as circuit steward Glenis Quible opened the door and awaited our entry. We said first hellos, then Alan helped unload our luggage. "Oh my . . . ," Glenis responded in a rising and falling musical voice as each bag made its way into the house, or perhaps that was my own sigh and sound. Glenis has sparkly dancing eyes, curly strawberry-blonde hair, and a lovely caring personality that helped put me at ease. Vernon Cracknell and his wife, Anne, arrived almost immediately to be a part of the greeting team. After we exchanged hellos, thanks, and goodbyes, our gracious driver went on his way, while the others gathered as a welcome party in the front hallway.

After guiding us through a brief up-and-down tour of the house, the two women went to the kitchen to put the kettle on, as we moved to the lounge; Vernon and I sat down in two large comfy beige chairs by the front window, while Davis settled in on the couch. Over our first official "cuppa" tea, we began the conversation. I'm not sure what I expected, but Vernon was what I would imagine a British Ichobad Crane to look like: tall and lanky, hair a little askew and wiry (balding on top), glasses resting on a slim pointed nose, a mouth shaping proper words but breaking into a hearty laugh pose easily and often. On this first day he wore a light blue short-sleeved shirt and dark grey slacks. Round his neck was a white ministerial collar, not an accessory I was accustomed to for Methodist ministers, but on him it looked right.

From the very first moment of conversation, we were relaxed and felt comfortable with each other. My head was filled with questions, so much curiosity about so many things. Vernon suggested we not try to cover everything in this first greeting time, but he and I were both eager to talk about the possibilities of the year.

He tilted his head back slightly as he spoke. "At the end of the day, we'll sort all this out."

"What does he mean, at the end of the day?" I inwardly thought, "I plan on being asleep then!"

Several times during the conversation, Vernon used the phrase, which I later came to recognize as a common saying here. At some point during these first weeks, the memory of that phrase from a different setting came back to me. It was the opening line of a song from the magnificent stage musical *Les Miserables*, known simply as *Les Mis*; my choir had sung it in our last Broadway musical review in Alabama: "*At the end of the day, you're another day older . . . .*" I can hear the rhythmic energy and drive of the tune in my head, the words bitingly sung by the chorus, one of many memorable songs from the musical. Suddenly it becomes a marker of the movement in my life, from a sung phrase to a spoken word, from days turning into years. But on this first day of my arrival, I would merely be happy to wait till beyond the end of this day to think and sort some things out. For now I merely remain in the moment.

"Here is your diary, with upcoming events penciled in," Vernon stated, as he reached over and handed me a planning calendar. I felt I was receiving a gift of the magi, holding some precious insight for the future. Quickly putting it to use, I began to add to his notes on the backside of the page. "You need to be in London by next Monday at 4 p.m. for your induction," he reminded me, and then suggested that we just relax these first days. He tried to cover the necessary topics, but I couldn't stop a few immediate questions for him:

"What is the first service going to be like? What are the churches like? Where are they? Do I need to wear a collar?"

My head was still turning with more questions, but Vernon wisely knew that they could wait. In his gentle way he was leading me into a new way of thinking, of life and self-care. His advice about relaxing was probably good, and the warm tea had just hit the spot. Recognizing that we were jet-lagged, our welcome team left for the day, and I felt myself quickly coming to a collapse.

Davis and I now had the chance to walk through and look around our new home a little more freely. Even though this is a lovely house, it felt so different from home, and though I knew I would love being here, in that moment of jet-lag fatigue, the house felt tight, close, foreign.

"Don't worry, mama, it's gonna be all right," Davis reassured me.

And the bed beckoned me for a closer encounter.

The Manse Becomes a Home . . .

NESTLED AT THE END OF THE STREET in a nice newer housing estate of two-story red-brick homes, Nine Clumber Close was purchased as the manse for the minister serving the Ripley section of the circuit. Now I become the second minister to live here. Although on that first day Davis and I both were wanting to rest, we also were becoming acquainted with the place that would be our home, my English home, for the next year.

The bedrooms are on the second floor, called "first floor" in England. Our two larger bedrooms on the backside of the house have nice big double-glazed windows that look out into the trees lining the back edge of the garden. With no screens, we can open the windows, reach out, and touch the trees. "Wow, just like a tree house, how neat!" we both think.

They have prepared the bedrooms with care. Soft comfy duvets on the double beds await us. Each room also has a nightstand, small chest, and wardrobe. My bed's duvet is a flowery coral pattern, edged with lace matching the light ivory of the walls. Pale billowy window-length cotton floral curtains frame my windows, and a lovely peaceful watercolor of a quaint riverside windmill scene and another of a stone bridge, both painted by church member Pat Rose, hang on the walls. Slightly below ceiling level a pretty flowered wallpaper border circles the room. This English home, like many others, has no built-in closets in any of the bedrooms; the wardrobe serves that purpose. I think of C. S. Lewis and wonder what mysteries the wardrobes hold for us. In my room the large light brown wood wardrobe fills the length of one wall, with a seated vanity desk and mirror area between the two doors of hanging space. As I was told in the letter, the master bedroom is *ensuite,* which means it has an adjoining shower/sink/toilet room. The shower works with motorized water flow. That is, you *must* remember how to turn it on and control it if you expect to take a shower.

Davis's bedroom is a bit smaller—for the moment his duffel and golf bags claimed the walk space. The room is decorated in a light spring-green color scheme, and his antique two-door wardrobe is a richly grained veneered dark-and-golden marbled wood. A low three-drawer chest sits against the front wall. When lying in bed, Davis can look through the large window into the tall trees behind the home. A great *Swiss Family Robinson* view for both of us.

The other two bedrooms on this floor are much smaller and have dual purpose. At the top of the stairway you walk directly into the front room serving as an office, filled by a desk and chair. The plain ivory walls would soon become a blessing wall, with signs and symbols of life here alongside pictures from home. With one very soft twin bed and a wardrobe holding extra towels and sheets, the other small bedroom on the front side of the house would be a guest hideaway for those who come to visit. Windows in these rooms overlook the cul-de-sac, allowing a view of the neighborhood.

The entire outside area, called garden in England, with grassy areas known as lawn, was just as the picture looked, complete with the palm tree in the front yard. I admit that since I was expecting a "typical" English flower garden, I was disappointed not to find established flowerbeds.

"Palm tree, in mid-England? I had those in Florida. Why would anyone want a palm tree in their yard here?" my mind wondered. I later realized that given the grey days of the long winters, a palm tree can serve as a hopeful reminder of warmer places.

Behind the house a narrow sidewalk bordered a narrow strip of lawn barely three feet deep, bound by a shoulder-high wooden fence and backed by trees and a vacant lot. A single spindly rose bush struggled to grow at the fence on the right end of the strip; it became my mission project to revive. We found a small side lawn between the house and the garage (with the accent on *gar*), consisting of a plot of green grass and an outdoor circular clothes hanger which folds up and down like a patio umbrella. At least, that's what we thought it might be, having never used one like that. We also discovered a sloped plot of grass belonging to the manse on the far side of the detached two-door garage. I began to visualize a few of my own flowers along the fence.

Inside the house again, it was strange to think of the living room as the lounge, but the names are actually not that different, both are words for the room to live in, to lounge and sit in. We discovered that the three-piece couch-and-chairs lounge suite was a traveling set for American ministers, now coming to us from the Belper circuit, where a Texas minister had served for the past two years. Five years later, when I returned to England, I discovered the very same set in another American minister's home.

The circuit had thoughtfully placed a lovely old dark brown upright piano in the lounge, pitched a step or two below the norm from its years of being in a chapel, but fitting my low voice. Delicate Staffordshire English china dishes and stemmed crystal glasses filled the shelves of a Danish-style honey brown breakfront; imagine giving up a set of dishes for a year. Heavy dark brown velvet curtains—a heating plus in winter—hang at the front bay window and across the sliding glass doors, which open to the back garden.

English ecumenism was evident in the dining room, with a beautiful dark wood antique table and six rich leather-seat chairs, donated for the year by the local Catholic monsignor, who had also sent a note with a welcome blessing. I could already imagine my family sitting around the table. I also envisioned that the three tiers of empty built-in wall shelves would fill with books and memorabilia of the year, and I looked forward to learning the stories of the china and linens I saw in the drawers and cabinets underneath, all graciously loaned to us by members of the circuit. The Polynesian Island tea towel certainly had traveled a long journey to be in this manse. The team had left a list of who provided what, but I knew it would take some time to match face, name, and item. A dark-framed triple window across the width of the back wall gives another view of the trees behind us. No screens anywhere on the windows. I have images of Julie Andrews hanging out of the windows singing to her heart's content.

An unusual picture hung in the hallway—a copper etching of the crooked spire on the church at Chesterfield, a large town north of here—giving us a glimpse into the mix of folklore and faith found in Derbyshire. Several legends exist about that spire: The devil once sat on it or kicked it in a rage, some say; others say that the spire itself twisted to see with its own eyes when a virgin married in the church and will straighten itself out when another virgin marries. I wondered what other interesting tales we would discover.

The kitchen, which sits directly off the hall across from the front door, is a narrow brown-and-tan walk-through room with cabinets lining both sides and a glass-paned door opening to the back garden, still only three-feet deep to the back fence. A front-loading washer, stainless-steel sink with window above, and brown gas stove/range line the left wall. On the right side of the room is a built-in broom closet, some counter space, and a small four-foot-high refrigerator. The kitchen seemed just the right size for someone like me, who did not spend much time there; the gas range would be a new experience. Later in the year, I once found Davis sitting on the kitchen floor, watching the washer go round and round and round, which may say something about the television choices here. On this first night we had a lovely evening meal of salad and other foods waiting for us in the "fridge"—another gracious sign of welcome hospitality. New to both of us, the dressing was the one mainstay dressing of England; simply called "Salad Cream," it is a cross between mayonnaise and Green Goddess dressing.

On the left of the entryway hall is a small toilet room, known casually as a "loo," where the control for the alarm system is mounted. Now that could be interesting. We had been told the houses here need alarm systems because of the high rate of robberies. Can you imagine sitting there, and the alarm goes off?

At the other end of the hallway, under the open stairwell of steps covered with dappled brown shag carpet, is a snug little cubbyplace to hang coats and umbrellas and to curl up and read. It did not take long to appreciate this little nook.

The stewards and circuit had worked quite hard to get the house and lawn ready for us—painting, cleaning, and gathering furniture, appliances, and household items from across and beyond the circuit for our year's use. They had created a place that immediately was ready to live in, reflecting warmth, care, and comfort. But settling into any new home takes a little time, and this was no different. Although the house had been carefully and caringly prepared, I was thrown askew by my own discomfort with the unfamiliarity of finding and using items. Things need to belong in a certain spot, and when it is a new place and new things, no drawer holds what you expect. Stress of change comes in small packages.

I also was in transition regarding size and space, which may also happen for other visitors from a country that does not regard frugal stewardship of space and size as important. In my tiredness, the house and garden felt strange, not home.

"It's nice, mama," Davis again spoke words of support and encouragement. "It's all gonna be ok."

He was so right.

The Town . . .

AFTER A LITTLE REST, Davis and I were ready to explore, so we walked the short blocks uptown to see our new community. In those first days, we learned that Ripley is a market town, a gathering place, which means: 1) there is a fresh market in the town square on Friday and Saturday during the day; and 2) all the young Britons congregate in the local pubs and streets on Friday and Saturday evening. We have been warned not to go out in the evenings and were informed of the importance of locking doors at all times. Robbery is a serious job opportunity here. Taking stolen items to carboot* sales on the weekend has become a vocation for a portion of the population.

We had our first look at places that would become a more familiar part of our weekly shopping routines, such stores as Boots pharmacy, Wilkinson's variety, Clarke's department store, the Co-op. The main business part of town is not that large, one or two streets going one direction, with three or four streets crossing them. Davis may not find much to do here; it would definitely not take him long to learn his way around.

The Car . . .

DRIVING WAS A REAL EXPERIENCE IN THESE INITIAL DAYS. For a left-handed person, I could not have comprehended how driving on the left side could cause stress and anxiety. It looks simple enough, but it is not. A few curbs and one lost hubcap later, I finally settled in a bit. I don't understand how so many curbs could get in the way. And I have no idea how that left hubcap came off when I tried to take the Eastwood exit off the A6 road. Davis and I parked and searched for half an hour in

* This and other British words marked with an asterisk are explained in the glossary on page 228.

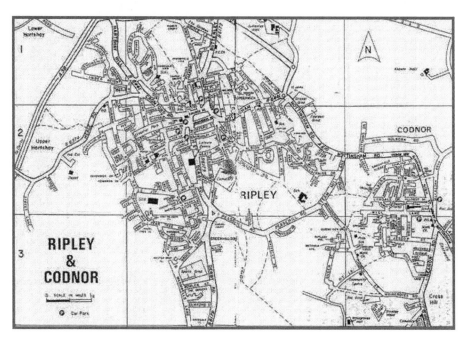

Map of the streets of Ripley

the scrubby grass and shrub along the curb. We found a hubcap, but it did not match the other three on my car. I could not believe this happened, as I wondered what a replacement hubcap costs, or if I could find a match.

In the first days, I walked the streets of Ripley often and studied the town map, to learn the one-way patterns and watch drivers and people. I never realized how much about driving could be learned by observing: cars move into this lane, stop at the double lines, pause left, pause right. I had also driven through the town centre*, but definitely not during rush hour. Soon I needed to go all the way to a meeting near the large city of Nottingham, which was feeling a long way away, quite a trip.

I also realized the emotional difference in driving as a tourist and as a resident. As a tourist you just do it, you don't have time to think about it, to be anxious, to anticipate. Being here for the long run gave me plenty of time to anticipate and acclimate. Davis couldn't drive the car because of insurance costs, so he served as my coach and navigator. I do not think I could have done it by myself. Having circled many a time round a roundabout as he helped see which exit to take, without him I would still be going around my first roundabout, afraid to get off. I had a good driving coach.

The Churches . . .

THE MOMENT I HAD BEEN WAITING FOR: A first visit to the churches. I have now ridden to all—note, not driven to—but have not been inside them all yet. Glenis Quible and husband Geoff kindly took me around in my car—would I really ever learn to drive it? I have learned that she is a primary-school assistant head teacher and he is a policeman. Geoff managed to fold his slim six-plus-foot-tall build into my little red Vauxhall and with a kind smile gently assure me that I will learn to drive here. For the moment, I appreciate being chauffeured. And now, to the churches: I saw their pictures in the materials Vernon sent, now I've visited them up close and for real. And they are as picturesque as I imagined.

CRICH WESLEY CHAPEL   In the lovely little village of Crich, Crich Wesley Chapel is perched on a high, high hill. I am told the village is the setting for the television series *Peak Practice.* Once we're up in the village, we turn left onto a one-lane side street, appropriately named Chapel Street, as are most town streets where the Methodist chapel is located. Driving up past the chapel's side, we pull around to the front and park on the slanted street. Around the other side of the quaint square two-story greystone church is a side garden overgrown with brambles and weeds,

Crich Wesley
Methodist Chapel
CJ Moore, 1992

offering an immediate gardening project. "This is the church where John Wesley once preached in the late 1700s," Glenis reminds me. How moving that is, to know that I will be preaching here. The older congregation is now comprised of fifteen to twenty members who still attend. As in most English towns, the predominant church in this village is the Church of England. People must intentionally choose to be Methodist or any other denomination. I see that on the front wall the sign awaits the name of the new minister.

NETHER HEAGE My circuit steward could not even find this one, how will I? Once we take the correct road from Crich village to Nether Heage, I discover another picturesque setting: a tiny single-story greystone chapel in a small village just beyond and below the village of Heage,

Nether Heage Methodist Chapel, 1992. CJ Moore.

thus the name *Nether* Heage. Sheep graze in the green pasture behind the church, and perched on the next hill is a white four-winged windmill, looking like an angel overseeing her animal and human flocks. What a delightful view! This membership is less than Crich. We are not able to go in.

WOOD STREET The largest of the five churches, this chapel is located in Ripley on a side street named, of course, Wood Street. In England Methodist buildings are called chapels, in contrast to the Anglican churches. This tall red-brick building was built in the mid-1800s. Parking is extremely limited on the narrow street in front, as the church is tightly fitted between residences. There appear to be two primary groups in the congregation: a young adult group, which includes the music band Oasis, united around contemporary-style music

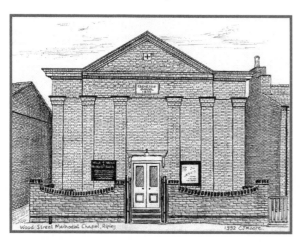

Wood Street Methodist Chapel, Ripley. 1992 CJMoore.

and worship, and the older traditionalists. This sounds familiar. Seventy-seven people are listed on the church rolls, but double that on community participation rolls.

WAINGROVES The little white chapel is in the midst of its own village within a town: Waingroves Village in Ripley town. This group is trying to raise money to remodel its old, worn building. During this first week, I went for a wedding rehearsal and found that the pews

Waingroves Methodist Chapel 1992 C.J.Moore

had all been moved around and the walls were decorated with children's artwork and homemade banners. A "Holiday Club" was being held this week, similar to U.S. children's summer Vacation Bible Schools. There was a sense of energy, activity, and flexibility, even though the program was not happening at that moment. The circuit plan shows forty-five members on roll, but again a much larger active community participation. I am beginning to see a pattern here.

CODNOR CHAPEL This chapel is in a small village named Codnor, only a mile away from Waingroves and literally flowing out of Ripley with little separation. When faced with the high costs of renovation of an old building, the congregation chose to relocate

and build a one-story multipurpose facility. Quite a change from the other buildings, this is Glenis's church, so I learn more about it. They originally built one multipurpose room plus a kitchen and recently added a Sunday School room. The chapel has a core group of middle-age adults with lots

Codnor Methodist Chapel C.J.Moore, 1992

of energy and an active children's Sunday School work. The church membership is at fifty, and again they have a much larger community circle of participation.

The People . . .

IN OUR FIRST DAYS, the circuit stewards and church members we have encountered could not be more gracious and welcoming to us. Americans are not commonly seen in Ripley, but I am reminded of the graciousness of people in my own Southern home state. Already things are feeling more comfortable, and the anxieties are subsiding.

An Orientation Time and a First London Visit . . .

ON MONDAY DAVIS AND I HAD OUR FIRST TRAIN EXPERIENCE, traveling to London where I had a fairly intense orientation session lasting until Thursday, while Davis had the chance to experience some of London.

"Hi, I'm from Perkins . . . " "You can't believe what we had to go through to get our papers . . ." "You are from Candler? Do you know . . ." "I am so excited about this." "We got here last week and worshipped at Wesley Chapel. It was great, but we didn't know *any* of the hymns." Conversation flowed freely during the meet-and-mingle time at the Foreign Mission Club as the orientation began for all the Americans and others from around the world serving in Britain this year. It was good to know that all shared a similar mix of excitement and apprehension. In the introduction to British ministry and life, I appreciated the wise words of John Simmonds, as he led us through the orientation and offered an approach to time management in ministry.

"Divide the day into three parts," he suggested. "Spend two of the three on work, protect the other for yourself. That way," he continued, "you will not burn out." What good advice, a sensible approach to a balance of time. I would carry this wisdom with me into my new work and world.

There were many new things to learn besides unfamiliar hymns, where I wondered how I would ever adjust to music notes on one page, hymn words on the other. We had conversations about funerals and weddings, church structure, cultural traditions. "This is baptism by immersion," I thought, trusting it would all sort out at the proper time.

During one afternoon's break Davis and I traveled down to Westminster Abbey, near the Thames River. Finding that it was being renovated on the outside and we could take a roof tour, we donned yellow hardhats and rode a scaffolding platform up to the roof heights. High above the trees, we could see all of London stretching out for miles, with the bridge-draped river twisting through the city like an artery of life. "Mom, look

Westminster Abbey
from the Southwest
on Abingdon Street.

at that!" Before we descended, Davis spotted high-level British humor in the form of small modern gargoyles on the Abbey rooftops, decorated with sunglasses and smirks, thanks to good-humored reconstructionists. I could not imagine a roof trip happening in the U.S.; liability insurance would not allow it.

One bright sunshiny day Davis maneuvered his way through London transport to enjoy a tour of the historic Tower of London, while in the training sessions my mind often wandered to skewed visions of him voyaging his way alone through London's transportation maze. Another afternoon we journeyed together to Hamley's toy store, which in itself is worth a trip to London, to see seven floors of toys, so many types of toys, so many lovers of toys. Established in the 1800s on Regent Street, the store's invitation is: "*Step over the threshold and you enter a world of joy and wonder.*" Another slogan for the year.

On one floor a huge spindly Tinkertoy ferris wheel turned and glowed in the middle of the area for building toys. Davis had always constructed things as a child, from Legos, paper, wire, or toothpicks and tape. Now here we were—kids in a construction area of an unbelievable toy shop. Surrounded by whirs, whizzes, buzzes, chimes, and human laughter, we drank it all in.

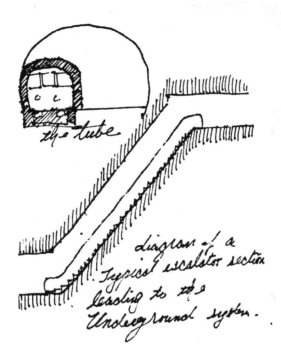

the tube.

diagram of a
Typical escalator section
leading to the
Underground system.

Filled with childlike joy and wonder, we exited and eventually headed for the closest tube station. Huge timing mistake. How quickly emotions shift. No one wants to be at Oxford Circus station at rush hour in such a body-packed face-to-back tight crowd. Forcing our way, pushing, moving, desperately hanging on to each other, we survived and finally arrived back at Islington Station and the Foreign Mission Club.

Our days in London came to an end. We boarded the train for the ride home to Ripley, our seats facing the other direction this time, looking backward as we rode, watching the scenery pass in reverse in a magical rhythm. So it had been in the days, scenes of new settings passing through. My mind now filled with new knowledge, I returned to begin the work.

❧

THIS HAS BEEN A BUSY, ACTIVE, CULTURE-ADJUSTING FIRST WEEK. Friday I started full speed on the job with a funeral, a wedding rehearsal, and a support group meeting. Davis hopes to begin some travel on his own soon, and I am settling into ministerial life here. I am also already realizing that I will love this work, this place, and these people. I have found time to weed the yard and definitely will plant flowers. That palm tree could go, though.

Ripley Town Hall

$\mathcal{S}$EPTEMBER: *Hello to a New World*

Every day is a messenger of God.
Russian proverb

$\mathcal{S}$uitcases unpacked and orientation ended, our new life truly began. Each experience, each day was a window into a new world as we became a part of the community, customs, traditions, and life here.

"Do you, take thee . . ."

VERNON HAD ARRANGED FOR ME TO ASSIST HIM in Saturday's wedding at Waingroves, offering a blessing prayer. I was grateful to be involved—not only was I participating in my first official wedding, it was a British wedding, with different traditions. This gave me an opportunity to ease into the process, learning from him.

On Friday afternoon, we went to prepare the forms. Each church has a safe where church records, including the marriage registers, are kept. At this church, the safe is in a little side room, on the floor underneath a shelf. In order to get the marriage book, Vernon knelt down on his lanky hands and knees, then sat on the floor. Hunched under the shelf like a toad under a mushroom, he reached over to slip the large key into the lock, then turned the handle, and heaved open the heavy metal door. So, in the future, I will have to crawl down on the floor under a shelf, manage the keys into the lock and hoist open the door to pull out the register books without hitting myself? This should be interesting, I thought. "Not all safes are under a shelf," he smiled.

Once the registers are on a table, he meticulously prepares each required form in pencil before the wedding, then he is ready after the wedding to ink them in. There are three forms to complete for each wedding: two register books kept in the officially approved church's safe and the certificate to be mailed in to the county registrar at the end of the quarter. "At the conclusion of the wedding ceremony, actually as a part of the ceremony, the bride and groom, their chosen witnesses, and the minister sign the books and certificate in the presence of all," he explained.

On Saturday the long wooden pews of the simply decorated little chapel soon filled with community folks as the pipe organ filled the room with sound. Dressed in our robes, Vernon in grey and I in black, we moved to the chancel and turned to greet the wedding party, first the groom and best man, then the bride leading in her attendants. With service books in hand, Vernon led the couple through the ceremony, and I offered the blessing prayer. Then we all moved to the cloth-covered table at the side of the room where the bride placed her bouquet down and we began the register signing, declaring the marriage official. Organ music swelled in conclusion, and the newlyweds recessed out of the church to a waiting vintage car. As the chapel emptied, Vernon finished inking the forms in the "proper" black ink, with his ink blotter handy. Already he was shaping me, with his fastidiousness and care for detail. And he offered another important word of knowledge:

"Although the ministers have a key for each chapel and each safe, do *not* become responsible for locking and unlocking the church. This is the job of the church stewards."

Note duly made.

The First Supper . . .

IN THE CHRISTIAN TRADITION the act of giving and receiving the bread and cup of Holy Communion is an ancient ritual shared by the community of faith. In this, my first official Sunday, I had not anticipated the emotion I would feel at serving my first communions here in first Sunday worship services at Wood Street and Codnor. Vernon led the service and I read scripture, as again he helped ease me into the work. In both settings—the lovely traditional communion rail at Wood Street and the hand-stitched cushions on the steps at Codnor—people came forward and knelt. I walked behind Vernon, pausing at each person, and offered the cup and words of grace with each serving, "The cup of God's love poured out for you."

I was looking into the eyes of people young and old, families, couples, individuals who would look to me as their minister for the next year, those who would uphold me in spite of my mistakes and shortcomings, who would regularly worship and meet with me, people I would soon know by name. Those who had welcomed me and greeted me now joined me in the community ritual observed by the church for centuries, the breaking of bread and sharing of cup, which in itself came from the ageless pattern of people gathering at a daily table to share bread and wine. In this first communion was the beginning of a lifelong act of community love and service for which I would never tire.

Words from one of my communion anthems sang in my head:

> Bread and cup on sacred table, reminders of an ancient blessing,
> invite the human heart to new covenant.

This *was* new covenant, new community, new caring. I thought of the days and months ahead, sharing the common meal with them, eating mushy peas and shepherd's pie together, drinking many cups of tea in their homes, being served at their table. One act is not complete without the other, has no meaning except with the other: the common table is to be holy, the sacred table comes from the shared ordinary.

The first Sunday had ended. And I was settling into the joy of life together.

Ashes to Ashes . . .

DEATH IS REAL. In the first week I assisted in two funerals and soon conducted one on my own. I quickly realized that Methodist ministers here are dealing with aging congregations and are also called upon to perform funerals for community people not affiliated with their churches, offering ministers opportunities to be connected with the great number of community people who do not come to church. Many deceased are cremated, perhaps because of scarcity of land. The funeral service is held in the local chapel or church, then the funeral entourage travels down the motorway or slim back roads known by the official drivers to the closest city where there is a crematorium, in our case Derby, where the service continues.

The casket is processed in and placed on a nicely decorated conveyor-type belt to the right of the minister. At a certain point in the crematorium service the minister pushes the button to close the curtains on the casket, then in what is a moving and emotional moment, the curtains slowly furl around the deceased.

Unfamiliar with this custom and practice, I was quite unnerved about that moment of responsibility, afraid that I might push the button too soon and totally disrupt the service and completely dishevel the grieving family. I made a yellow sticky note for my service book saying *"Push the button NOW!"* That sticky note was in my service book for every funeral I ever conducted. Actually, to make it worse, on the podium at this crematorium are two buttons, one to close the curtains and one to start and stop the recorded music.

"OK, which one is it, which one is it?! God, do not let me push the wrong button," an inner voice bartered. In all my time there, I do not remember ever pressing the wrong button, nor did the conveyor belt malfunction and catapult a newly claimed angel directly up to heaven, for which I am eternally grateful.

As I conducted the first funeral service at Codnor by myself, I appreciated that I had been on family visits with Vernon; his caring way helped shape my pastoral understanding of that home-visit time. We would sit in the lounge, with delicate china teacups lightly resting on our knees, and listen to family members share stories and memories as Vernon offered just the right support and gave the needed spaces and silences. His sincere presence and unhurried manner were a balm to the grieving. It is such a fragile gift we are given, to be present with families in this time.

In this early stage of my work, I did not yet recognize all the cultural traditions, still thinking about getting through the British service itself, saying names and places right, reading the correct passages from the service book. People stand as the minister leads the coffin in, reading scripture sentences while walking. Much respect is shown the body, by both the funeral directors and the minister, with slight genuflects while walking in and out. There are traditions of greeting the family and of the congregation standing at the words of commendation. And always, hymns are sung by everyone, with "The Day Thou Gavest" and Crimond's—it must be the Crimond tune—"Twenty-third Psalm" being favorites. People here know tune names of the hymns and know which one they want to sing.

The funeral director, male or female, wears a formal grey/black mourning suit and top hat and occasionally carries a tall regal plume-topped staff as he or she leads the procession with much ceremony. At a cemetery procession, the director and minister walk down the driveway in front of the limousine to the place of burial. And leaving the cemetery, the minister must remember to sign the burial book, or it might not be a "proper" burial.

At a service's conclusion the family gathers in a home for a time of visiting and tea, and ministers are invited to come by. This tradition reminded me of Southern hospitality, where loving church members and neighbors bring casseroles and dishes as an act of pastoral care.

This particular service went smoothly, *except* that the electricity went out at the chapel immediately before the service, so no lights; then a local men's choir of about fifty singers showed up to sing for the service, of which I did not recall being prewarned; and then just at the close the rain descended like justice rolling down from the mighty heavens. This occasion was not to be forgotten; we were sharing a ritual of life, and I would appreciate the widow's support and friendship for the rest of my time there. As it turned out, the last wedding I performed while in Ripley was for a member of this same family.

In the first week, I had shared sacramental life with these communities—in weddings, in communion, in funerals. Life takes no time for "learning to drive." The journey has begun.

Journeying Together . . .

Whoever receives one whom I send receives me . . .
John 13:20a

RAIN HAD FALLEN FOR MOST OF THE DAY but stopped by evening, leaving a blanket of grey haze over the town. Although the service did not start until 7 o'clock, people began to arrive early, stacking coats and umbrellas along the back wall. Chatting and greeting others, they flowed into the sanctuary, into the middle pews, then to the front, crowding into the back seats, even up into the balcony. By 7 o'clock all seats were taken, and the room was filled with the warmth of the energy present.

People had come from all eleven churches to Wood Street chapel for this Friday evening gathering, the circuit induction service for the new minister, who is appointed to the circuit, not to an individual church. Sounds of voices continued to swell. And then the singing began. No dependency on choirs here—let the people sing! And oh, how they sang, lustily and heartily, worthy of John Wesley himself. After a rousing opening hymn, the organ led the people into the second song, new to me but soon to become one of my favorites. In quiet reverence they began:

Be still, for the presence of the Lord is moving in this place . . . .

When the last note ended, a quiet stillness and beauty lingered in the room, letting the song remain in the space. Then Vernon stood and introduced our preacher for the evening, District Chairman Geoffrey Clark, who had come to be a part of the welcome. I had been told how good a minister, leader, and preacher he was, admired and appreciated throughout the entire British Methodist Conference, and I soon saw why. With his gentle manner and soft voice, he began the words of his scripture text, John 13:12–20.

After he had washed their feet . . . he said to them "Do you know what I have done to you?
. . . Very truly, I tell you, whoever receives one whom I send receives me; and whoever receives
me receives him who sent me."

"We are called today," he said, "to follow the example of Jesus, wash each other's feet, do as Christ has done for us, share life and blessing, and to receive this one who has been sent." In the frame of these words, Vernon and I moved to join him as the congregation stood for the formal welcome covenant. With the rustling sound as of a covey of doves taking flight, they rose and in one voice spoke their words of covenant to their new minister:

"We will work with you and pray for you."

They were speaking to *me*. A gathered congregation ready to love, work with, and pray for this white-headed, white-skinned, middle-of-life-aged Southern woman from the colonies across the pond. How can we not have meaningful work and good life together in this year? And I had been inducted by a second British minister whose gentle grace was reflected in his action and being. From that first act Geoffrey continued to offer support and encouragement. He was a softly spoken servant leader and friend throughout my years of ministry in England. I returned five years later to work with him in his final year of ministry and wrote an anthem for his retirement celebration.

As this service ended we all sat back down for their tradition of a closing moment of silence, then we remained seated for the postlude ringing forth from the organ. When the music ceased the crowd rose and moved from the sanctuary through the side doors of the chapel down the little hallway into the back schoolroom, where tables and chairs had been set up for tea and a finger-food reception. As I moved around the tables, welcome words flowed into conversations, with folks telling me more stories of the churches and community than I could ever remember: "I was a member of the old Methodist Chapel on . . . ." "We've been a part of our chapel since . . . ." "Our chapel decided to . . . ." "We hope you will . . . ." In these words and stories I was sensing and seeing the nature of care and community of the people here. With his sweet smile and good heart, Davis also listened and received words of welcome and insight from all who gathered round him, including some suggestions regarding the local golf course.

Steward Patrick Dawson called for everyone's attention and presented "our new American lady minister" with a personal copy of *Mission Praise,* the contemporary songbook used in worship. As a closing gift, Jean from Wood Street handed me the lovely bouquet of yellow and white daisy mums from the evening. Fresh flowers for the home and blessing. What a good welcome to my time here. Journeying together.

So, What *Is* an Outdoor Show Service?

MY FIRST PREACHING EXPERIENCE ON ENGLISH SOIL occurred outdoors, Sunday at 9:30 a.m., with a bunch of clowns on a playground. Waingroves village was holding its annual autumn weekend celebration called the "Outdoor Show." Clowns in full red-nose regalia welcomed us and showed folks to the folding chairs set up on the concrete play area of the school grounds for worship—even dogs were welcome. Through the trees the lively music and games for the main show on the neighboring lot were gearing up in full volume, adding to the fun-filled cacophony. "Can I preach over that?" I wondered.

When the chapel's music group led the singing time, I was ready with my new songbook to follow the unfamiliar melodies, while the congregated crowd sang with great gusto. With the bright blue sky overlooking us, small fluffy white clouds billowing by, kids coming and going, crazy painted faces staring back at me, I preached.

As we became acquainted in this setting, I thought, "So these folks are my congregation at Waingroves. I wonder if I will recognize these clowns without their red noses and yellow hair." Who said English church was stuffy!

And in the Afternoon, Other Firsts . . .

I LEARNED FROM KEN CRESSWELL, Wood Street's pastoral church visitor, that one of their oldest members was celebrating her ninety-fourth birthday. In the early afternoon we drove up the road to the neighboring town of Alfreton to the retirement home where she now lived. Ken bravely rode with me, which meant I had someone else's life in my car. We traveled up to the town three or four miles away, through the intersection—*"Which lane? Where to turn?"* my mind cried. *"Stay left!"* then right to the retirement home, into the parking lot. *"Breathe now! I must remember to breathe when I drive."* Alice was delightfully healthy. She welcomed me, thanked us for coming, and I returned Ken safely home.

Later in the afternoon, Patrick drove me up to Crich for tea at the home of Cheryl Love, the chapel lay leader at Wesley Chapel in that village. It is good Patrick drove; the regular road was filled with construction work, so we traveled back lanes—single lanes to be exact—small, winding single lanes, with thick tight high hedgerows on either side. At one point when we met another vehicle, one of us had to back up to what I learned was a necessary passing place in the road. I was grateful that I was not driving; I had no idea how we got there. My evening prayer included the following request:

May the construction please be gone by the next time I need to drive up here.

Cheryl lives in an intriguing two-story manor house of dark stone down a block from the chapel. I felt as if I were entering another world. On the little dirt lane leading to her home is the public sign **DANGER! FROG CROSSING.** An ancient black steam engine and a colorful gypsy wagon are parked in front of the home. Inside the entranceway, old clocks tick and tock, part of a collection scattered throughout the home. Obviously Cheryl's Derbyshire-born husband Graham has many fascinating and diverse interests, though I must admit I could not understand much of what he said on this first visit; I had to watch his mouth when he spoke, until I became more familiar with a Derbyshire brogue.

During tea Cheryl spoke about the little chapel and its unique history, the connection to John Wesley, its long past in the village, and its struggling present, with aging members and declining membership. "But God watches over us," she said, as her deep love for the church shone through her voice, eyes, and being. In her simple phrase for living, the words of an old hymn I had heard so often in my past came to my mind: *"Be not dismayed, whate'er befalls, God will take care of you."* How much that was true for this little chapel. We continued the conversation as I gained a picture of the congregation and community. After sharing a final cup of tea in front of the warm wood-burning fireplace, we crossed the road up to the chapel for the evening Harvest Festival.

I had driven to Crich earlier in the week to see the chapel and meet some of the congregation, but this was special—my first service in the chapel where John Wesley had preached. A powerful sense of history is present here. In the chancel area a tall staircase leads up to a yellow wooden gate door, which opens into the tall pulpit with its original candle sconces on either side, the pulpit rising up over the congregation. Brilliant red-, green-, and yellow-paned glass windows flank each side of the pulpit. A dark wood balcony, which wraps around the back and sides of the sanctuary, is no longer used except on rare occasions of community or circuit service, but the old doored pews up there are reminders of the chapel's earlier active life.

The room is a mix of old and new; in an effort to modernize, the congregation had at some time added light-colored wood panel sheets around the sides of the balcony. A sprawling Christmas cactus mixes with plastic and silk flowers to adorn the chancel area. The small, antique glass-paned cabinet by the back wall holds treasures of the Wesley heritage, chalice and patens of earlier days, ceramic cups, and an anniversary brochure.

This is the congregation of Bessie, Alan, and Joe, folks who have been coming to this chapel all their lives, who do not want to see it end its time and place in their village.

Also present were a few people who, as the village had reached for its future, moved here to retire in an idyllic Derbyshire location.

Cheryl had prepared the altar with a simple and beautiful setting—a large piece of coal, a clear pitcher of water, a loaf of bread. These are the symbols of the harvest of this community, a coal-mining area where most folks have been in some way connected with the mines. They have been closed for a few decades now, but the area still struggled to recover. I recalled Vernon's comment in his letter regarding where the communities were in that recovery. More Harvest celebrations were to come, with a chance for me to better understand the traditions of the festival. But on my first Harvest service, here in this small rural village, the altar symbols could have represented life for similar places in Alabama, towns that knew the declines and changes of the times. As we ended the service, the church stewards brought tea in delicate china cups and saucers on a tray from the kitchen, and we shared tea and friendship on a Harvest evening.

An Ever-expanding Circle

"OK, THIS IS IT." I started the car motor and drove out of the estate, armed with a map and instructions but dreading the morning crossing of the M1 junction that lay between me and Ravenshead.

The day had come for me to drive to Ravenshead in Nottinghamshire for a ministry probationers' meeting, to venture out alone in the car for a longer distance. Driving was still an unnerving experience, and this trip took me through a busy crossover of the M1 Motorway, but I was learning and feeling more confident. As I drove into Ravenshead, a distance of seventeen miles though it seemed much longer, I noted a difference in the look of the community. Houses were more diverse in architecture, larger, with more trees. The village felt welcoming and inviting, built around a small walker-friendly shop centre. Finding the home nestled in a small cul-de-sac, I parked the car and walked to the front door.

"Welcome, do come in!" Hostess and district probationers' committee member Sheila Hawkins and her husband, Ken, greeted me and immediately helped put me at ease, with their cheerful laughter and comfortable hospitable manner. In my later years in England, Ken and Sheila would become close friends when I worked in their circuit, and their home a favorite visiting haven. The probationer group included other mid-life-age men and women making career changes into ministry, so shared interests and questions became a bridge for conversation. I was glad to be meeting people at this gathering who would be a part of my year's work.

Judith was a local magistrate who had now made the move into ministry. As we stood together chatting, she told me more of herself and family, her experience of English ministry. We discussed such things as whether we would wear clerical collars as is the custom for Methodist ministers in England but not for us in America. I had decided that unless it was an issue I would not; it is not in my tradition to do so. Talk flowed easily, then the group soon moved into shared conversation and topics.

Sheila's dining room has large picture windows facing a beautiful terraced rock garden with a miniature windmill. In that picturesque setting, lunch became another opportunity to become more familiar with English food, with pasties* and pâté*, as I learned more about the probationer's program. One thing that impressed me was their emphasis on ministers reading and experiencing beyond the theological world. Reading and media resources to be explored during each person's probation time were to be broad-based—from culture, world events, movies—an approach that was unique for the mid-1990s. Imagine having to read fiction or go to movies as work. I also appreciated the emphasis put on taking care of self and taking time for preparation. This would be a good component of the year. I looked forward to other retreat/gathering times.

On the return trip, I found myself less worried about the driving, as I reflected on conversations and expectations, on women in ministry here and what that meant, on enjoying the day. Happily I made it back across the junction and leisurely drove home.

Observations at the End of the Day . . .

ABOUT THE PEOPLE

I DO BELIEVE THESE PEOPLE LIKE TO MEET. With tonight's annual circuit meeting at Crich, I have been here only a week, and I am meeting'd out. But I have learned that time over tea is an important ritual of any meeting. And no styrofoam cups here, proper cups and saucers, with everyone, men and women, pitching in for the much-practiced ritual of wash, dry, and put away.

Whether in meetings or daily encounters, the people continue to be very warm and gracious, quickly accepting and receiving me, and Davis as well. In each of the churches, there is an active core of leadership, there are a few older folk who simply want to be checked on occasionally by the minister, and, where present, the younger adults are full of energy. The singing is great everywhere, with each church favoring a particular hymnal—the *present* Methodist Hymnal, the *old* (the *real*) Methodist hymnal, the *new* Mission Praise book. Hymnbook arguments abound internationally.

Lay leadership in the churches is strong. In a circuit such as this, the people see the minister only once a month in some places, so they do the work of the church themselves. With three excellent circuit stewards, and Vernon as the superintendent, their care and support have helped place any culture shock of the town in a better perspective.

AND ABOUT US

SHARING OUTINGS TOGETHER has been great fun. Last Saturday as Davis and I drove down the back way to the outskirts of Derby, we came across a McDonald's, and I suddenly found myself craving McDonald's. It never tasted better—a taste of home. A simple hamburger and fries were like manna from heaven. For that moment, we were transported. And I don't even like McDonald's.

Later in the week we drove up the A6 road to Matlock Bath, a postcard-pretty little town built on the banks of the Derwent River where it bubbles and cuts through the tall limestone hills. Locating a car park close to the train station, we purchased our parking sticker and placed it on the car window, so as not to be tire-clamped. From the swingy cable cars that travel up the steep cliff side for the Heights of Abraham, we looked back down on the lovely pastel buildings set along the river's curve, resembling a picturesque Swiss village, and enjoyed the green patchwork vista out across the Derbyshire countryside.

On the mountaintop is a nature park with a small challenge course. We paused for Davis to enjoy the challenges. The caverns of the Heights of Abraham are said to have been the source of lead mining since the Roman times, with a heyday during the seventeenth century. These days they offer a chance for modern folk to re-track the paths of miners and to view impressive underground caves existing for millennia. Inspired by our mountaintop experience, we decided to hike back down the ledge, following streets that should have led to the bottom. Under Davis's adventurous leadership, our descent passed through sections of town we would have missed otherwise, perhaps streets known only to their residents. After a great walking workout, we arrived at the bottom and found our way back to the car park, thankfully before the ticket expired.

The week held room for one more family outing, an important occasion. On Saturday we located the local golf course, Ormonde Fields, just on the edge of Codnor village not far from the ruins of Codnor Castle. Davis played his first English round of golf as I walked alongside, enjoying the undulating hills and expansive views of open fields. There were not many other players on the course, just a few men playing their usual Saturday game. I did not even think to ask if it were acceptable for me to walk the course with Davis; since no one accosted me, it must have been alright. These days, more women are actually playing courses. I will stick to walking.

We were still discovering new insights of our English home. We both looked for and could not find the music rack on the piano and just concluded that it must not have one, how strange, only to discover it folded inside the top. It is good we did not complain about it. In going to get library cards Friday, we learned that the library had been broken into the previous night; again we are reminded that theft is a major problem here. We did get our cards a day later and promptly checked out books. Davis possibly is headed to Scotland for a few days.

AND ON LIFE

MARLENE FROM CODNOR brought lovely orange-and-coral blooming pansy plants and a planter, so after a little dirt-mixing, small mounds of color now greet visitors at the front door. How lovely that little bit of color is. Perhaps that is why gardening is so important to people here—to make small places into containers of beauty.

We have found the Co-op grocery within walking distance and the nicer Sainsbury's supermarket a drive across town; in visiting those stores we have discovered how different the shopping is here. Products that are the same have different labels; for example, P&G soap products are called by other names. There is no pickle, as in pickled cucumbers. Jello is jelly, and jelly is jam. The coffee pot is not, unless one has a cafetière. Instant is in and perked is out. Items are sold in small amounts. Fries are chips, and chips are crisps. And there are more flavors of crisps than one can imagine; plain is hard to find. Grocery shopping is a great adventure. We must allow more time for searching in our shopping.

We have hung two loads of clothes out to dry on that circular clothes tree, then forgotten them both times and had them rained on, so we had to wash them again and hang them on the radiators and in the drying closet. The iron blew the circuit, so we now have a wonderful new one, thanks to help from Patrick. And I can now print from the computer. Still no modem hookup—a few *minor* problems related to compatibility.

Harvest Festival . . .

Lord, you have been our dwelling place . . . .
From Psalm 90

GOURDS AND POTATOES, FLOWERS AND FRUIT, baskets and wellies*—
Sunday sanctuaries were filled with the signs of colorful harvest festival celebrations.
Harvest festivals occur in the autumn, or the *fall* as we Americans would say, usually in
the month of September. They are one of several important church occasions, along
with Church anniversaries and flower festivals. For this festival, churches have a long
tradition of bringing the bounty, the harvested crops, to church to give thanks for them
and to decorate the sanctuaries with them, and then to share them in some way with
the people. Some produce has been grown in home gardens. Other, particularly as
fewer folks grow vegetables these days, are bought at the local markets.

Harvest festival could be compared to our Thanksgiving time, yet with more
emphasis on the harvest itself: an occasion to be communally grateful for the produce
of the earth and to be mindful of the needs of others and of the needs of the earth.
Beyond the Sunday service, congregations also have a harvest dinner on a preceding
weekend night or the following Monday. Guest preachers are invited a year prior to
the event, and special entertainment is arranged for the dinners, where tickets may be
sold for the dinner and guests invited. The event is a great time for the churches; it is

also an occasion for addressing the hunger needs of the world and the environmental challenges of this century. I may not have quite comprehended all this in my first experience of Harvest festivals, but I thoroughly enjoyed the beauty, energy, and focus of the events.

At Wood Street Chapel the young adults had decorated the front of their sanctuary beautifully. This in itself was a step forward for the church, relinquishing the visual interpretation tradition to the younger group, who were wonderfully creative. The rich brown woods of the rails and pulpit furniture stood as background for a colorful palate of vegetables and fruit, including one I did not recognize, a marrow, a large, long green gourd. Their bright display even included communion elements of bread and juice in the bounty, as well as tools of the farmer complete with wellies, shovel, and hoe. The chancel was filled with color.

"Come ye thankful people come…" As we sang the opening strains of the first hymn of the service, ten to twelve young children processed down the right aisle, bringing baskets of fruit to the altar table. Later a youth tambourine band stepped into the front space and moved to lively music by English rock band The Who. Tambourines and ribbons danced all around: High, low, around one side, then the other—shake … tap, tap, shake, shake . . . . In all my years of music I never had a tambourine band in church before. Perhaps a product of the influence of English Salvation Army bands, it was great! Following The Who rendition, the boys and girls of the Sunday School program presented two children's skits with much gusto, I gave a *very* short sermon, and we all had a great time. It was good to see the commitment of these adults to the young people, and to be a part of such life and energy in the service.

Evening Harvest Service at Nether Heage was equally beautiful but in a totally different setting. The little chapel there is warm and inviting in the evening lights, with its multicolored windows and intimate space. In an interesting design, the pews are raised in greatly tiered rows, each row about a foot high with perhaps four or five tiers up, looking down on the chancel area and the lovely little boxed pipe organ where Evelyn Bamford sat and played. Under the caring leadership of Frank Hackman, who besides being a local preacher and the lay leader of this chapel was a talented flower arranger, the small group had lovingly prepared a beautiful altar table of vegetables and fruit and had intertwined fresh flowers and greenery around the communion rail.

Several community members attended, making the crowd a little larger than usual, placing it in the high twenties. After the service, the bounty was sold, with the money going toward mission outreach projects.

"Welcome! Welcome, love!" With his bright smile, church member Keith Taylor joyfully greeted me at Codnor's Saturday evening Harvest Festival celebration. I was glad to be able to be with them for a part of their festival activities. Laughter flowed freely in this warm and fun group. Their women's music ensemble Codnor Connexion sang, and for the first time since arriving I recognized a majority of the songs used in church. Of course, these happened to be primarily older favorites.

I was not with Waingroves at all for their Harvest weekend, but the focus of their festival was the plight of the homeless, and the speaker for the day was a person working at a homeless shelter in Derby. Crich's service the preceding week had a similar setting: coal, water, and bread on the table, symbolizing the challenges of the community and the world; they held a Saturday bake sale in the Crich marketplace. The overall diversity of the Harvest Festival celebrations in all the churches reflects the diversity among the churches themselves, each able to celebrate uniquely.

The Harvest Festival celebration is a wonderful experience, built around tradition, care, and concern for the environment, creative beauty, fellowship, and fun. Perhaps it lacks our family emphasis at Thanksgiving and its focus primarily on giving thanks, but Harvest celebrates the rhythm of the seasons and nature in a festive and thoughtful way.

I thought back as the daughter of a man who made his living in Mississippi helping the farmers with their cotton crops, as they knew and experienced the changing seasons, the successes and failures of crop production. Farmers would show appreciation for Daddy's work with them by giving us corn, peas, and butterbeans from their vegetable gardens, which Mother then put up in the freezer. I felt an inherent appreciation for the English church's recognition of the harvest season, much as our secular county fairs do. What better place than in church to both honor the earth's bounty and to hear the voice of justice and fairness for all people and for the earth itself?

Melodious Sounds from the Minster Grounds . . .

OUR OFFICIAL REASON FOR THE TRIP TO SOUTHWELL was to attend synod on Saturday. Once past Mansfield, Patrick drove us eastward on lovely country roads, eventually arriving at the beautiful small minster town, a hidden jewel. Leaving the last country turns and entering the town, we located our meeting place, which was at the local school building. Synod is a biannual meeting of the entire district, which might be compared roughly to a church denomination's regional annual conference. It is a time for business, but also for friendship and visiting, with folks coming from all over the two counties of Nottinghamshire and Derbyshire. It was interesting to see business conducted English Methodist style and also to recognize the delight for everyone in greeting friends and colleagues. Like home, there is concern here about the declining and aging Methodist congregations.

At the lunch break, those who knew to bring a sandwich enjoyed their mealtime. Patrick suggested we walk over to see the minster there, so we wandered through the cobblestone streets of the town down to the entry to Southwell minster, a marvelous beauty of a structure set in lovely tree-framed grounds not far from the centre of town. Walking across the grounds, we discovered that inside the minster, by delightful coincidence, a wedding was taking place. *"Da-da-da-da Da-da-da-da, Da-da-da-da Da-da-da-da,"* the pipes of the organ pealed forth. Widor's *Toccata,* shades of home! What glorious fun to hear this majestic organ work being performed in the minster.

As we continued to stand outside and listen, up and out floated the angelic sound of the minster choir singing John Rutter's *"For the beauty of the earth—, for the glory of the ski-i-i-es . . ."* Cherubic voices soared as they sang: *"Lord of all—to thee we ra-a-a-aise . . ."* Did I order this moment in time from heaven? And if that were not enough, at the end of the ceremony a bagpiper tuned up and led the bridal party out, with the groom and his groomsmen dressed in Scottish plaids. Lucky enough to receive this surprise gift of tradition, ceremony, and beauty, we stood by and enjoyed every moment of the occasion, uninvited but grateful guests.

Then it was back to the business of the day, but what a marvelous interlude. The synod continued through the afternoon. I had reached my absorption point by the end, but I returned home with a musical memory of my Southwell minster unexpected gift, a lovely September song.

A Lovely 'ello

A GYMFUL OF ONE HUNDRED SIXTY scrubbed, polished, and uniformed seven-to-eleven year olds greeted me. "Good morning boys and girls," spoke the Deputy Headteacher.

"Good mor-ning, Miss-es Jo-o-nes. Good morning, Rev-rand Mu-tert. Good mor-ning, ev-ery-o-one," intoned the children in unison.

And from the first greeting we had a wonderful visit. In contrast to U.S. schools, where religion in schools is an issue, here the local ministers come regularly to share in the morning devotionals. Just think, multiply this visit times four communities with schools, and add that to my diary! We had a great time together. Later when I was in Codnor, some of the children passed me and recognized me, shouting, "There's the American minister!"

As I was leaving this first visit, teachers quietly commented to me:

"Oh, I hope the children didn't misbehave too much!" "I'm so sorry if they were restless." "How did you think they were?"

"You've got to be kidding!" my mind instantly responded. The kids had filed in single file, without talking. During the fifteen-minute assembly, they sat cross-legged on the floor in straight, close rows and hardly spoke or moved the entire time, even when I tried to loosen them up to interact with me. At the end they stood and filed out single file, shyly looking my way and some speaking quietly a soft "ello." Compared to some classes I had in my music teaching years, this is the dream team. *You have got to be kidding!*

"They were lovely," with a smile I replied aloud.

Dinner with the Monsignor: A Welcome Colleague

"MAY THE LORD BLESS THEE," began the printed St. Francis blessing that awaited me upon my arrival. Monsignor Jonathan Moore, the Ripley Roman Catholic priest, had attended my induction service, had loaned the beautiful antique dining room table and chairs for the manse, and along with the blessing card had sent us an invitation to dinner at his home, with other guests from the area. Now the night had arrived, and Davis and I experienced a delightful evening.

The Ripley Catholic Church is a beautiful little brick church, set in a large sloping plot of land, which seemed somewhat unusual compared to the other non-Anglican local churches. The church parish includes perhaps four hundred members. Pulling into the drive at the top of the hill, we found an attractive two-story home at the backside of the church. The Monsignor had invited another priest from a community down the road and an American church member, a young woman who had married a British doctor. We all gathered in his cozy lounge for a predinner getting-acquainted chat over sherry, with friendly conversation and a few jokes from our host. Msgr. Moore is a gracious, warm individual who enjoys entertaining and has a grand memory for jokes. He and his home-keeping assistant Sylvia even published a joke-and-recipe book titled *Laugh . . . and grow fat!*, with a foreword statement that Sylvia's recipes injected "just a little good taste into a collection of Msgr. Moore's jokes!"

"Dinner is now ready," Sylvia invited, so we moved into the dining room and took our places around the formal table. Seeing his home filled with beautiful antiques, I was grateful that he shared the dining table for my manse. Sylvia had prepared an elegant roast meal, and we leisurely enjoyed ourselves through all the courses, down to the last sip of coffee from the cafetière, the closing to a most relaxing evening. In my limited experience of ecumenical clergy camaraderie and my awareness that I was the first female Methodist minister to serve here, I found this warm reception by Msgr. Moore to be delightful and welcome, and I looked forward to working with him in the year.

In the two hospitable events of this day, I realized I was finding my way and settling in to these new communities as home away from home. Children on both sides of the ocean are comfortable befrienders. And a gracious home of hospitality is a welcome sign in any town.

Cornwall Calls

"TheLordbewithyou...liftupyourhearts...inthenameofthefather,son,andholyghostamen."

THUS ENDED THE SUNDAY-NIGHT SERVICE AT WOOD STREET, which included the fastest communion great thanksgiving ever said, knowing that we were trying to make a train in Derby twenty minutes away. Davis and I flew out the door and jumped into Patrick's car; he was driving us because he thought it not safe to leave my car parked at the station. When we arrived, we jumped out of the car, ran up and down trying to find the correct platform, heard the "All aboard!", and quickly boarded a train that then sat in the station for forty-five minutes. The consistency of the British trains is found in the delays. I could have breathed in-between paragraphs in the communion liturgy, if I had known. Finally the train started up and headed to Plymouth. We were off to this southwest end of England. It was worth the wait as we started another train-ride adventure. I felt like a kid.

Plymouth is a fascinating maritime city full of history and story. I learned that in WWII this was one of the English cities that was greatly destroyed by bombing raids, but it has completely rebuilt with modern architecture and layout. Plymouth's history dates back so much earlier than the last half-century's war, and this is evident in the many memorials created there. We located an inexpensive hotel, The Grosvenor Park, near the train station, then walked down through the large town mall with its concrete sidewalks and open spaces, and found our way down to the Hoe and the waterfront, passing the harbor lighthouse Smeaton's Tower and Sir Francis Drake's statue. Locating Barbican Pier, we came upon the very spot where the Mayflower ship departed, heading to a new world. For us as U.S. citizens, this was a moving moment, to stand at the top and look down into the dark waters that led to our land and story. Though the steps were demolished shortly after that departure, they have been rebuilt and are in use today. The narrow stone steps led into the water where the Mayflower would have been docked. Down those steps the Pilgrims descended and departed. Davis, Carl, and I had visited the U.S. Plymouth Rock on a trip to Boston; now we stood at one of the beginning points from the motherland.

In the waterfront area we discovered an exhibit of Plymouth's history. Paying the entry fee, we entered the enclosed area and immediately noticed a disturbingly unpleasant smell. Trying to ignore it, we finally commented to each other:

"Do you smell that awful smell?" " Yeah, it smells like something rotten. I wonder what it is." "Seems like they wouldn't let an odor go like that!" "What is it?" "I don't know why they don't do something about it."

After about the third room, we realized this was an English 1990s version of virtual reality, odors and all. It was the street smell of earlier centuries. We both were certainly glad we did not live back then.

Penzance was next on our little excursion into this Celtic corner of England. A beautiful bay to discover, for us it first became a departure for our ultimate goal, Land's End, the westernmost spot of England. Davis hoped to travel from one end of England to the other during his stay. We treated ourselves to a bayside hotel, left our luggage, located the route we wanted, and boarded the upper deck of a double-decker bus that carried us the ten miles in a ride that took one hour. It happened to be a foggy day, so upon arriving at Land's End we did not actually see America. As if we could on a clear day.

There is a certain beauty, mystery, and appeal about the place. With its steep granite cliffs and roaring sea, it carries legends of Arthur and Lyonnese. Even when there is no view, the smell of sea, the caw of gulls, the mist of ocean spray pervades the famous spot. Leaving the grey misty corner, we traveled back to Penzance to enjoy the calmer view and waterfront at the hotel.

The next day we wandered through town, then set out for a walk during low tide across the causeway over to St. Michael's Mount, a castle on a little tidal island in Mount's Bay. Once a Benedictine monastery, then a fortified castle, the place had ties with its French counterpart, Mont St. Michel, but it has been for many centuries the home of the St. Aubyn family.

Even for one unaware of the historical context, there is something mystical and timeless about being able to walk out to the island, knowing that the tides control your going and coming. Beyond human manipulation, just move with the rhythm of the sea. Enjoyably, we were able to walk out, linger, and return before the tides came in.

The train returned us to Plymouth, where we walked down with our luggage to the waterfront and found the charming Devonia Hotel right on the bay, complete with pink ruffled bed skirts and lace curtains. In the middle of the night, we were abruptly awakened by the wildest noises imaginable and looked out the window to view a crazy massive gull gathering in the bay at low tide. The strangest guttural sounds emitted forth: "Haw, haw, haw, haw, haw." I had been reading a Daphne du Maurier book earlier that evening; when I awoke I truly wondered if I were in dream mode, if this were some surreal reenactment from *The Birds*. Thank goodness, only birds in the bay.

All too soon morning arrived, the end of a quick glimpse into a great corner of England. Davis and I reboarded the train for a return journey to Derby and Ripley, where at home I discovered that I needed to chair the local preachers' meeting because Vernon was ill.

Chatsworth

I AM NOT SURE WHO FIRST TOOK ME THERE FOR A VISIT; I just know early on it became one of my favorite visiting places, and a first stop for all my American visitors arriving at Manchester airport and traveling the A6 route to Ripley.

Nestled at the edge of the Peak District National Park in the Derbyshire countryside, Chatsworth is the estate home of the Duke and Duchess of Devonshire. In a unique situation, the home and gardens are open to the public for a fee—the surrounding grounds of open fields and riverside paths, pastures of grazing sheep, deer, and elk are available for all to enjoy. The elegant home houses remarkable collections of art and furniture, all that you expect in an English estate home, well worth several visits to absorb. But the gardens and open grounds are what draw people back for ongoing walks, picnics, and excursions. The entire estate includes several small villages, a farm shop at one end, a garden shop, and a tea room at the other end. And truth is, the sheep are the lords of the land, lazily grazing and watching the bypassing human hikers or haughtily crossing the road in defiance of any oncoming cars who forget that the sheep have the right of way.

Each season holds its own beauty at Chatsworth, both in the gardens and on the hillside grounds. The rich colors of autumn paint the hillsides with its rustic palette of hues, the hardwoods changing as the temperatures drop. Winter offers a blanket of quiet peace on the scene, with bare-limbed trees revealing a vulnerability of visibility to the visitor.

Spring brings the joy of lambing season; now the little ones begin to rule the roads, as signs appear along the way reminding the humans of the priority: **CAUTION! LAMBING SEASON.** Bluebells nestle underneath the tall trees; flowering gardens within the walled estate burst into spring pastels; and peacocks, proud roosters, and plump feathered hens walk among the topiary kitchen garden scenes.

Summer gives opportunity for games and sports scattered throughout the grounds; people everywhere enjoy long days of relaxation and recreation. Children play hide-and-seek in the maze; parents hoist kites in the open fields; couples stroll hand in hand.

A cup of tea in the stables-turned-restaurant, a stroll along the bubbling river, a hike in the woods, and the body and spirit are refreshed, a person now ready to return to the calls of life beyond the sheep.

OCTOBER AND NOVEMBER:
A Change of Seasons

For everything there is a season . . .
a time to laugh . . . a time to cry . . .
from Ecclesiastes 3

$\mathcal{L}$ife was settling into what was beginning to be a comfortable routine: ongoing church responsibilities, getting to know folks and communities better, letting the house take on our presence, becoming more familiar with the area and all it had to offer. Davis was traveling some, exploring farther afield.

I had been busy with the many church councils that occur at this time of year, these semi-annual official meetings of each congregation where necessary business and decision-making is dealt with. Having them occur so soon upon arrival brought me right into the workings of the congregations and the circuit. Vernon had planned to cover some with me and to have me cover some alone. I ended up chairing all those in my section.

The harvest festivals brought me into the life and traditions of the church; church councils brought me into the work and challenges of the church. There were typical celebrations about good things and struggles with the harder matters such as buildings and money; people excited and people tired, wanting others to step forward but not always wanting to give up ownership; and questions about how to look to and prepare for the future or how to survive in the present.

I had also moved into the pattern of meeting with couples regarding spring marriages; performing infant baptisms almost weekly, which meant visiting with those families; and there was an ongoing happening of funerals for both church members and the community. I saw these opportunities to be with people other than the active congregation members as something needed for sure—as a connection of what was happening within the church with the people and life events outside the church communities. I sensed already that we needed to find ways to be out in the life of the whole community if we were to live out the calling of faith. I was also beginning to see the challenge of that, when these faithful people were doing all they could to keep their church lives and activities going.

Back in Alabama, Dan's birthday was in early October. We chatted and visited on the phone that day. Then Daddy's birthday came later in the month, and again, the telephone lines connected us from afar. I decided not to worry about those international phone bills too much; I had found a good rate. I was also looking forward to my first family visitors in November—my sister Ann's family from Alabama was coming, the first of family and friend visits planned for throughout the year.

An Unexpected Turn

EVENTS IN THE CIRCUIT OCCURRED IN THESE WEEKS in a way no one could have imagined. There is a big gap in my journal during this time, perhaps because of the events of those weeks. Life took an unexpected turn. What had begun as a wonderful experience, a great ministry relationship with Vernon and the circuit, moved into a scenario that felt unreal, except that it *was* real. Circumstances moved so quickly that most of us had little time to realize what was happening.

Vernon had not felt well at my arrival, a slight flu bug, which took some of his energy. So I had occasionally filled in for him at a meeting or two, had supported him as needed. I look back on my calendar to sort it out, for in my mind facts blur into feelings and fuzzy memories. There was a wedding at Sommercotes, not in my section; Vernon invited me to participate as he had done at other functions. Where is it on my diary, where are the events that pointed to this? It's as if life goes on, with meetings and baptism families and committees. What are the events that stand out in my mind, which help me remember what happened?

THERE WAS A WEDDING .... The Sommercotes church worship area was a small open room, decorated for the wedding. Vernon and I stood at the front together, he in his grey robe and I in my white. He was not feeling well. The table for signing the official register was placed in the front, with chairs available for the bride and groom to sit down to sign the book. We moved one of those chairs closer to where we would stand for the ceremony.

At one point in the ceremony, Vernon had to sit down to continue, and I performed a part of the ceremony for him. Together, we made it through the service. At the end, he did as he had done before, meticulously filling out the forms, but even then, he moved slowly and weakly, a definite sign that something serious was wrong with him. This flu bug had lingered for too many weeks now. He had been to the doctors on more than one occasion, but nothing more than the flu had been diagnosed.

Finally, in the next weeks, his energy was gone. On a Friday evening in the latter days of October, as I arrived at Swanwick to attend a women's network meeting, I was told that Vernon and his wife Anne would not be there. He had been given some blood tests, and the doctor had come over to the house that day to say he needed to go to the hospital as a result of the test findings. So, in his place, I was asked to give the opening prayer for the meeting.

In the next days, I went to visit Vernon at the hospital down in Derby. Over the weekend there was no word, then on Monday the doctor shared the news. The blood test results revealed that he had pancreatic cancer, already spread throughout the body, and there was nothing they could do for him.

I recall visiting with him in the long open ward of the old hospital—all the beds there together, lined up, person by person. The hospitals themselves were a new and strange experience for me—the open wards, the lack of privacy for patients and families. It all felt like an image out of an old black-and-white war movie.

He was sitting up in a chair at the side of his bed. I think we talked of what had happened in just these few days. Vernon's emotions came through in his words of how uncaring the system had seemed in sharing such news. Head barely tilted back, he spoke with disbelief: "No chaplain, no preparation, just the news: it's cancer; there's no hope; go home and get your things in order." Do I remember correctly? Was it really that cold and abrupt? I think Anne would say so.

And that is what he did.

In a few days, Vernon went home, and in the next precious weeks, he lost energy and strength and life. Anne, Alison, and Elizabeth must have felt like this was some strange masquerade, some unreal chapter in a story. Their loving, gentle, strong husband and father was in a matter of days dwindling away from them. The circuit was in shock. Vernon had chosen to come to them, to a little place called Ripley circuit, eleven churches, with money for only two ministers. In just a year's time, he had given them hope and energy for the future, a future led by this kind, insightful encourager. Now, in what seemed to be only days, he was being taken from them.

I recall that on one visit to their home I asked Vernon if he would like to receive communion, as I was sharing it with others that day. He declined, replying that he was used to administering it with others, how strange it felt to be thinking of receiving it in this setting, but perhaps another day. How deeply my question must have touched him. As a minister, Vernon was loved and cared for, ministered to in these days by his pastor, District Chairman Geoff Clark, while his many ministry friends also called on him.

In just a short time, his health declined. As much as everyone hoped and prayed for his recovery, it seemed clear that his life and energy were leaving him. How can anyone be ready for that day? Not spiritually, but ready to let go of dreams, of family, of unfinished goals, of life?

IN THE MIDST OF THIS, the life of the circuit went on. Meetings and gatherings continued. Such events as the national Guy Fawkes Bonfire Day on November 5th were observed. My sister's family from Alabama arrived for their visit, and we were able to share some of the highlights of the area in day trips to Chatsworth, Nottingham, and other spots. Ann and Bobby's adult children had come on the trip, and this was a chance for them to meet their son Darrell's Spanish girlfriend, Nuria, who would later become his wife. The family got to worship in my churches, to meet the people, to see the countryside I loved. At Nether Heage, they almost doubled the attendance. It was a good visit, yet framed by this life-holding situation. This was their first trip abroad as a family, a very special occasion, a splurge for the family. Later I mailed the Christmas newsletter to friends at home, looking back on these weeks and giving some word about the illness, as well as sketchy insights into the wonderful family visit.

These two worlds—life-and-death with Vernon and the circuit and the anticipated fun-filled tourist days of the first family visit—seemed to stand against each other, yet this is the fabric of life itself. I did not want to spoil my family's vacation time over here; I did not want to remove myself from the crisis of ministry and life occurring in the circuit. It was perhaps my first experience at the difficult rub of life in which ministers—and all people—sometimes find themselves: life stops, life goes on.

I WENT TO VERNON'S HOME on a Saturday night, aware that this was both a pastoral visit and a personal visit. It was likely that he was now in the last hours of his life. When Patrick and I arrived at the home on Hickton Road, Anne and the girls were there, as was Geoff Clark and a few close friends.

My time in those hours was divided between sitting downstairs with the girls and sitting upstairs in the room with Vernon, Anne, and the nurse. This was a home of such deep love and sharing of life. Now the family was sharing in the experience of death. The girls and I sat in the middle of the floor in the downstairs hallway, as they told stories of earlier years, funny stories as minister's children, special times with family. The talk and chatter often came fast and light, yet we were all aware of the movement and sound from the room above us.

Occasionally, I moved upstairs and sat in silence with Anne. At one point as we talked, Anne spoke of how they met: "It was in a Methodist youth group many years ago when we were both young." And how their lives and years in ministry came together—she was a part of his ministry. Mostly, we sat quietly, wanting and waiting now for the pained struggle to end.

After a while I would move downstairs to visit with the girls, standing and visiting in the kitchen over a cup of tea, sitting in the floor in the hallway as we looked at music books and they talked of their many church music experiences—this family that loved music. Then we would move to the living room to sit in the chairs and talk as Tessa the dog came to be loved and assured. She, too, was aware that something unsettling was happening. Alison was sure that her father would not die on Saturday, for it was his deceased mother's birthday; he would wait until the day was over. In his unconscious state, Vernon seemed to live out that fact. He continued to hold onto life. I returned upstairs.

In the early morning hour, we sat on the bed, listened to each breath, and waited. Aware that I had three services the next day, Anne suggested in her quiet voice, "You go on home, you have responsibilities in the morning." I struggled inwardly with the decision to stay or go. I was aware of two pulling thoughts: Death was very near, and I did not want to not be present; yet, the family might need privacy in these last moments. His breathing moved to the irregular rhythm of a slowing pattern. Together, in the silence punctuated by the sighs of last life, we prayed for peace and rest.

I went down to the girls while Anne sat with Vernon, waiting. Together, sitting on the floor, we prayed and hugged, then Patrick and I left, and a close friend remained with the girls. Vernon died twenty minutes later, at five before one on Sunday morning.

THE FUNERAL SERVICE WAS HELD at the end of the week, the day after my sister's family departed for the rest of their visit to other parts of England. Vernon had been able to plan what he wanted in the service led by some of his lifelong clergy friends, with Geoff Clark offering the eulogy. Ministers and friends from all around came to remember this gentle shepherd. Vernon had chosen one of his favorites, Psalms 121, as the Psalter reading.

> *I will lift up mine eyes unto the hills . . . from whence comes my help?*

We enter into pastoral care bringing our own vulnerabilities and needs. In that home of love and care, I perhaps needed to be there, to be a part of the ending that seemed so abrupt and unreal to all around, including me. My first ministerial colleague—alongside whom I worked, who guided me in these first months of ministry here, who had been there for me and had shared a model of ministry I would not forget, who in a brief time was my friend—was suddenly gone. The minister who in one year's time had become loved by all was now no longer here to give the vision and direction to this circuit. His death would obviously shape my work and ministry for the remaining nine months in England.

I had tried in those days to minister with him. And yet in his dying came his offering of ministry to me. This presence at death was an experience I had not known before. I had not been present at the death of anyone before, yet time and time again in my ministry of the following years, I was called upon to be with someone in that moment. I officiated at twenty-plus funerals during the rest of my year in England; while there I would face more deaths, some of which seemed a result of time and some a vicious cruel turn of fate. I returned to America to a ministry setting of aging congregations, where I often faced the oncoming of death on many occasions.

And then in my own life, my personal family would also know sudden illness, unexpected death, and deep loss. Eight years later, our oldest son Doug had a very brief flu-like illness that was also an undiagnosed cancer, and then only a week later died from it; we too sat by his side, stunned and unable to do anything except to sit and love him. Being there with Vernon, Anne, Alison, and Elizabeth helped shape me for my own future.

In a jubilee year of life, I began to see my own mortality in a more realistic light. Life itself is both fluid and fragile. In your thirties and forties, unless you have faced a major crisis, do you sense the terminality? I'm not sure I did. But now, in the sudden change of life circumstances of a friend and mentor my own age—who was too quickly and too soon taken from his family, his ministry, his intended future—life and death take on new meaning.

Life Goes On

THE SHOCK OF VERNON'S DEATH continued to move within us all, yet the events of November continued to play out.

As Thanksgiving approached, Davis and I realized that this traditional occasion is an American observation. Though this was not their holiday, people in the circuit sensed that this was a time for reaching out and supporting us. And so, Thanksgiving took on a fuller face. An occasion for only two became a rich time of sitting at the table with many as cards from both sides of the ocean welcomed the day.

For our Thanksgiving Day feast for two, I attempted to locate the ingredients we needed for a proper observance meal but discovered that what we Americans take to be readily available items are not necessarily so in England. The shopping trip in our small town to find ingredients for our American traditions was an adventure in itself. We did not have pumpkin pie, because we could not find cans of pumpkin. We did not have cornbread dressing because I could not find cornmeal. Our very fresh turkey still had a few feathers in it. And the can of cranberry sauce was not to be.

Davis and I celebrated the day by cooking a turkey and whatever creative trimmings we could find and having a delightful sit-down meal, just the two of us. Feeling fulfilled in our meal, we talked with family during the day. Patrick and Jacque Dawson invited us over for a Friday Thanksgiving dinner, where they and the Wood Street young adults surprised us with a full Thanksgiving meal, complete with pumpkin pie made fresh from real pumpkin. Karen had worked to make the pie from scratch, a feat I had never done. The side dish of baked potatoes came with English condiment of slaw. A lovely mix of English and American, it was a welcome surprise and another gift from caring folks. Thanksgiving weekend came to a close, and we eagerly awaited family's arrival in December.

A Heartwarming Experience

REV. MICHAEL MOOKERJI, the Anglican vicar at St. James Church in Codnor, had invited me to preach at the annual community civic service held in the last week of November to recognize the civic community leaders, who come with official medallions and titles. I had given adequate work on the sermon and felt good about it. When the time came in the service for me to ascend to the pulpit and begin to preach, I started off with great energy and enthusiasm. Soon I noticed that folks were stirring, leaning forward, beginning to show great interest. This did not seem normal for the English congregations I had experienced, but perhaps, I thought, a little Wesleyan fire was beginning to burn. So I took on the communal energy and lifted the sermon a notch.

Then I began to notice that, in fact, folks were looking beyond me, to the chancel area. Turning to see where the object of their attention lay, if it were not my heartwarming sermon, I discovered that actually a candle placed too close to the altar curtain had kindled a small smoke screen that would at any second break into full fire flame unless immediately deterred.

"Could someone please extinguish that candle?" I humbly inserted into my sermon script. A willing choir member instantly responded, and with the fire of the spirit snuffed out, I continued a somewhat subdued and less expectant charge to fan the flame of love in this community. It was a night to remember.

THE FULLNESS OF TIME, of fall known as autumn, of falling leaves and changes of life, of settling in and sudden startling, had brought us through the season. The changes brought changed responsibilities, changed needs and priorities. The rituals of baptisms, wedding plans, and unexpected funerals, the beauty of family and community bonding and holding together, all was becoming a rich palette of life. Still reeling from the circumstances, now we moved into December.

Holy One of before life, of life, of death, of after life, touch and bless this dear family in their loss and life, be with this circuit in its ongoing, be with me that I might not expect more of myself except to offer your presence in this place and to feel your presence in the journey. And even in the midst of the pain, how thankful we are for your child and your servant, Vernon. May we never forget his spirit, his care, his faith witness. In the midst of loss, may memory and love prevail.

Watch over my sister's family, as they have shaped memory, have experienced this land and place, have opened their circle of love to include another, and have blessed me with their visit.

In this season of changes, this time of life thanksgiving, the meaning of love, of family, of life's preciousness deepens. May these hills around us lift our spirits, may the occasions of joining together in joy, commitment and blessing, in sorrow and remembrance nourish and strengthen us, binding us together in love.

CHRISTMAS GREETINGS TO FAMILY AND FRIENDS, FROM ENGLAND

Christmas will soon be here, an English Christmas awaits. The last two months have been quite busy for me and have thus passed rapidly. The fact is, we move into the Christmas season in the midst of all the mixed realities of life.

In my seventh week here, my colleague Vernon Cracknell, age 51, was discovered to be very ill and died three weeks later, on November 12. That obviously has impacted the nature of my work here. We have reassigned circuit administrative/ministerial matters, a neighboring superintendent has assumed responsibilities as acting superintendent, and a retired minister has picked up pastoral responsibilities for the other section. But for everyone the grieving, healing process continues. Vernon's wife Anne and college-age daughters Alison and Elizabeth, who welcomed me so warmly, are now facing their future steps. Keep all in your prayers.

*We also celebrated the first much-awaited family visit as my sister Ann and family spent a wonderful week with us in November, where, as typical Americans, they covered the whole of England in a few days' span. They were able to visit some of my favorite places: North to York and its Viking history, a local walk in Robin Hood's Sherwood Forest and Nottingham city, south to Warwick Castle, Coventry Cathedral, Shakespeare's Stratford-on-Avon, the Georgian city of Bath, and mysterious mystical Stonehenge. Then we told the family goodbye as Bobby drove them on to London and its perilous traffic. While here, Steve the architect created a marvelous memory journal of picture and word as he sketched his way through the adventures. Kenneth arranged a guided tour through the city hall of

Nottingham, seeing jewels and all. At the end of the visit Darrell and his guest Nuria headed back to Spain, while Ann, Bobby, and other family flew home. Ann says this was her first but definitely not her last international trip—she's coming back.

*Davis has been to Scotland twice and to Ireland, and now has become one of those crazy left-sided drivers, stick shift and all. The first snow has fallen, last week while I was at a retreat at Bath and Davis was out on his own on the roads, discovering Oxford. Following the retreat, in a sweeping circle we dashed to Glastonbury, headed home, and have had snow ever since.

*We have begun to share Christmas customs and carols and have learned that we don't sing the same carols, at least not the same words or tunes. *"What Child Is This"* is not on their best-loved list; they know it as the folk song *"Greensleeves."* We have services of lessons and carols to look forward to, and I have been invited to bring the word for the Christmas Eve Midnight Mass at the Anglican Church.

*AND, soon more family comes. Saturday the 16th Carl and Dan arrive, joined on the 23rd by Doug, Becky, and Collier. After that, as Becky says, I can just sit and hold the baby. Carl flies back on the 1st, Davis on the 4th, and the rest on the 6th. I will be home in January for an all-too-quick week, when I hope to see some of you then. Davis will reenter the wonderful and challenging track of studentdom.

We wish each of you a joyous Christmas, a marvelous Boxing Day, and a happy new year!

Love,
Kay & Davis,
and the arriving family members

$\mathscr{D}$ECEMBER: *A Christmas to Remember*

But Mary kept all these things and
pondered them in her heart.

Luke 2:19 KJV

$\mathscr{I}$t is a fact of life that no one can anticipate what any month, any week, any day will hold. This community that had known a difficult loss in November would face a December containing both joy and, again, sudden surprising sorrow. By our very living, we are invited to face each day, each new dawn with hope and expectation, and to face each new challenge with the love and communal support upon which our inner faith is founded. So it was here, the joys of the season, the unpredictable pain of circumstance. Is that not a reality of the Christchild story? But first, the family arrived.

A Family Christmas to Remember

"WE'VE LANDED!" THE PHONE CALL CAME.

Davis and I had looked forward to the gathering of all the Muterts for the holidays, and the time had finally come. Carl and Dan arrived first, landing at London Gatwick after an almost-missed plane and a marathon trip over. By midafternoon they were in Ripley, driving up the same hill and curve Davis and I had taken four months ago. Before they barely settled in, Carl and I were out again for the evening.

Codnor Hens and Roosters had invited us to join them for their annual Christmas dinner, this year at a quaint little French bistro in a charming eighteenth-century building in Wirksworth village. A group of couples and friends who have shared life, laughter, and story over many years, the women of the Hens and men of the Roosters each meet on a regular basis and often go on yearly holidays as a group. They had already included me in their gatherings and now extended that hospitality. Glenis and Geoff arrived at our door right on time, and once again I left the driving to them.

The quaint bistro glowed with candlelight, sparkling lights, and bits of holly, silver balls, and ribbon. Sitting around the white-clothed tables in our warmly lit dining room, we were served the several courses of food everyone had selected weeks earlier. As we ate, we all chatted comfortably of flights, sports, weather, life, even their minister, as the group made Carl feel welcome. We sipped the final cups of coffee, said goodnights, and headed home in the cold winter night's air. Stars twinkled overhead. Padded with good food and a warm blanket of air from the car heater, we had a sleepy ride back to Ripley, both glad the Quibles had driven us for the evening. While we were gone, at Nine Clumber Close Dan crashed deep into the cushy lounge couch—not a sound was heard from him until morning.

Our first days of family holiday began with Sunday's rhythm. A silver tinsel Christmas tree decorated with its blue, red, and green balls greeted worshippers arriving in Wood Street's sanctuary for morning worship. Gathering in the sanctuary as the congregation does every Sunday, people on this day extended extra warmth and greeting. From the greeters at the door to the young adults, from the left and right—all made my family feel welcome. They too had looked forward to having these visitors.

People settled into the pews when Tony's prelude called us to worship. At communion time I was very aware of my family's presence. With other worshippers they moved out of the pews, walked down the side aisle, knelt at the rail, and waited to be served a first communion from me in my new role.

"The body of Christ is broken for you."

I looked into their faces, seeing beyond the jet lag to the love in their eyes. I hoped that in this setting they somehow could feel how much I loved them yet could also understand my love for the work I was now doing. The transition of one's life touches the lives of all around. I had felt supported in it, but this trip combined both the expectation of family fun and the occasion for them to witness my new work and this new place that had beckoned me.

After worship, standing with their teacups balanced in saucers, folks continued to welcome and greet the family. Of course, conversations about golf and golf courses floated in the air. "Are you going to St. Andrews?" some wondered. "Depends on the weather," was the reply.

For Sunday lunch we drove out the A6 into the Derbyshire Dales to the picturesque ivy-covered greystone Derwent Hotel, which is situated at the turn of the road before the bridge in Whatstandwell in the dale by the River Derwent. A chalk-written black slate board out front announced that Sunday roast was on the menu.

Across from the car park, the entry unfortunately led into a cigarette smoke–encased jukebox area, a given of many pubs in those years before smoking bans. After moving past that smoky entry, the setting is nice. The food is good here, and beer is served in traditional pint glasses with fill markers etched at the top—two of them take-home souvenirs from the owner.

Following a tasty roast lunch, Dan wanted to go for an English countryside walk, a good thing after a day of flying. The steep, winding, narrow hillside road led several miles up from Whatstandwell to Crich village, at the top of the hill, where my afternoon service would take place. Located in this village is the Memorial Crich Stand, a landmark that can be seen from miles around like a candle in the darkness. A rarity on inland cliffs, it is a beacon light stand situated 340 meters above sea level and dedicated to the fallen soldiers of WWI from the Sherwood Foresters Regiment, from the counties of Nottinghamshire and Derbyshire. According to the family's wishes, I let them out there. Their plan was to enjoy a leisurely stroll back down from Crich Stand to the inn while I led the Crich Chapel midafternoon worship service.

"No problem—this will be great!" they proclaimed. After my service I would collect them back down at the inn. Without two essentials of English walkers, walking boots and an official marked ordinance map showing public paths, the guys tackled the steep descent through pasture and farms, through bog and muck, sheep and cow and bull, more bog and muck, down, down, down. When I arrived at the inn to collect them, they declared that they had now officially retired from English walking trails. The entrancing aroma of pasture lingered on their shoes.

With evening descending, we drove to the little village of Nether Heage, with its lovely guardian windmill, which this year only had four sails on it; two had been removed for repair. Inside the chapel, the dozen or so villagers present for communion warmly greeted my family. Carl, Dan, and Davis moved up the high steps of the little chapel to the top level of pews and settled in the golden glow of the interior to again experience the worship of these little congregations. What different worlds they came from, my American family and these village worshipers, but again the welcome was good.

Monday brought the first opportunity to experience their great love for golf here in the area where I lived. And Davis now had his regular playing partners to play with.

Morning skies were blue and clear, the weather crisp but not cold. Breadsall Priory is located only a ten-minute drive from Ripley in a beautiful pastoral setting, found down narrow winding roads. Lovely old priory grounds have been converted into an elegant resort that includes a first-class golf course and a workout spa area with pool, steam, and sauna. It was evident they would repeat this journey.

A biting-cold grey Tuesday did not deter the plan for another golf outing, this time at Allestree Park down toward Derby. The Allestree course is within a large country park I had not yet seen, with three hundred wooded green acres surrounding Allestree Hall. Visiting it via the golf course in December grey may not offer the same beauty as on a clear spring afternoon when all is in bloom, but we still felt as if we were characters in an English epic scene. In the bitterness of the winter day, I walked as they played the course with great energy. It was an invigorating, actually a *shivering*, round of golf by guys with Southern blood; none of them wanted to admit to the cold, but all were glad when the round ended.

"Should there be severe weather, the service will be held in the Methodist Church, Mill Lane."

The backside of the printed program stated the alternative location for the evening's Codnor community Christmas carol sing, something I looked forward to very much. Although the event was scheduled for outdoors at the marketplace where the village clock stood, the cold wet of afternoon had turned into falling snow, just the right touch for a picture-postcard English evening, but increasingly heavy snow led us to move indoors. I arrived to a magical setting of flakes flurrying down, folks young and old bundled in brightly colored woolen scarves and mittens, sounds of laughter and greeting, hugging and chatting, with people pouring in until the rooms were overflowing with the energy of Christmas, a joyous Dickens moment.

The carols began. From up front where I was helping lead the singing, I saw the family arrive in the crowded back of the chapel, as friends from Hens and Roosters eased through the mass of people to welcome them. Representatives from the Anglican church and Methodist chapel read the traditional scriptures, and everyone sang in the lovely four-part singing I had come to enjoy here:

"O little town of Bethlehem, how still we see thee lie . . . ."
"Once in royal David's city . . . ."
"O come all ye faithful, joyful and triumphant . . . ."

As the caroling ended, the hospitality team began serving steaming hot chocolate and biscuits. Warmed in spirit and body, folks were prepared to go back out into the still-falling snow, with cars now covered and footprints long gone in the deepening layer of white.

And the Family Christmas Continues

As a family we had planned to drive south toward Dover for a Channel crossing and a few days in Europe. After all was sung and said and crowds had dispersed, Codnor church folk were concerned to see us off at that hour in such increasingly dismal weather. But in the darkness of the evening and lateness of hour, we left on an unforgettable midnight drive down the M1. The wind was whirling; snow, sleet, and hail falling; visibility was minimal; yet still we drove on, heading to the white cliffs of Dover. We traveled in two cars—Dan and I in my little red Vauxhall and Carl and Davis in the rented car. We are most fortunate that we arrived anywhere, as we struggled to see and maneuver.

"Turn here!" "Watch out! That truck isn't slowing down!" "There! That's the lane we need, over there!"

We made it, but not without gratitude for safe arrival.

Leaving my car at the port, we now traveled in the other car with Dan as navigator and Carl driving. In a memorable mere two days we saw Belgium, Germany, Luxembourg, and France, and then it was time to travel back to continue our English Christmas. Regrounded on English soil and glad to see that my car was still at the Dover port, we reclaimed the two-car entourage and moved inland to Canterbury, where we located a comfortable inn right in city centre.

Canterbury is a magnificent old city, full of ancient tales and holy places. Its twisting old lanes and narrow streets eventually lead to beautiful Canterbury Cathedral. Passing through its entrance gates, we faced the well-known elegant edifice silhouetted by a pale grey evening sky. As in past visits, I marveled at the cathedral's great ascending-to-heaven lines and intricate carved lacework. The grounds surround and protect the building with a peace and subtle tranquility built on centuries of guard. Pausing to view the elegant spires from the approach, we then walked farther into the entry drive and took a quick evening tour of the open areas. There would be daytime visits for the interior, but the visit by night catches the shadowed image of its long and dramatic history.

As we left the grounds and re-entered the energetic evening life of the town, along one street I realized we were passing Canterbury Methodist Church. Still under the shadow of the mother, it was not quite the minster, but it too had a stately exterior. Later in the evening we enjoyed the city itself; we older ones headed for a little Italian restaurant, while the younger guys went to discover more of the present-day city life. Back at the hotel, the many night street sounds never interfered with a good night's restful sleep.

Doug, Becky, and Collier's arrival day had now come. Before leaving Canterbury, Carl and Dan unloaded their car into mine, making space for new luggage, and traveled across southern England to Gatwick to pick up the arriving travelers. Lingering in the city, Davis and I returned for a closer daytime look at the minster, which continued to reveal its beauty and grace as the day's sunlight highlighted the lines and crevices of the pale beige cathedral. On a city side street, we discovered *The Tales of Canterbury*, a pre–virtual reality sound-and-smell experience of the legends of the city, although the smells here did not come close to matching the aromas of our Plymouth travel-back-in-time. We were then off on our way home.

The preceding day, after driving to Dulles airport from their home in Virginia, Doug and family had barely made their plane but then waited forever on the runway. At the end of a long over-the-Atlantic flight with a baby, who was a great little traveler, they finally arrived at Gatwick two hours late and discovered that their luggage did not make the flight. But the waiting welcome car greeted and transported them home to Ripley.

In the early winter night as darkness had fallen, both cars arrived safely home at Nine Clumber Close. The house soon was filled with the chaos of family, and it liked the feeling. Our exhausted travelers, baby Collier included, bedded down and began to catch up on sleep. The fact that they were suitcaseless did not seem to matter. With the sweet smell and sound of a baby, breathing sighs of tired bodies, creaks of extra footsteps up and down the stairs getting ready for the night, all gradually settled into a restful lull of sleep and silence.

But as my family settled in here, I went up to my office to check phone messages and discovered shocking news about the family of a friend and church member.

FROM THE INITIAL TIME I met Ruth as one of the funny-faced clowns in my first preaching visit at Waingroves, I had appreciated her life and sparkle. She was active in the church and the community and was a teacher at a local college in the field we used to call home economics. Her husband, Dave, was an officer in the Derbyshire police force, and their two sons, Matthew and Andrew, were a part of the Waingroves chapel youth. I did not know them well, but I remember clearly a conversation I shared with Ruth one autumn Sunday.

She had come to church that cool grey morning wearing a full-length navy-blue wool winter coat. Ruth and her friend Maureen were standing about halfway back in the chapel, on the right side as I faced them. Ruth wore a red AIDS ribbon pinned to the lapel of her coat. The only other individual I had seen over here with the small crimson looped symbol was Judi Smart, my ministerial colleague from the South Normanton circuit. I had a particular concern for and response to the disease represented by the red-looped ribbon.

Our own family had been touched by this devastating syndrome, when a decade earlier, someone very dear to us had died from the complications of AIDS at a time in the early 1980s when blood donors were not yet being tested for AIDS. Her death had been a part of the path leading to my recent transition into pastoral ministry. The spring before coming to England I served an internship with an AIDS clinic in Alabama, where I was involved with the establishment of care teams for people living with HIV/AIDS, an experience which meant much to me. In a time when society was not sure about HIV/AIDS or the patients who live with it, I appreciated people who showed awareness, care, and concern.

So on that particular Sunday morning the sight of the red ribbon on Ruth's coat immediately drew me to this woman with wonderful smiling eyes and a lively face framed by her short honey-blonde hair. As we chatted we discovered that our common interests sparked a good conversation and a connection. I knew I would enjoy getting to know Ruth better; I had surely discovered a kindred spirit. Our experiences of teaching and similar concerns gave us many things to talk about, establishing a natural bond between us. But my schedule had not provided much more time for us to visit.

Now came the word of an accident that involved her family.

The Holiday Accident

RUTH'S HUSBAND DAVE, eleven-year-old Matthew, and nine-year-old Andrew were traveling on a Christmas-gift purchasing journey to Manchester to the Manchester United football team shop when their car was struck head-on by a truck attempting to pass in the early morning fog of the Derbyshire countryside. Dave and Andrew were killed instantly; Matthew held on to life, but only precariously. Ruth was notified of the accident at her home by one of Dave's friends from the Derbyshire police force, where Dave had served for many years.

When Ruth and her friend Pam traveled to Manchester Hospital, she was faced with the fact that Matthew would not live. In those long difficult hours at the hospital, Ruth decided to donate Matthew's body for organ donation, an act which ultimately gave five other children an opportunity for new life and health and five families a new lease on life. This act of caring reflected the beauty, spirit, and heart of a remarkable woman, who even in her own loss was willing to give the gift of life.

It is hard to realize that well-known routes, which hold treasures of history and beauty, can be highways of destruction. To get to Manchester, the family had to drive across the Peak District on two-lane roads. They could have traveled on many routes. That day they chose to go by A523. I was gradually becoming familiar with the road network through this beautiful but somewhat barren area, and I later recognized the route Dave had chosen. While traveling in that moment of time, they encountered another vehicle, with a driver making instant decisions. What had been a great Christmas family outing had turned into a tremendous tragedy.

After a few telephone calls and learning more of the situation from acting Superintendent Colin Reasbeck, who had offered his ministerial support in those days, and from church steward Mark Ratcliffe, who also was a close friend of Ruth's, I immediately went to visit with Ruth at her home on Pit Lane, my mind and heart trying to encompass the proportions of the accident. Here I am, celebrating the holidays with my family, and Ruth has lost her entire family in a holiday outing. My heart, my soul ached and grieved for her.

I remember entering her foyer, where we embraced in silence and then moved to the lounge to quietly sit together on the sofa in her softly lit lounge, the fireplace step reflecting the flames of flickering candles as she began to share with me the story of the past two days. Fumbling for words and apologizing to her that my family was visiting and I had not been here at the time, I was rethinking the family plans we had made for the next few days.

I will never forget her loving reply:

"Enjoy your family while they are here. Right now I am surrounded by the love and care of my friends, of my family, of this community. I know I will need you later."

These words were spoken from the heart of one who even in her own shock and grief offered love and grace to me. I was completely ready to change our plans, and she offered a wisdom that touched and guided me for all my ministry and years to come. She and the community needed time to just be together, to come to grips with what had happened. We talked about how even thinking about what was needed needed time. The funeral service would not be held until after the holidays, offering everyone space to reflect upon what that service needed to be, the date to be set for a day in January. My days with my family would not impede upon the planning of those community acts of faith and support.

And so, trusting her mothering gift of words and heart, which must have come through such a numbed core of body and mind, I returned to share the presence of my own family in those brief days they were there and to treasure it with a new appreciation of each moment shared. Ruth's words of grace to me in the midst of her deep loss allowed my family visit that Christmas to become a precious memory that would inevitably deepen in its own meaning for us as a family in the years to come. In the light of our Doug's death in later years, this Christmas visit became an occasion to cherish. Significant memories of life shaped in seemingly simple and casual settings become deep treasures when the tragedies of life occur.

This gift also helped shape what I would try to live out in my ensuing years of ministry and life: the word to all that there is nothing more meaningful, precious, or fleeting than the simple present time of life together with loved ones. A family or community held together in love has the capacity to *be* love to one another, held in God's love, in the time of the simplest joy or in deepest grief and loss. This community now moved to live out that understanding of their faith, their love and care.

The days following this convoluted mix of the accident within the holy holiday season were difficult, holding deeply cutting emotions felt by so many: children's fears, pain, questions, and anger, all mirrored in the adults within the community at such a loss. Easily recalled words did not fit these wounds. "How could this happen during Christmas?" the question burned for many. Somewhere in the abyss of reflection in my mind rose the unsettling story of a Christchild birth story built around the slaughter of innocent children, a part of the story not honored in today's world memory. Yet the pain and loss of those families was as real as that felt in this community. And no easy answers come for either.

This event reached far beyond the community into the many corners of the nation touched and pained by it. Children questioned what had happened to those their age, to a father. An entire regional police force grieved the loss of one of its own. Adults dealt with guilt that their children lived while Ruth's family was gone. All questioned how such loss could ever be faced. Ruth's deep faith and inner strength supported others around her, but such grief cannot be contained. How devastating life had become, and no one could change that. This close-knit community simply poured out its love and care for her and for each other.

There are no good answers to the difficult questions of a time like this. In such a situation traditional faith verbiage fails. The only response is to hold each other in love, honoring the myriad feelings present and to somehow believe that the God who loves deeply grieves deeply also. Only a God who had lost a child could offer presence to see Ruth, to see everyone, through, one day at a time. I had not anticipated such losses as these in my first year of pastoral ministry here. But beyond my life as minister, my mother's heart knew that there is no greater grief than this loss of the very ones carried in the womb. How *does* life go on?

These weeks reminded us all of the way the joyous celebrations of life and the difficult profound losses of life walk parallel and hand in hand, with no controls for when or where they intersect. As in my sister's visit coinciding with Vernon's death, the occasion of Christmas adventures was now placed in the light of such a loss as occurred in these days of the holy season. Again, for all, life stops, life goes on.

The remaining months of my time in the circuit were bound together in love deepened by the turns life here had taken. After two major sets of losses, the Ripley Methodist communities of faith took their pain and moved through the season into the months to come, traveling together into the Lenten walk toward the cross seeking Easter resurrection and healing. And for me, Ruth became a dear friend, an *anam cara* on my own journey, as throughout the ensuing years we shared occasions of joy and meaning, of pain and healing, laughter and love.

> *In the Mystery of life and death, which is beyond any comprehension, may sacred presence be with a community in its grief at the presence of cruel death, with a mother and wife in the depths of the valley, with me as I live in ministry and community with the people in this place and time. So may we all be upheld.*

Christmas Eve

IN THE LIGHT OF WHAT HAD HAPPENED in the life of the community, to tell of continued family experiences seems abrupt, a juxtaposition of conflicting emotions and events. Yet it is the way life occurs, timing not always making sense, or coming easily. In the decision that family plans would move forward for these days, we as a family began to share the traditions of both home and here, of personal and communal, in the weavings of the holy days, the anticipated family experiences and the community events.

My family had all been apart for the past four months, since the goodbyes at the Atlanta airport; it was hard to realize that the family was now here, all together for Christmas Eve and Day, gathered in Ripley, England. At the Sunday morning service, I had shared the news of Doug's family arrival without suitcases; soon after lunch, in true Christmas spirit, folks began to knock on the door of the manse, bringing gifts of food and clothes for the baby and parents.

These special times of Christmas Eve and Day were a spiritual rhythmic pattern I had observed all my life. I loved the sense, sound, and aroma of Christmas Eve gatherings, whether in early evening or late night, whether as a formal high celebration in a massive sanctuary aglow with magnificent Chrismon trees and hand candles held high or as a simple home gathering around the Christmas tree to light the final candle of a small Advent wreath and tell a well-known story. Now I came to this moment in England, where it was shaped by the loss of a family, the presence of a family.

For the late-night hours of this Christmas Eve, I had been invited by the Codnor Anglican vicar to help lead the traditional midnight communion service at St. James

Church. To be a part of this holy English Christmas Eve service in the setting of St. James was a unique and memorable experience, and having the family present added to the meaning. I went on to church early, and then near service time the Muterts arrived and filled the back pew of the chilly and dimly lit stone sanctuary, coming to hear a sermon and service led by mom. Ruth had also indicated that she planned to attend the service; this was where she wanted to be. As worshippers gathered I watched for her, then moved back to speak with her as she arrived with a friend. The sanctuary continued to fill with people from throughout the community coming to share in the beauty of this late-evening observance.

"Beloved in Christ..."

So began the bidding prayer of a ritual shaped by the tradition of the years. Together, we and the congregation created the familiar rhythm of alternating litanies, songs, and readings of the night. Again in this pulpit I brought the meditation. Then Rev. Mookerji, celebrant of Holy Communion, stood before the high altar and prepared the elements as I knelt at the side. Silently, I gave thanks for his inclusion of me in the life of his church, for this moment and occasion. After reciting the prayer of thanksgiving, he and I shared the elements of bread and cup. The warm heady bit of wine in my mouth brought a warm taste of the mystery of the sacred, a sense of the holy presence in a story meant to intersect with our own stories and lives.

With the aromas of old stones, burning candles, and rich wine mingling in the air, Rev. Mookerji and I moved to the rail and began to serve the congregation as the choir and organist provided a beautiful blanket of music. Starting with the front pews, the congregation began row by row to stand, walk up the stone steps through the blessing of choral sound from both sides of this split chancel, and approach the communion rail. With others, Ruth and Maureen rose, joined the pilgrimage, and knelt down. These elements of wafer and cup were our reminder of the deep stirring spirit of holy Love of all time and place present in this moment, present on this evening, present to uphold and embrace, unseen, unheard. Bringing her grief held in her faith, coming in the fact that in a moment life was changed, Ruth knelt alongside others, who brought their own brokenness, their own needs and joys, to the rail in this Christmas Eve hour.

A few minutes later, all the Muterts stood, moved from their pew down the long centre aisle, walked up the stone steps into the chancel, and knelt at the communion rail. I gazed upon them and realized how blessed life has been for this family, so filled with opportunity. Now we shared the gift of this *kairos* moment, a time beyond time envelope. Rev. Mookerji led the way in serving them, pausing to offer blessing on little Collier, and then moved down the rail.

As I stood in front of Doug and Becky, I laid my hand on my little five-month-old grandson's curly head and offered a blessing; on his first Christmas Eve, Collier was doubly blessed. The practice of blessing infants at the rail in communion, a privilege I hold dear, now became a deeply personal opportunity, to lay my hand on my first grandchild, this five-month-old tot who had traveled with his parents to this place. Feeling his little black tousled hair under my hand, I knew that this was a moment to be cherished. In the same flow of connection I served Doug and Becky as they knelt with him, then moved on to each of the others in turn—Dan, Davis, Carl—offering silent, unseen blessing on each, as all of the family knelt and shared this midnight holy communion at the table. The service ended, but another memory was etched in my heart.

Our two cars traveled home, and then most of us quickly settled into bed. As in all the preceding years of Christmas Eve preparations, I found it hard to go to sleep. So in the pattern of other years, I sat on the carpeted floor of the dimly lit lounge, doing last-minute wrapping and stocking gathering, as the Christmas tree lights blinked rhythmically on and off and played little tinkly tunes of the season. Nutcracker ornaments for each member of the family sent from America by our dear family friend Emily magically danced in the light and sound, keeping me company in the wee hours.

Finally sleep came, but not without thanksgiving. Here, in this little English town of Ripley—where I had begun my new work and found it to be right and rich and meaningful, where I saw life in a pace and focus that was changing me, where I had faced traumas that taught the precious gift of each day lived—here now my family was present in this home, to share love come down at Christmas. The stillness of the night rested on this place.

On this Holy Night, may blessing, love, and protection surround my precious family as they have gathered to be present here. May the one who has just experienced such tragedy, dear Ruth, know the power of love that does not end, in the difficult incomprehensible losses of her precious family. May this community know a presence of love come down at Christmas in a way that speaks to the hurt of all who grieve. May peace be possible in hearts. And may the deep meaning of Christmas break through.

Christmas Day

"MERRY CHRISTMAS!" our morning at the manse began, as sleepers stirred to greet the day. Collier was allowed to follow his own schedule, and it took all our time and energy to get everyone ready for the morning celebration. Stockings and presents would wait until later. Their luggage had arrived, so Becky dressed Collier in the little Christmas elf outfit bought just for this occasion.

"Happy Christmas!" the greetings came. "Merry Christmas!" we Americans replied. And Wood Street came alive for the 10 o'clock Christmas morning informal service. With great joy and energy, young and old gathered in casual clothes and style, greeting and wishing Christmas cheer. The weather outside was crisp and cold, grey winter skies bringing possibilities of snow. Wood Street's sanctuary was filled with the warmth of worshippers gathered to share this Holy Morning. News of the accident had spread to all the churches, and here as elsewhere Ruth was held in love and prayers.

This time the whole Mutert family sat on a pew toward the front, buoyed by Collier's gentle snoring, which he also had shared the previous night at St. James. He would occasionally waken to the sounds of other young voices around him. Excited children who brought their shiny new toys with them to church were eager to skip down the aisles, take a place on the front pew, and tell about their new treasures in a lively show-and-tell moment, showing off cars, dolls, sweaters, a few electronic devices, more dolls, with no end of energy and excitement. We sang familiar carols, and then came the moment for the Luke story, which everyone gathered here knew but loved to hear:

"And there were shepherds gathered in a field, keeping watch over their flock. . . ."

I continued the story to the familiar closing line:

"And Mary kept all these things and pondered them in her heart."

Ah, Mary, how I understand your heart, your pondering. This season itself calls me to think of you, the young mother of the story, the one who was called into a strange and difficult pregnancy, who birthed in a place of straw and hay, who was called to raise a child only to lose a child, to stand by and see his death. In this area, where the rate of teenage pregnancy is high, where living conditions are not easy for some, where a mother has just lost her children, where a mother celebrates her family . . . . Mary, your story is not fully known, but for yourself and for all mothers, you ponder this gift of new life, of that life's journey, of inevitable life's ending. This story we tell on a Christmas morning is your story too.

The small simple gathering in a Methodist chapel, shared with family, came to an end. Collecting our coats, blankets, and sleeping babe, we returned home, the last of my seasonal services now done. The combination of settings—community services, caroling, a beautiful Christmas Eve communion, and informal Christmas morning—had all shaped a memorable experience and observance. Now I turned to share in family activities.

Late afternoon, the tantalizing aroma of turkey floated throughout the house, places were set at the dining table with the Evesham china loaned for the year, and we all gathered round in just the way I had imagined, in anticipation of our Christmas feast. I looked around the table with gratitude, as we joined hands and gave thanks. Then came the English tradition of pulling Christmas crackers. In good English fashion, we picked up the small gold cylinders, pulled on each end, and popped our paper poppers with loud snapping cracks, sending our prizes of small plastic toys and games flying across the room. Out of each broken container we pulled the joke page and the folded paper crowns, donned our colorful king's crowns, and read our jokes aloud to each other. It was a sight to see—the Mutert wisemen here in Ripley. Throughout the years I had collected magi sets for our little wisemen, now here they were, donning these colorful paper crowns, in real life. The scene topped off a picturesque day. Becky spoke in later years of remembering the fun of the crackers.

As the evening continued, we moved to the lounge, all still wearing crowns. We settled into chairs, on the couch, stretched out on the shag-rugged floor, and shared stockings around the tree. Little Collier, in his red-and-green one-piece elf suit and cap, sat propped up with pillows balanced on the couch and ruled the roost. Even when he shared a projectile of milk onto the couch, no one minded. It was Christmas Day in England. Colored lights blinked on and off, while tinkly music from the silver bells played on and on, providing musical accompaniment for what was a very special celebration of family together, in a unique moment and place.

THE NEXT DAYS SHAPED MANY MORE MEMORIES of this Christmas family journey. We had determined that yes, we would go ahead and travel; our time together and the travel were needed gifts for the family. With blizzard snow and power outages in Scotland, we decided to sleep on our decision of which direction to go, but south certainly sounded warmer.

Boxing Day and Beyond

NO ONE AROSE EARLY, NOT EVEN COLLIER. After a good night's sleep, we awoke to Boxing Day. December 26 is a uniquely British holiday, the day on which gifts were given to the English service folk in boxes, thus the name of the day. In the present day, English folk plan family walks and rides in the countryside, perhaps to walk off Christmas meals, and visit friends for tea and Christmas cake, in a holiday observed by all. Some things are important to remember in this country; the closing of everything on Boxing Day is one of them. On holidays stores and banks are closed tight. So, some intended shopping for our own journey did not occur. Checking the weather report, we decided to go south to Stonehenge. Somewhere around midday, six adults, one infant and car seat, four sets of golf clubs, and many American suitcases fit into two cars. And the after-Christmas experience began.

En route to Stonehenge is historic Oxford, the well-known historic bastion of learning. We took a long walk around the campuses, then decided that the best place to visit at that hour might be the local favorite pub of the college crowd. It was filled with energy, noise, and group conversations, giving us a good taste of the atmosphere but not serving food. Directly across the street was an attractive Italian restaurant, complete with red-checked tablecloths, where Doug and Becky graciously treated us to a delicious English Italian dinner.

The mystic energy of Stonehenge was calling us on, as we continued our journey through the winter night. The magnetic pull drew us to Amesbury, close to Stonehenge, as we each anticipated the experience of the awaiting day. A local Travelodge offered us a good night's sleep, which would have us ready for the next morning's visit to the mysterious circle of time-chiseled stone. In our own way we were each pilgrims on a journey—modern pilgrims draped in sweaters, jackets, mittens, and scarves, each at different stages of encounter with the human story. A few hypotheses were formulated

Stonehenge - from the Southwest
10:00am, Nov. 16, 1995

upon the origins and meanings of the site, in a manner typical of our family, with our narratives, our journeys, our storytelling, our hypothesizing. Soon at the end of a long day, lights went out—this time the snoring was definitely not little Collier's.

In time such as this, each day has no name except *the next day*. This was vacation time, and vacation time can melt into unnamed days and places like pats of butter on a warm waffle. As the next day came, we arose for a midmorning English breakfast at one of England's better-known chains, Little Chef. The warmth of food fueled us for the short ride to Stonehenge, but the bitter cold did not go away.

In the midmorning mist, we crossed the short, flat section of the open fairway plain between Amesbury and our destination. Our cars came to a split in the road, where we glimpsed our first sight of the grey megalithic structure, surrounded by grey air, grey clouds, grey cold. In this first frame, the well-known place seems much smaller than it should be. The road leads up to the right, passing close by the formation. A parking sign took us beyond the stones into a lot that offered no other preliminary look at the monuments. In the biting cold, we piled out of the cars while we piled on as much clothing as we could find, stuffed stiff.

From the parking lot, the circle still cannot be seen. English Heritage has fortified the access with an entrance leading down, under the road, and around back up a ramp whose walled murals offer information about the history of the place. We had received our audios; each of us was armed for audio action. In the rain-shaped mist, headsets on, buttons sorted, umbrellas in hand, we began the walk into the past.

There is for me in each visit to Stonehenge an anticipation, a sense of wonder, an energy about what awaits. This is a thin place, both numinous and visceral, stirring emotions and imagination. It is a spot needing some solitary, lone-walking time. No longer are you allowed up close to the stones, as we were on our first visit several decades earlier. The thinking, viewing, circling, wondering now comes from farther away. Fortunately, on such a cold day as this, there were not too many adventurous people filled with wonderment for the past wandering about here. If we could endure the cold and wet, we could at least do it without being pushed and shut off by crowds.

Our large striped golf umbrellas served as shields of weather protection. Doug was "great with child," as a pregnant father might look, with Collier nestled snugly inside his jacket. And each person was free to walk, look, shiver, and ponder at the amazing place and its story.

Our land of America has a history as ancient, but much of it is unknown to many of us, with stories of the past only a whisper of knowing. Yet the visit here leads us back to wonder about the stillness, the silent story of the early civilizations of the Americas as well. The world has so much to tell, or to keep secret, of its age and inhabitants, its science and sacred. Stonehenge is a visual reminder that instant grits is not the only way humans have existed.

We had missed the winter solstice by less than a week, which if the stone circle were a giant solar calendar, would spot the sun right at the apex point on that day, although the sun may have been as hidden on that day as this. But we have been able to grasp a feel for the bitterness of the plains in the grey of winter and to circle and photograph the moment, umbrellas and all. Great grey stones stand on circling ripples of bright green grass, with mounds in the hazy distance, marking a linear track to this site. City and county planning existed long before it became a degreed career—only the blueprints are missing.

The cold had crept in to our head, toes, and body through the many layers of warmth, bringing in all a chilled readiness to move on. This place is indeed amazing. And our little Collier is amazing for having endured it. I wondered if the imprint of sacred place and layers of time entered his cloud of unknowing.

After a chilled connection with ancient minds, we moved on to the steaming waters for ancient bodies, historic Bath. From the plains we traveled west, into rolling hills, lovely farms, and forests. The country road led us up, around, and then steeply down, curving between homes built on the descent to the city, offering a great entry to all who traveled through the centuries to this place.

The street from the car park led down into old town Bath, following the arrows of the street markers. Once there, Becky and I entered a little millinery shop on a side street and selected hats to help shelter us from the cold. Becky chose a black brimmed felt; my royal blue fuzzy floppy remained with me throughout the rest of my England stays. Now we were ready to sightsee in this Georgian city.

Signs led to the not as ancient as Stonehenge but older than most things Roman baths. Wandering and turning through ancient winding tunnels, the amazing labyrinth of waterways is a marvel, ending at the warm baths with hot steam rising into the cool above-ground air. Collier was snuggled like a little warm potato beneath Doug's winter jacket; someday he may gaze at their picture by the side of the bath and wonder where he is in the photo. After a great meandering, we could have lingered at the visually warm poolside, but it was 4 o'clock, and soon time would be up on our parking meters.

As we moved back through the town, we could only manage a fleeting glimpse of Bath Abbey. "Quick, look at those great carved ladders with kids all over them, climbing up and down," someone offered. Bath Abbey's exterior is worth even a short occasion to view, with its ascending and descending cherubs on the front façade. After a glimpse at the outside and a fast walk through the inside of the abbey, it was time to move on.

Bath Abbey Transept

With the help of the maps, we drove west to Bristol's Redwood Lodge, which could have been named the Southwest England YMCA resort. This was definitely this family's kind of place—a sports extravaganza with basketball, ping-pong, workout room, swimming, sauna and steam, and squash courts—truly a great place for a family holiday. Like other families, we shared the fun of activity and competition as a part of the family fabric of memory.

Somerset was an unfamiliar county, but we decided to travel to the seaside town of Minehead, which sits on the edge of Bristol Bay at the foothills of the national park. A wonderful ride around curvy roads, over sea cliffs, through the hedge-fenced fields, brought us to this lovely seaside town. We stayed at the beautiful Northfield Hotel, nestled on sloping landscaped gardens overlooking the bay. This was the perfect place; in the extreme cold weather of the day, their amenities of pool, sauna, and steam room sounded very inviting.

Afternoon tea in the Victorian drawing room proved to be a delight, with the whole group sharing English tea in an English manor. In gentility fashion, Davis and Dan moved to the table by the windows and became engaged in a brotherly game of chess, while the rest of us went for a ride into nearby Minehead village, a medieval moment captured in a place.

"Listen!" Doug's ears picked up the faint chiming of the bells ringing "In the Bleak Midwinter," the beautiful tune that we know for Christina Rosetti's moving poem. In a mercantile store we met an old gentleman who was born in the room above the store and still lived there. Responding to the cold, we completed our late-night shopping with purchases of tights and bootwarmers. Back at the hotel we found our young intellectuals engaged in the same game. Dinner, then coffee around the table in the drawing room, and a family game of trivial pursuit ended the evening.

When morning came, the freezing weather remained settled over the coastline. But as loyal golfers the men decided to weather the weather and went for a game on the links course. Becky, Collier, and I braved the weather on the streets of Minehead and Dunster, then found Cleave Abbey and its ruins. Becky videoed the abbey for future enjoyment in a warmer environment. Leaving Minehead at evening tide on treacherous icy roads, without a reservation for the night's stay, we ended up returning to the Bristol area. Rather than returning to the Redwood Lodge, we tried to find a quaint B&B in Bristol, traveling over the suspension bridge and back, through the back streets of Bristol, finally checking in at the local Travelodge with a morning breakfast at Little Chef, two not-so-quaint institutions of England. Saturday morning brought even more ice than the night before. The road was a virtual skating rink, as the Mutert road trip came to an end. We were on our way back to Ripley, with one weekend to go.

It was good to be home. I prepared a favorite back-home meal of chili, and in good family fashion, the boys said it tasted great. The BSE scare (commonly referred to as mad cow disease) did not stop anybody. The clothes washer might not have been prepared for the sudden barrage it was receiving; we encountered a small drain problem in the kitchen sink. After we solved this problem, dishes were washed the old-fashioned way, carrying the water to the bathroom to pour out.

"No, not in the toilet, in the drain!"

"Oops."

We as a family now knew what happens when the toilet gets too much water in it. The plumber was called to come the next week.

New Year's Eve

ON THIS EVE MORNING, I prepared a home-cooked English breakfast for all, the aromas of baked beans, grilled tomatoes, rashers,* eggs, and toast enticed all to the table. My kitchen was getting quite a workout in these days of visiting family. Weather was not great, but no one lets that stop them in England. Getting folks and dirty clothes into the two cars, we drove into downtown Ripley to drop off the laundry at the one laundromat in town, run by a friendly and helpful lady who received our loads with enthusiasm. Then we proceeded into the countryside via the A6, for a drive up to the Matlock area. Parking the two cars in the large Matlock car park by the train tracks, we placed our parking stickers on the windshields and walked across the little stone bridge into Matlock Bath. After a leisurely stroll along the River Derwent, tea and scones at a little main-street restaurant just hit the spot, while we planned the rest of our afternoon. By now we had developed a good pattern for a plan of action. The cars would separate, each going our own way.

Becky, Collier, and I buckled into my little red car and drove up to Chatsworth, where we found the estate closed, but in the grey mist it held its mystic beauty even from the road. We drove the curving narrow lane through the pastures past the house drive and then turned left into the little village of Edensor, site of the estate village church, where Becky wanted to see Kathleen Kennedy's grave, which is located there. Pulling the car over to a curb, we bundled Collier again, and in the crisp grey mist crossed over into the church grounds up to the back hill where the family graves are located. It is a compelling story, how Kathleen Kennedy found a new life for herself here at Chatsworth, leaving all the glamour of the American Kennedy clan, even to permanently rest in this little English graveyard following her early death. I understand a bit of her heart, in loving this place, this land.

When we walked back to the car, an elderly gentleman, whose attire included a clergy collar, was strolling down the street. Being the village vicar, he shared in a wonderful but too-brief conversation of a few stories of life there. Visions of possibility danced in my head. What a place to serve. I wonder if the sheep who roam and own the fields get blessed.

As we all returned and re-gathered at the house, I realized, it is New Year's Eve in Ripley, with no groceries in the house, stores closed, and probably not too much to do. Good fortune prevailed; by telephone we located a restaurant that could take us, Denby Lodge, known for good steak. Nothing could have been better for New Year's Eve, the evening the family has always celebrated Carl's January 1 birthday, than to be sharing steak with his sons. Local folks considered this restaurant a good place to be also, because the place was packed. People here make reservations very early for holidays like Christmas dinner and New Year's Eve; this time we were lucky. Full and content, we drove back to Ripley, and the old year ended.

In the wee hours of the morning, as I looked back on this year, I felt overcome with emotion at all that had occurred: a year of turning fifty, a first grandchild, a move into a new *vocatio,* a life in another world, the facing of sudden and unexpected events, the joy of family sharing… each New Year's Eve brings endings and beginnings. What a year this had been. I thought of all who were a part of my life and all whose lives I had now become a part. The celebrations and tragedies of this year were a mirror of ongoing life itself. I was grateful for the journey I had traveled and for those who journeyed with me.

> *God of love, I give thanks for these dear family members who have traveled a long distance to be with me, who have supported me in this year. I see the pain of loss of those in this community in this year, and so hope for them the mending touch of the new year that lies ahead. In this wide world as the old year ends and the new begins, may the light of love dawn. May my family, in their various stages of life, know the possibility of the new yet to be. And may I live into the calling that has brought me to this moment. So may it be.*

A New Year Starts, and Goodbyes Begin . . .

AS THE FIRST NEW DAY IN A NEW YEAR DAWNED, trips home began. With all that we had squeezed into these two weeks, everyone was tired. I always find departures and goodbyes at the end of a visit sad, and as this time I was the one being left alone, I suppose I felt each goodbye the most. I continued to be so appreciative of the community here, who knew what it meant for me to have my family with me for these few days. Even in the middle of the accident and the holidays, they had given me space to enjoy this special time that would become a lifelong memory. I had stayed in touch with Ruth and was grateful for those who surrounded her with love.

Carl was the first to leave, on his birthday January 1. Packing the rental car, he then drove down the long M1, back around London on the M25 circle, and finally arrived at Gatwick where he turned in the car, by way of a curb and a lost hubcap on the way into the car return. That story seems somewhat familiar; maybe it's a family thing. Did he make it to Alabama? Yes, but not without another round-the-country flight, a snowstorm, and a fogged-in Memphis on the way. His holiday was now over. He would begin to prepare for the January PGA show in Orlando and the start of another selling season.

Doug, Becky, and Collier packed up in one suitcase; I would bring the rest of the luggage down to London in the boot of my car. They had juggled their several bags throughout the visit, so now they enjoyed a brief taste of a lighter way of traveling. We took them to the train station at Derby, where they boarded for Coventry and an afternoon excursion around that great cathedral. The train carried them on to Warwick, where they located a B&B over a little pub and enjoyed a relaxing evening on their own.

Medieval Warwick Castle held a mix of colors, sounds, sights, and stories to enjoy; even little Collier was a real trouper. He would return many years later to see it again in its festive glory. For now, the seed of medieval adventure were planted. After a great visit, they boarded the train for London, where we would meet them the next day.

Dan, Davis, and I went north to the huge Meadowhall Mall outside the large industrial city of Sheffield. I had not yet visited it, but Dan had read about it and wanted to see an English shopping centre. To get there, we rode the train from Alfreton up to Sheffield town centre, then took a second line directly delivering us to the mall. A ramp from the train guided the crowd of shoppers into a commercial wonderland, complete with twinkling lights, singing bears, fabulous food courts, and lots of stores beckoning. The high energy of the Christmas season was still there, with bustling shoppers returning gifts or hitting the sales, friends just congregating in an indoor place to visit, and children on a family outing. After a few hours of high energy ourselves, we re-located the station, again boarded the train for the return trip, and traveled back

WARWICK CASTLE

through Leister to Alfreton. No looking for the car in the mall's huge parking lot or delays out of the lot onto the motorway or backed-up traffic on the southbound lane—we corporately decided that trains are the way to go in England.

As Dan and Davis spent their next day in front of the television relaxing and playing video games, my thoughts began to return to the work of the community, making several visits and contacts. Our night was a packing evening, as I savored this final evening of family being in my home and knew that soon there would be quiet singleness within the manse.

Morning came, and with it the time for last departures from Ripley. Davis packed up all his belongings plus a few new items back into those blue duffle and golf bags. We fit them into my little car and drove up to Alfreton train station for the beginning of his journey home. Oh, my, this mom did not want to see him go. He had been my support, my family, my company in the house. I had cherished the opportunity to spend time with one son in this way. He had heard about church councils and hard days; we had shopped together and adventured together. He had also sprouted his own wings of adventure, growth, and risk-taking; had traveled and learned to face new experiences alone; to solve problems and to create alternatives. Of course, he had also watched a lot of English television and washing machines and had sometimes found nothing to do, with few friends. He was probably ready to be back in down-home Alabama, but I was not ready for him to leave.

The train pulled into the station, and in the next moments, Davis loaded up with heavy bags and waved his last goodbyes to Derbyshire. I wondered if he loved the countryside like I did. He spent his last English night at an airport motel in Manchester so he could catch the morning flight home to the US, where he would resume his university studies in Alabama.

When I returned to the manse, Dan and I took the tree down, with him guiding the way and doing the hard work. After clearing the house of lingering decorations, we loaded the boot and back seat of the car with our luggage, the golf bags, and the other pieces of Doug and Becky's things, then headed out for the last of our road trips— destination London. With Dan at the map and Kay at the wheel, we made it down the M1 into the heart of London itself. Was I really crazy enough to say, "Sure, I can drive in downtown London into areas I don't know?"

Driving into Islington we located the London Foreign Mission Club and rendezvoused with Doug and Becky, who were back from a morning visit to the Tower of London. Doug's tour there at age twelve with Grandma Dody had floated back into his memory, and he recognized even the placement of street vendors from that earlier visit. Collier's little five-month-old memory might not be so vivid. We caught our breath, then went out again to see London at night.

The iconic view of London's Big Ben and Westminster at night is beautiful, even on a freezing-cold winter night. Warm golden lights bring all the buildings aglow, with shimmering reflections dancing on the city's famous river. Ben reaches up into the sky, and you wait expectantly for him to sing in his mellow voice, "Tah-da-da dah . . . dah da-da tah." In the chilly night air, we strolled out onto the bridge over the Thames River and stood, enjoying the moment and the view. Collier was quite comfortable bundled inside warm jackets. Our evening stroll continued around the Houses of Parliament, up Whitehall via No. 10 Downing Street, on to colorful Trafalgar Square for a taste of the energy of its bustling nightlife, and back via Charing Cross Station. As the full day ended, heads hit the pillows at the Foreign Mission Club for a heavy night's sleep.

I awoke thinking that hopefully Davis made his plane in Manchester. The rest of the clan was ready to tackle the rest of London, literally. Doug, Becky, and Collier made another wonderful excursion, this time Hampton Court, a place Becky had wanted to visit. As Dan and I were in charge of planning an evening at the theater, we decided to try for theater tickets for Les Mis before we saw the Tower of London. Skipping the half-price line, we tried the corner ticket agent.

"Excuse me, you advertise twenty-nine-pound tickets, but all you have are thirty-seven-pound-a-ticket seats? Where are they? Excuse me, what do you mean, you can't say until I buy them? Thank you, but no thanks." We went directly to the Palace Theater, where they say that regrettably the only tickets available are limited view for £6 a ticket. "Where?" Dan asked. "A box over the stage? We'll take them!"

Feeling heady from our success, we journeyed to the Tower of London, enjoyed a great audio tour there, and then traveled to the British Museum for lunch. This site holds more history than could be absorbed in a lifetime. Dan and I covered five or six thousand centuries of history in the next hour. Doug and Becky met us later, and after a few more quick visits to some of the significant displays at the museum, including Doug's stop at the Hammuradi scrolls, we moved on to a meal at Pizza Hut and then walked to the Palace Theatre. What an unbelievably grand experience, this box with limited view over the stage. Collier had room for a little bed on the floor, the adults could lean over the ledge and see the entire production, we could stand up and stretch—what more could we want?—and all at £6 a ticket.

At one point I eased down onto the floor with Collier and lay beside him as the melodies soared into our special VIP booth: *"At the end of the day you're another day older …"* the magnificent chorus sang. *"God on high, hear my prayer …"* Jean Valjean's beautiful mature voice floated up to the spine-tingling last notes of this tender plea for watchful eye over his young beloved one, as my heart silently embraced my first grandchild and this dear family I loved so deeply, each in their own unique place in life. How much we want to protect and uphold our young loved ones, whose lives are shaped on expectancy and possibility. We can only pray and hope that safety enfolds and good life prevails, midst the reality of the turmoil of any time in history, of any moment in any day. Certainly the events of these few months here had brought home to me the reality of the vulnerability of life. This night, this story, this occasion was a time to remember. Finally, a late-night tube ride returned us to our lodging for a night's rest.

On the last morning of our family holiday, while I attended a meeting at the British Methodist Office on Marylebone Road, the others ventured out on their own to discover last bits of London. Doug and Becky visited St. Paul's Cathedral, while Dan located the Bank of England, then all enjoyed a little taste of London shopping. We rendezvoused later at Hamley's toy shop and wandered down Carnaby Street, dashed over to Harrod's for an evening meal and last-minute shopping, and then exhausted, we headed out to Gatwick. Stirring in my own head was the realization that the visit would soon end; folks were returning to their lives in the US.

Doug, Becky, and Collier took the train to the airport hotel, while Dan and I returned to our lodging, loaded up the luggage, and headed out through the heart of London. For whatever reason, we did not have a map with all the streets on it—shades of our European vacation. And with my limited night vision, we wandered through London's black streets in the dark of night, unable to read signs and street names; finally, we

St. Paul's Cathedral
London.

found and crossed the Thames River. Success, "We're almost there, now!" Wrong. Two hours and many near mishaps and side comments later, we have never been so glad to see Gatwick signs in our life—we are there, we think. Wrong again. In an incessantly increasing dynamic of stress, the conversation continued: "What terminal?" "What lane?" "What direction?" "What motel?" When we finally arrived, we warned: "Doug and Becky, don't dare say a cheerful word about what time you got here!" Dan and I totally collapsed. Ah, the joys of travel. I would miss the frolicking fun driving excursions shared with Dan on this holiday visit.

Morning arrived. The motel van carried us to the train for the terminal; after a long wait for Doug and Becky in the luggage check-in line, it was now time for the last of the Muterts to walk through the international flights door. Dan would quickly be resuming his studies at Alabama; Doug, Becky, and Collier were returning to law-school life in Virginia.

What a trip, what a family, how much I love each one of them. How much I appreciate what each person contributed to our Christmas together and Carl's commitment to have them all here. There may not be many other new parents who would dare fly to and travel across England with their five-month-old child as Doug and Becky did—or any built-in foursome who enjoyed the golf courses as much as this group did, even in the cold. The experience would have been incomplete without the presence of each member of the family.

Actually, the trip was not really over. Carl flew back, but flew right out to New York, where he got snowed in. Doug, Becky, and Collier flew to Washington but ended up spending a few nights in a Virginia Holiday Inn before the roads were cleared from a major snowstorm so that they could return home to Crozet. And there was still plenty of house-straightening to do to return the manse to its ordinary order.

The pictures, memories, and stories of this holiday would remain in our minds and hearts. Funny stories became treasured sagas of the family playing together. Balances of personalities while traveling are magnified images of the dynamics of different individuals joined in family relationship while moving in new surroundings. Each one of us, including little Collier, added to the story.

Following Vernon's death, I had looked forward to being with family. This holiday was a chance for us to claim precious time together as lives were changing, young men were growing into adults, a young family was still a part of the larger family, and I was so far away. Through it all we were fully conscious of the fragility of life, of Ruth and all who were hurting, as we inscribed the joys, even the stress, and all the memorable moments of these days into our lives. No one ever knows what lies ahead; we can only encounter the present with the choices of how we claim it. I would be forever grateful for our time together.

This unpredictable month had again held such pain and loss, juxtaposed with the joy of the season, the meaning of my work here, and the gathering of our family. For all that it had known, it was a Christmas to remember.

Eternal love, watch over my family in their travels, their work and studies. May I always claim a grateful heart for the gift of these precious people in my life, near or far. May the trip linger in our hearts as a time of joy and laughter, of memory and insight. For this memory, I am thankful. For those who have graciously enabled us with this time, I offer gratitude.

In the difficult realities of life, may we live incarnate love. May we honor the pain of loss felt beyond any manner of speaking. May some ray of light offer direction for all in the year now beginning and memory of the good in the year now ending.

$\mathcal{J}$ANUARY: *A Time of Covenant*

. . . wherever you may place me . . .
from the Wesley Covenant Service

$\mathcal{H}$ow quiet the drive home on Saturday felt, as the last of my family flew home. I came back to enter a sadly silent and empty but fairly messy house. The boys had helped take the tree down and out, but there were still pine needles to loose from the carpet, stuff throughout the house to sort, and the reshaping of the home to single occupation.

I knew that the week ahead, which included the Hogarth Memorial service, would continue to contain difficult emotions for the community. To begin the week and the year with covenant and communion was a meaningful preparation for whatever lay ahead.

A Day of Covenant . . .

I am no longer my own but yours.
Your will, not mine, be done in all things,
Wherever you may place me,
In all that I do and in all that I may endure:
When there is work for me and when there is none;
When I am troubled and when I am at peace.
Your will be done when I am valued and when I am disregarded;
When I find fulfillment and when it is lacking;
When I have all things, and when I have nothing.
I willingly offer all I have and am to serve you, as and where you choose.
Glorious and blessed God, Father, Son and Holy Spirit,
You are mine and I am yours. May it be so for ever.
Let this covenant now made on earth be fulfilled in heaven. Amen.

The Wesley Covenant Service was an event I had looked forward to since first thinking of my year here. For Methodists the first Sunday of the new year means the Wesley Covenant Service. In a Methodist tradition dating back to 1755 and John himself, we begin each new year by renewing our commitment vows with God through a particular set of covenant words and prayers that Wesley had attributed to the puritans. I now was to share three such services on this day, in three unique settings and situations.

In the quiet cool of the Sunday morning air, Waingroves' church family gathered to love and support each other in the still-new grief process. Others from the community had joined us for the worship time together. Those present spoke the covenant in a new realization of its meaning. When there is nothing, "You are mine and I am yours."

We had shared covenant words together; now we prepared for the communion gift of bread and cup. Ruth and Maureen had been scheduled to be sacrament stewards for this day and had chosen to do so. From the back they entered through the door and slowly walked down the centre aisle of the chapel, carefully holding the covered bread and cup in their hands. Embraced by God's love, which knows no boundaries of joy or grief, we met at the communion table, eyes speaking, as I reached across the communion rail and received the elements. Ruth's presence again spoke silently of this place and community, this God as a haven in the storms of life. These elements were that visible sign of the love by which they lived their lives. In the quiet, I offered blessing and thanksgiving, silently raised and broke the little bread roll, then lifted the cup. Together we tasted the reminders of Love's presence, then moved to serve others who came forward.

In the blanket of covenant words and bread-breaking reminder of the brokenness of this community, Ruth's presence was a witness to her deep faith, which sustained her. She was not there out of any "should be"; she was present where her heart called her. The covenant words were a chance for all to express belonging, to acknowledge the brokenness of life, to hunger for understanding, to be held in communal love. The holy sacrament became nourishment for moving into the emotion of the next few days for this community and the memorial services that lay ahead. In a painfully unique setting, the words and acts of the ages brought life and meaning.

After the service I stood at the back door greeting people as they left. Longtime member Fred Grace shook my hand in a grasp so tight I could barely focus on his words as I felt my fingers curling within his strong grip. I knew to expect this and always tried to prepare and protect my hand for such a strong greeting. Fred and Edna were pillars of the church; Fred was a local preacher and a well-known community leader.

Their son John had followed their footsteps of service and commitment. Fred knew the roots of his tradition; he knew the value of reclaiming covenant words. His was a life of service, this strong-willed, tall, straight-backed, gruff-looking gentleman now crushing my fingers and offering a good word for this covenant day. Even with his hearing escaping him, Fred missed little. "Good service!" he growled as the church family left this place of love.

Crich's afternoon service at Wesley Chapel went a markedly different direction. Driving west past the Excavator pub, then turning right under the stone rail viaduct and up the steep hill, I moved past the cottages and stonewalls bordering the curving road, farther up into the little village sitting at the top like icing on the cake. As I made this drive and eventually turned left into Chapel Lane, I realized the expectancy and anticipation I felt. Like the first time I had preached at Crich, knowing then that this was a setting where John Wesley had preached during his ministry and lifetime, I now eagerly awaited the opportunity of saying the Wesley covenant words in this historic little place.

When I pulled into the small parking area outside the chapel and quickly entered the door with little time to spare, church steward Cheryl Love met me, escorted me into the small vestry room at the back, and spoke.

"It seems the covenant service books are missing," she informed me. *"Calm, now, quick thinking is needed,"* my mind said.

"Not to worry, my dear," Cheryl suggested. She then walked to a storage shelf and pulled out old service books I had never seen and went dispersing them to the waiting congregation, handing me one as I walked down the aisle and up to the lectern. And so the service began, with the first notes of the organ. *"Please let him play a long introduction,"* I uttered my own inner invocation.

The congregation stood and enthusiastically sang the verses of the opening hymn, while I began comparing the services: *"Not the same, immediate drop back and punt moment!"* The cold air in the sanctuary was not the only chill I was feeling. We negotiated through opening prayers and collects, then, as the congregation sang the next hymn, I flipped through pages to find the next section. Thank goodness for hymns.

"Now turn to page seventeen," I confidently announced to all. Who can preach a sermon when you're wondering where to turn next. There is a definite advantage in already having done a sermon earlier in the day, albeit in a different setting: at least the words have a familiar taste.

We were then into the covenant itself. Now, what page, what line, what word? Remarkably, we made it through together, sharing the Wesleyan words in full unity. For the second time of this day I listened and heard the voices speak as I too spoke:

"I am no longer my own but yours . . . ."

With these historic familiar words now spoken in this space and in hearts, we were able to continue in the planned routine, moving to the communion books. Cheryl had taken the beautiful old silver-weathered communion pieces from the antique Wesley cabinet for the occasion, giving us another way we felt connected to the roots of this particular Methodist story. This little church family who had known two centuries of church life and activity and who now struggled to find the energy and support to continue as a congregation, moved to the rail to receive bread and cup and give thanks for God's covenant love and grace. In the fullest sense, we had witnessed to the reasons for having this particular tradition.

The final covenant service of the day was at Codnor's evening worship. With their usual energy, commitment, and love of liturgy, they enthusiastically embraced the worship occasion. By that time, family goodbyes, covenant fatigue, and general exhaustion were settling into my brain and body.

At the end of the day, I was certainly feeling "poured out." These new people in my life had already lived all our first months in covenant to receive and accept me with all my acts of humanity. As in the words we had spoken this day, God's covenant love would see me through to be present with them in the last half of my ministry here.

In these covenant words was much to consider. What does it mean to be no longer one's own, to offer all one has to serve as and where the Unknown chooses? Work . . . none, troubled . . . peace—the terms used in lines of the prayer call forth realities of life and point to a renewed way of living, no matter what the life circumstances. In this year, as in any, it is the new year's glimpse into ongoing living with a covenant Being.

Holy one, when I find fulfillment and when it is lacking, when I have all things, and when I have nothing, I hope to offer what I have and who I am to serve your centered being of love. In creation, redemption, sustenance is life. May it be so forever. Let this covenant now made be fulfilled in endless time.

From the Journal

Come unto me, all who labor and
are heavy-laden, and I will give you rest.
Matthew 11:28

7 JANUARY, AFTERNOON

I AM TIRED, AND I HAVE ONE MORE COVENANT SERVICE TO DO. At the Waingroves morning service, of course all are still heavy there. Even in the heaviness, their love, faith, and care shine through.

In the afternoon I visited with a member whose granddaughter, age twenty, died of mastitis over the holidays. That has something to do with the breast. She was breastfeeding her week-old infant, and it seems that neglect over the holidays may have contributed; the doctors did not check on her. What a painful loss that is.

Then, another member spoke with me about a fifty-year-old niece in the hospital critically ill, needing dialysis, and she wants him to give her the treatments at home—a decision he is trying to think through. How much that will add to his life and responsibilities, but I know his heart.

Tomorrow I have a morning appointment with a Codnor mother who doesn't even know Ruth but is herself distraught over the tragedy. I will also travel to Derby to visit the niece in the hospital, attend a pastoral care group night meeting that they forgot to tell me about, and visit with Ruth later in the evening.

For right now, I am trying to find the energy for this last night service. But, I know it will come. And so will rest. May all these dear people who are hurting and grieving also find rest.

A Village Joins Together in Love

WAINGROVES' STEWARDS HAD PREPARED THE CHAPEL for the funeral service. The Derbyshire police force organized the processional.

As the day and time came, villagers, friends and neighbors, coworkers, young and old, gathered along the way in Waingroves to share their love. The police force lined up in honor brigade on the main road as it ascended up the hill, forming a holy road to the chapel. With overflow fullness inside the little white chapel that meant so much to this village, loudspeakers offered the outdoor crowds the opportunity to be a part of the service. Voices from within and without joined in the songs, listened with love and memory to the stories, and shed tears in the loss felt so heavy by so many.

Following the service, our motor brigade moved slowly through the green hills and winding curves of the Derbyshire countryside to the Derby crematorium, where once again, the county police force lined the drive. Again a chapel overflowed with people who had come to support Ruth, to express love and grief in their own hearts, to show care and love from the community. The sacrament of goodbye for Dave, Matthew, and Andrew found its way into the hearts of all who attended.

Much later, in a quiet moment, the ashes were laid to rest.

Across the Ocean and Back

I WAS SCHEDULED TO MEET WITH the North Alabama Methodist committee on ordination during their January convening, thus I had planned a trip to the United States in mid-January. It was a whirlwind time, seeing family, meeting with the group, having doctor's checkups, including an annual mammogram. I was to fly back on Friday, arriving in England on Saturday to prepare for three Sunday services plus host the Service of Christian Unity. Late Thursday afternoon I received a phone call; I needed to immediately schedule a biopsy and possible removal of a suspicious cyst before returning to England. In a panic, I rescheduled flight, made a couple of calls to England, and planned to have it done first thing Friday morning, then fly a day or two later if all were alright.

With Carl out of town, Davis had planned to take me to Birmingham to the airport Friday; instead he took me to a hospital there for the procedure. When we arrived, the doctor met me and with apology said, "I looked at the films again. We don't need to do this." Unbelievable. Relief, anger, decisions to make . . . . I appreciated the doctor's caution and concern to deal with something before I was overseas again, and then I trusted his word not to act, but what a rollercoaster. I made immediate phone calls, we drove back to Tuscaloosa for luggage, and then back to Birmingham. I got back on the Friday flight and headed back to England. Most folks there never knew my day of send-off. In a twinkling one's life can change—or not.

A Softer Way of Life . . .

The abbeys, the streams, the fields call.
Come into quiet reflection . . . come to be still;
come to be renewed, the wind whispers.
Come to create, to play, to dance.
And humans hear and respond, and come and follow the heart.
In time which was deemed to be meaningful, refreshing, and needed,
in place touched and kissed and shaped by the glory and beauty of nature,
we gathered.
The church ordained it so, compelled that we go,
called us to clear our calendars, walk away from the demands of the work,
and come . . . to the quiet of the countryside, the silent singing stones of the
abbeys, the fresh aromas of the field.

Retreat time,
for letting go of stress, for hearing the still-quiet voice of care, for walking
in green pastures with sheep and cows, and singing joyfully with friends
or standing in sustaining reverence among the polyphonic chorus of
nature's sounds, the polychromatic palette of earth's colors surrounding us.

And so we gathered.

For a week's retreat, a weekend away, a quiet day
At Willersley Castle, at Morley Retreat House, at Ammerdown Centre . . .
in settings attuned to God's creation scattered throughout the countryside.
We walked and talked, baked bread and picked flowers, painted and reflected
and sometimes even dared to dance.
Then we returned to the places of our calling, more able to care for ourselves
and others, more attuned to the song of life.

I recall the life of one who walked on earth in the countryside,
along the mountains and lakes,
who spoke of the lilies of the fields and the birds of the air.
I think of countless saints dedicated to the rhythm of abbey life throughout
the history of this land, people who did not have easy lives but who chose
the joy of sacred space and place in the midst of natural beauty.

I am thankful for the gift of quiet retreat I am learning here,
of expression for the soul's sake rather than performance sake,
of valuing time spent in creation as a worthy use of presence.
I am grateful for conference leaders and for congregation friends who
encourage me to experience holy life in this way.
May I return to my homeland to share the joy of slower living,
to offer the quiet of renewal to people running to keep up.

WINTER into SPRING

$\mathcal{F}$EBRUARY: *Journey to Spring*

In the cold and snow of winter,
there's a spring that waits to be . . .

Hymn of Promise, Natalie Sleeth

$\mathcal{I}$ had a sense that February began the journey to spring, even though the cold winter was by no means past. But the move beyond Epiphany toward the Lenten/Easter cycle seemed to call us all toward new awakenings and healings, in the shadow of the autumn/winter starkness and the hope of Easter dawn. Such is the rhythm of life.

A Memorable Memorial

THIS WAS THE DAY OF THE CHESTERFIELD MEMORIAL SERVICE for Dave and the children. The Derbyshire police force were the core initiators of this gathering. It feels that such a long time has passed since the accident, a length not common for us in the US, but certainly needed for all in this situation. The morning has been a very moving time for everyone involved, with memorials and tributes given to each by people who knew them so well. As anecdotes both funny and poignant were told and music that was special to each was heard, the community has been given a chance to remember together the living story, the songs which Dave, Matthew, and Andrew liked, the memories they had been a part of creating. The day marked the end of official memorials for now, a last opportunity for the community to express its love and care, though there would be concerts and golf benefits held later in the year.

These weeks had been such an emotional experience for all touched by Ruth and her family—for the church, for me, for the community, the school, the police force. In its own way, this time had bonded people together. Even people who didn't know them grieved with them. Mothers who didn't know Ruth directly carried guilt that their children lived while hers had died. I am not sure any community is prepared for such loss, regardless of the connection with those who are immediately affected. Memorial services grab the emotions in such a strong way, pulling us back to other times and places, other stories and life. Yet the unfairness of death too soon, as it has happened here, cuts so deep for us all.

> *Holy One of love that does not end, watch over Ruth, watch over these communities and all whose grief extends so deep. Lead us on into the unknown future, where you await us.*

Singin' in the Rain . . .

NEWS FROM THE USA: GENE KELLY DIED.

In reports about his death, the one thing repeatedly shown from his movies was the *Singin' in the Rain* scene. I love that scene—rain pouring down; a black umbrella that becomes a part of the dance; a handsome man with wonderful laughing eyes and a soft easy voice was soaking wet, but smiling, singing, and dancing "in the rain." As a child I grew up dancing and wanting to dance forever. Gene Kelly was one of my movie idols.

Several years ago, on an earlier visit to England, we saw the musical on stage in London. Of course the dance scene wasn't quite the same, but it got the point (or the dance) across: a water-filled wading gutter stretched across the stage, and on cue, the actor (not Gene) splashed through it. That great scene illustrates that which is lasting, something we all share in, a life moment. Wonder how many of us have lived that scene. It's enough to set us singing and smiling for the day.

Thanks, Gene. We will miss you, but your dance will linger on in our souls.

A Little Self-pity Warms the Body; A Balm Warms the Soul

I JUST RETURNED FROM THE CRICH AFTERNOON WORSHIP SERVICE. My hands are so stiff from the cold that I can hardly type. I am aware of furthering stiffness in them and have a feeling permanent damage is happening to my body, in the cold, in old damp churches, in not exercising. I see again and again that this weather, these old buildings must surely add to the health problems of people over here, along with the limited exercise that occurs. Americans are considered exercise addicts; well, some are, unfortunately not all of us, in particular not me, but some healthier conditions here would surely contribute to healthier people.

I can't believe how many words I have had to retype and correct; my hands are still frozen. I marked Tuesdays at two on my diary for exercise, which is when a group at Codnor gets together. Last night Patrick and Jacque warned me again about not going out walking on my own. There is such a caution factor here; it is hard to know the OK choices, but this cold weather has made it more difficult to intentionally walk to places anyway. A news article this week spoke about what poor eating habits the British have and what poor health condition they are in. Maybe I'm becoming British.

Turning from care of our bodies to care for our souls, Sunday worship services brought such good yet unanticipated responses. At Codnor's morning family service, when all the children stay in for the whole service and families are encouraged to come, the day was designated Education Sunday. Worshippers filled all sides of the open-room chapel like a star-filled sky on a clear winter's night. Following the education theme, I used the story of Jesus as teacher, then moved into an overview of the Christian year, which they seem not to have practiced here. As we introduced each season, a child placed a colored streamer on a banner pole—blue, white, green, purple, gold and white, red. Then, with Gill directing them, the children lined the steps and recited and sang with great joy. "Twinkle, Twinkle Little Star" has never been more spiritual, with little human-hand stars reaching for the sky and twinkling everywhere.

In presenting Lent, I acknowledged the reality of hurt and the hope of healing, taking a small bottle of lotion and explaining what balm was. Singing quietly the American spiritual "There Is a Balm in Gilead," I eased through the rows of people, gently touching the hands of some and sharing the lotion. At the end of service during the singing of the last hymn, the beautiful new "Hymn of Promise" by Natalie Sleeth, we handed each person a ribbon of the various seasonal colors.

Shaped by the energy and enthusiasm of the children, our Codnor service had gone well. But I was not sure how the same service would adapt to the older adults at Crich. I drove up to the village with that question in my mind.

After turning left into the little chapel lane and parking the car in the open space, I entered the building and saw that we had only ten or so people sitting in the chapel. I decided to follow the same general service outline. In the beginning I was not sure whether to do the Lenten sharing, but in the moment of the service it seemed to be right to do. With so few people, I approached every one, offering lotion on the hand in a small stroke. As I walked among the pews, we all felt the spiritual power of the moment, in what became a very moving experience for all. With faces and hearts tuned in to the healing act, each person received the balm with deep feeling, with tears gently flowing down cheeks like healing streams. And the words of the song became the road of the journey:

"There is a balm in Gilead to make the wounded whole,
There is a balm in Gilead, to heal the sin sick soul."

We closed the service with the bread and cup of communion. The whole worship experience became a beautiful special time for everyone present in that lovely old chapel that has known so many seasons and with people who have known the hardships of life. A service prepared for children met the deepest human feelings of these folks of many years, who know and live in the wilderness loneliness. A simple bottle of lotion became a tool for healing and meaning.

At the end of this day, a membership class gathered at the manse. I have enjoyed this series very much, getting to know these folks better and talking faith matters with them, but membership is still a challenging item for people here. I will see these groups through but will not push membership anymore, because it seems to be a difficult subject. Perhaps the next minister can address why there are more on community rolls than on member rolls, but does it matter, beyond numbers and figures? Are we not all a part of the body, working together for the health of the heart?

And finally, time to read the newspaper. In an interesting headline article in Sunday's *Telegraph,* a group of Anglican bishops, including a few archbishops led by Desmond Tutu, were calling for ordination of homosexuals. That may be the final blow on splitting the Anglican Church, which is why Methodists over here say the Anglicans may be ready for a merger. I wonder why we choose the issue of sexuality to be the current divisive hardliner marker for the church. We know so little about the physicality of it, yet it has become the burning matter for so many denominations. On our trip to St. Andrews, at the aquarium I saw a fish species where the males carry the eggs. Nature doesn't seem to quarrel with itself about the nature of beings. Is that human ability a blessing or a curse for humanity? Where is the balm here?

I settle in for the night, weary from the fullness of the day, grateful for the encounters with young and old, for the connection with those familiar with and those new to the faith. And I make one more feeble promise to my body to do better.

Thoughts from a Day in February . . .

Sometimes I wonder: Did everybody else know this all along?
Did the story of God's unconditional love get understood by
    people all around?
Was I the only one who heard a message of judgment and rules
    and conditions?
That if I did the right things, God would love me?
If I opened the Bible up to the right passage
    I would find the answer?
If I only listened hard enough
    I would hear God's voice?
Was there this deeper understanding of God's grace and love
    out there that others have known about?

Then why didn't they shout it from the mountaintops
                for all to hear?
Why didn't they speak as loudly as the voices in my head?
Why are the walls and the rules there?
How could someone know and not tell others?

I offered a touch of soothing ointment last Sunday—
a day to share with children God's healing love.
And in the sharing came healing for all.

Are we all so wounded that we don't know
the cooling balm offered by the healing one,
the lover of us all?

Prayer is a mystery to me.
    Insights come in mere moments of thought:
Perhaps the answer to prayer comes in
            the opening up of oneself to possibilities
not yet considered.

IT SNOWED TODAY—beautiful white lacy snow, crystalline ballerinas floating down onto earth's stage. I am still enamored enough with snow to enjoy the rhythmic mesmerizing billows of white. Sticking to my commitment as I watched the snow stick to the ground, I drove over to Codnor and exercised with the group. We debated about canceling the night's workshop but decided we would go ahead with the plan. I was actually quite tired, from a restless night, but had rather have the meeting than reschedule it. Eight people besides myself attended; no one was stopped by the weather. A pragmatic way of life this is, and an enjoyable evening; they each are so committed to the children.

Earlier in the day I saw a young woman who helps with children at Codnor. She reached in her pocket and pulled out her purple ribbon from Sunday's service.

Synod and Story

"I AM THE BREAD OF LIFE . . . ." With its rousing, rising melody, the ministers heartily sang the communion song to close the biannual synod ministers' meeting in Nottingham, which went on this week in spite of the weather. It is always a joy to see Geoff Clark's leadership style at these meetings. He is quiet and affirming but definitely in control, guiding and balancing like the deep rudder of a ship. His presence benefits all those who work with him. An obituary read for Vernon at the meeting reminded me of how much he too is now connected with my image of ministry and with others. Both men have carried such a gentle caring manner into their ministry.

This group holds a familiarity and collegiality for me, as I am equally aware of friends from home who also travel this road. There is a shared camaraderie and friendship that comes in a connectional system. Hearing the ministry candidates speak, I thought of my own shaping factors, years in music education, the many years in church music, each place a lodestar for life's journey. I thought of the people from childhood, then from the various stages of my life, friends, colleagues, and mentors all along the way. My work had moved back and forth in a comfortable rhythm according to the situation at the time.

At one point, I faced the decision whether to give up the work of teaching music to children in schools to come to the music ministry at a church. I felt both positions to be important and both to be a fulfillment of my *vocation*. Then things fell into place, with a university teaching assistantship and the church job, and the next decade took shape, as I continued to find fulfillment in both arenas of life, finally moving fully into church work. Then in the time at my last church, working with a wonderfully talented group of folks, loving my music and worship work, I also recognized the joy of facilitating small Bible study groups and the meaningful experience of helping form the AIDS care team there and walking alongside our first care team friend Fred Rutledge as he lived with the ravaging disease. And my focus began to change.

Like the people who spoke at synod today as they stood at this transition point in their lives, we each have stories to tell, of people who touched our lives, events and situations that changed us, strengthened us, challenged us. Whatever our occupation or work, we share our understanding of life, our faith basis through our acts and our words, our being. And on occasion, again like this group at synod, it is good to tell our story, to put words to our understanding of who and how and why we are.

So here I am, still finding ways to fulfill my calling, now in a new way in a new place. It is not an either-or thing, this journey of life. The experiences we each uniquely have, the steps our lives have taken, the gifts we have been given are threads woven together, joined in our past, looping our present, loosely open for the future, waiting to see how they will take shape. Metamorphosis does not occur out of nothing, it takes what is and recreates into new richness and beauty.

SOMETIMES I HAVE TO WONDER ABOUT *THIS* YEAR, this time and this place, the circumstances that are a part of all these people's lives. Eighteen-year-old Jenny just called me; she had thought things were fine from a breast biopsy. A tall, energetic, and outgoing brunette, Jenny is a delightful and gifted young person in the Swanwick congregation. She is active in the circuit youth work and is very talented in the arts, planning to major in music in college. They confirmed today that she does not need surgery, but they had not prepared her for the idea of a treatment process. She must take chemo and radiation for eight months, beginning with chemotherapy on Tuesday. They suggested she take the next year off from college to recover. This diagnosis now began to change her life. We found a time for me to come visit with her, and I offered to be available to go with her for her first treatment, if she would like. I recall those early days of my first chaplaincy at a Chemo/Breast Imaging clinic as a part of my work at Candler. Not sure what to do or say, not yet realizing that in such pastoral situations there can be little needed to be said, I may not have realized how much those days were preparing me for days like this. I will hold Jenny close in my heart as she starts this new road.

IT IS STILL A SNOWY DAY, with the weather predicted to remain bad until Saturday. The night's meeting ended early, then the phone rang. Everyone at Crich is sick. Tomorrow evening's church meeting only has two healthy people, so we cancelled. I plan to open the beautiful jigsaw puzzle Davis gave me for Christmas, spread out the pieces on the dining-room table, turn them all over to the picture side, separate the edge pieces, and let the Rafael cherubs begin to come to life.

On Music and Life . . .

I SAT AT THE PIANO with pencil in hand this weekend, feeling a desire to do some music composition work. What a lost feeling. A new song came forth, a setting of Brian Wren's welcome words:

"In the name of Christ, welcome, in sadness or gladness, welcome . . . ."

Someone dropped a package through my mailbox. I heard the clunk and went to the front door, opened it, and discovered one of the men in the membership class just walking away. Laying on the carpet was a tape recording of John Rutter's *"Gloria"* and *"Requiem,"* pieces I had conducted. I placed the tape in the player, turned up the volume, and listened to the *"Gloria."* I must say I am glad my curtains were drawn. I sang, conducted, danced, and cried my way through it—how I do love music! I would like to invite folks over one evening for a Rutter night of listening. I find it ironic that someone would, without in any way knowing, bring me something which I love so deeply.

The *"Requiem"* is emotionally difficult to hear right now; it is a reminder of that which I put behind me. I checked out the scores to it last week when I was at Chesterfield, thinking there might be a place for one of the movements during Lent. Who knows— perhaps there will be some opportunity like Jacque's re-connecting. She chose to quit her dance outlet in her life, pursued her local preacher's work, and now five or more years later, as I have asked her to consider dancing to one of my compositions on Ash Wednesday, she is finding new life in claiming both as a reconnection of spirit. It might be only this single time of returning to her artistic gift, but even that is good.

How many times does the creative energy die, and then gently rebirth? How often do we tune out the stirrings of new creation, instead of inviting it to be, just to be, until the new Genesis moment occurs?

And Order . . .

THEY DO NOT USE PRINTED ORDERS OF WORSHIP in churches here, no yearly bound bulletin books. Coming from print-oriented churches, I find it strange; it stirs some organizational pondering. There are those for whom ordering comes naturally, whether printed or not, those who need a printed order to feel secure in knowing what comes next, and those who hold the pieces of the kaleidoscope in their hearts, able to order and reorder with fluidity and flow. I have established files as: *Past orders of worship; past sermon work; current sermon work; sermon resources.* But the question lingers: How to file sermon and order of worship, separate or together? It seems strange to separate orders from sermons. I work to weave the two together—the Word is more than the word. I suppose order has multiple meaning. Interesting how in changing focus of work, such things as filing and organizing need to be thought out anew. Or maybe there is just not enough good English television to watch.

THIS IS UNBELIEVABLE—I have been ecstatic all morning because there has been sunshine. I have opened curtains, cleaned house, worked at the desk. I've been highly productive, energized by the golden rays.

And what is it doing now? Snowing! Between songs, classical radio kept talking about snow and winds. I assumed it to be for other parts of the country. But here it is.

Life Is for Dancing . . .

AT THE END OF THE DAY Jacque came to the house, where in the small space of the lounge we began to shape the dance to "My Life Is in the Love of God" for the Ash Wednesday Service. First we talked about music and dance, how they each had been a part of our lives since childhood, and how for each of us the power of dance enhances and interprets the text and song. From the age-wise piano, I played and sang the song for her, allowing it to fill the space of the room, while from the couch she listened and then simply visualized the transfer of sound to movement. Two hearts each molded by a love of creative beauty.

"I'm not saying I'll do it," she shared, "but I'll think about it."

"Even if you don't dance for the service, what a gift this has been for me," I replied.

Jacque had studied ballet in formal training and moved with a grace and beauty that reflected those many years of study, even though she no longer danced. I understood about leaving a craft you loved.

After she had gone, thoughts lingered on the joy of dance, as another time and place came to mind:

"Life is for dancing. Music is playing, and we must move."

I remembered a dance that took place a decade earlier in a former church the year the youth week theme was "Life Is . . .", taken from a set of words written by the minister. During an August Youth Sunday morning worship, in a beautiful sanctuary framed by brilliantly colored stained-glass windows and grounded with a rich red carpet, the music ensemble sang "Life is for dancing," then spoke lines from the Psalms during instrumental portions of the song. They were providing the backdrop for an unforgettable moment of expression, as right there in the chancel three youth shared their own unique style of dance: Catherine in classical dance, Penny in modern dance, and Brian in breakdancing. As they danced I accompanied at the piano, letting the mood of music change with each style of dancing. We each will always remember their time of dance in the church and the minister's pastoral words following it, giving grace and blessing to the moment.

The creativity fire is reflamed each time a person finds her own chance to bring the life story alive in her own language, as Jacque is doing on this occasion with her beautiful dance gifts. At the end of the day, I am grateful for such a day as this, from sunshine and snow to the soaring spirit of dance and music. The last line of "Life Is . . .": "To stay still is to betray the beat of life."

Creative spirit of snow, sun, song and dance,
may we never forget the beauty and joy of the dance of life.

Thoughts about Bumps of Life in the Christian Community

AS IN ANY GROUP, there are occasional conflicts within the congregations here, disagreements about how or what to do. It would make life easier if those bumps did not occur. I imagine Paul thought that, too, in the early church. Perhaps maturity in pastoral leadership comes in learning to accept things as what has been and is, without feeling you have to fix it all.

I am also aware of the hurt caused when liturgies and prayers reflect a lack of concern for inclusive language or sensitivity to women, particularly when worshipping with the larger church community. It is true many Christians have not heard the story except through old images that not only exclude but also miss the richness of other images of the full character of God, both male and female, as well as human and otherly. These are not new images but are actually Biblical: "God is our rock . . . like a mother hen . . . ." Wonder how folks have missed that?

But then, to counter balance, I had a good time at the primary school with the children. Such is the rhythm of life.

A Visit at Ferndale

FROM MY HOUSE ON CLUMBER CLOSE, I walk up the street toward town, round the corners until I arrive at the next to last little walkway to the left, where the sign above the door reads FERNDALE. I turn into the walkway. On the right, in front of the windows and behind the brown front stonewall, the tiny front garden space holds lovely, long light green fern fronds in season.

I move down the walkway into the covered space shared with the neighbor, leading to both residences' doors. On the right I knock on the Pells' door, and Ada soon greets me with a lovely smile.

"My word, it's good to see you. Come in, do come in."

From the entryway we walk back into the dimly lit but warm and cozy lounge, and I am greeted by Mr. Pells—somehow "Harold" feels too informal. He is always glad to see me, and I am glad to be visiting here. Ada is an accomplished pianist—her dark wood upright piano sits in the front room. She has served as accompanist at Wood Street Chapel, but since Harold's increasing health problems, she is not so able to go and play. She is a dignified, stately woman, with a soft round-cheeked friendly face, short strawberry reddish curly hair, and a strong straight-back posture. Always a gracious hostess, she offers me a cup of tea. Of course, I accept.

Mr. Pells comes from Wales. Hanging on the wall above the heater is a picture of the bridge of his hometown, the town with the longest name in the country. Forget trying to spell and say it. He tells me of his town and the bridge there, a double-decker one with trains traveling on one level and cars on the next, and of his growing up days. At Mr. Pells' request, Ada stands and gets the memory albums, then the couple shares with me wonderful old sepia and black-and-white photos of times and places past. And I feel good just for being there. Mr. Pells is not able to walk much, and his illness is getting the best of him. But in this moment we sit and enjoy the conversation.

After a while, I suggest we have communion. Ada and I pull up a little round wooden table with a lovely white doily on it, and I open the small black communion carry case and set out three little glass cups and pour the juice. Then I place the little bread bits on the tiny silver plate. This carry case was given to me for such a moment as this. Because I know they love the words of the traditional service, we use the service books I have brought. Together we read the words:

"The peace of the Lord be with you."

"And also with you...."

Ada sits tall in her seat; Harold cannot sit so straight. I offer to each of them and for myself, the act of communion.

Together we take the bread.

"The body of Christ..."

And now, the cups.

"The cup of God's covenant love, poured out for you."

Together, we drink the juice in our small glass cups. Then sit in a few moments of silence. I offer a blessing, and it is time to rise and go.

"Thank you, my dear," he says to me, this once-firm and sure man, now weakened and wounded by age and illness.

"My word, oh yes, thank you," says Ada, one who deeply loves and sorely misses the beauty and ritual of the church, as she sees me to the door. Before leaving, I try to say what the visit has meant to me.

As she bids me out, Ada benedicts me:

"Do come again, when you can, any time. My word, we love for you to come."

I step out through the front doorway, from the warmth of the moment and the room, and move into the street. Time starts again. In the rhythm of life, I am grateful for the peaceful, quiet interludes such as this.

My word, thank you, Ada and Harold, dear friends, for who you are, for your hospitality, for the sharing of bread and cup.

A Derby Day

SHORT OF BURNING PALM BRANCHES MYSELF, Derby Cathedral store is the closest place to purchase ashes for the Ash Wednesday service. Driving into Derby is always a challenge, with the double roundabouts and quick turns on and off circle roads. You can easily end up going out of town on another road. But I made it to the town centre parking deck and then I enjoyed the stroll through town centre up to the Cathedral store for the ashes. Derby Cathedral is an interesting mix of styles. It uses wrought iron in the chancel, and its baptismal font is made of stainless steel; these both reflect area industries. Isn't that how a cathedral should be, coming out of the surroundings?

Besides buying the ashes at the cathedral store, I also found a couple of new books and tapes from the Iona Community and looked forward to becoming familiar with them for use in worship. Little did I know at that time that this purchase was the beginning of lifelong work with the community, later spending time on Iona and continually helping others discover the resources and intent of the group.

Meandering back through town centre toward my car, I stopped for lunch on the second floor at Bennetts department store. One of the oldest stores in England, it was established in 1734 and still offers shopping for elegant living; the restaurant on the mezzanine level is a lovely setting for lunch or tea. Sitting alone at my little round table, as my pot of tea steeped, I felt the conversational chatter of the twosome and threesome seated around me, folks who had also stopped here for a noon interlude; I was a part of them, yet I was in my own world.

Glass display cabinets in the china department are filled with beautiful treasures, particularly featuring Royal Crown Derby, a fine bone china made in Derby since 1750;

it is always fun to browse here. After a good walk-through, I then detoured through the marketplace building to enjoy the buzz and energy of the marketeers.

"Would you like to buy ... ?" "Two for one ..." "Try it on, see how it looks ..." "Fresh tomatoes ..." From slabs of meat to flowers, sewing goods, makeup, purses, and other accessories, vendors wait to sell their wares. Whereas at a restaurant it can be hard to catch the eye of a waiter for service, here the vendor watches intently with beaded eye, waiting for the moment to pounce for the sale. Any city marketplace is a lively visit.

The drive between Ripley and Derby takes only twenty minutes via the A38 road, so it was easy to be back home with time for a few more errands. I mailed Brian the composition I had worked on at the piano, the musical setting of his welcome words. At the manse I settled in the lounge and began to read the new books purchased in Derby.

Recognizing Roots

THIS LAND OF ANCIENT AND NEW OFFERS a rich environment for exploring new yet ancient realms that represent the human spirit in search of meaning and truth, such as are found in the new books about new/old ways. I think I am Celtic at heart, thought I am not sure I can say what Celtic at heart is. It is just an innate interest in Celtic heritage and story, a sense of connection with Celtic music and imagery as I am beginning to know it. Certainly in Celtic history, there is more claim of the feminine God, more connection with earth and all creation, more respect of human worth. Perhaps the connection with this story is natural, with the sense I feel toward it and the knowledge that Mother and Daddy's roots both go back to southwest Ireland, one area of Celtic life.

In a short quote from one of the books, the author writes of John Bell[1] of Iona Community: "John and his group have written wonderful hymns songs and liturgical chants drawing on Celtic spirituality and the Celtic feel for the creation."

The author asks about that. John states:

> It is a wee bit difficult to talk about Celtic spirituality because it is a rare breed.
> Something which emerges from fragments of poems and songs written by
> unknown lay people, before the Reformation, around the tenth or eleventh
> century, who had within the culture of the West Highlands, as in Ireland
> and Wales, kept alive some theological insights which the Celtic Church of
> the sixth and seventh centuries shared in these remote parts of the British Isle

1. M. Matthews, ed., *Finding Your Story* (London: Darton, Longman & Todd, 1992), p. 16.

with regard to creation, i.e., the Celts saw God as being totally thru creation, as
creation being charged with the goodness of God. Not that they worshipped
stones or flowers, but that in them they saw the carefulness of God's intention
in making this a beautiful place, and so they wanted to have a reverence for
all the life of the world and not just for human life.

Bell writes in music of the "kindness of the creator." And he quotes from old Celtic prayers about peoples asking that they have the "smile of God." And he emphasizes the feminine aspect of God. All of this speaks to the hearts of many, I think.

When I later planned and led a first Iona communion service for my congregations, the event was very well received; the language of the Iona service speaks to hearts. Reading further in the Celtic saints book, I found it to be so meaningful. I, like others, have discovered voices from my spiritual heritage. The more I read, the more I appreciate.

When the language used does not speak, when something feels disconnected, not authentic to personal life, then the deep archetypes of being stir within, and the journey to roots begins. This year of work abroad has in a sense brought me closer to home.

ON A MORE MUNDANE LEVEL, I have not been productive today. I intended to go to Crich to visit but admit that when I do pastoral visits a good bit, as has occurred this week in catch-up, I appreciate a break from dealing with the seriousness of the illness and aging matters. The people who are ill and aging probably would like a break from their matters too. I worked on the Raphael angel jigsaw puzzle Davis gave me ... and just got up from the table to realize that it is 3 p.m. Hey, it is Saturday. What was that formula given to us in the beginning training?

"You Can't Let Them Stop Your Life"

GLENIS PICKED ME UP AT 5:30 IN THE MORNING to go to the Derby train station for an early-bird-price day trip to London. It had snowed again in the evening, and I was not sure about being in London in bad weather.

The weather was only a small part of the memory of quite an exciting day. I did not hear news of two IRA London bombings on the preceding day; I saw news headlines only after we were already there in London! Once arriving, we walked everywhere, in a hurricane-type wind, all over downtown London. While I attended a meeting at Methodist Headquarters on Marylebone Road, Glenis walked down toward the Tate Gallery but took a wrong turn, and at one point was met by police armed with machine guns. They had stopped a blue van and had the occupant out beside it. They looked her way and stated, "Madam, could you please cross over to the other side." "Oh, my, of course," she replied and quickly crossed, walking on just in time to hear the changing of the guard band play "Happy Birthday" to Prince Edward. She was having quite an adventure while I sat in a meeting.

When I finally finished the planning session, we both walked down to Piccadilly Circus to window-shop, then walked back up Shaftsbury, past where all was roped off at the spot the second bombing had occurred. "Oh, my, what are we doing here?" I worried. "You can't let them stop your life," Glenis pragmatically replied. During dinner at the Bloomsbury hotel, we looked out the window and saw it begin to snow. By the time we walked back up to St. Pancras in the falling snow, the ground was covered. Our train left on schedule at 9 p.m., then was two hours late arriving home, because of weather. We arrived home at 1:30 a.m. Oh my, what a day!

A Holy Day

ASH WEDNESDAY HAS ALWAYS BEEN A SIGNIFICANT DAY for Christians and a meaningful occasion for me. This day that begins the season of Lent gives us time to reflect on our humanity and on God's eternal grace and love. So I had eagerly anticipated the observance in this year. We were holding a circuit service at Swanwick; this was a relatively new experience for them. I planned to offer communion by intinction, the process of dipping a piece of bread in the wine of the cup, and I soon found this was a total first for them. I had shaped it with three stations at the front, one in the middle for anyone who wants ashes, a pair of people on either side, with bread and cup. Jenny on cello and Tony on organ would provide the music during communion. Jacque had decided to dance, and we would close with the song "Until" as benediction. Wanting to avoid service book pages, I planned an informal prayer of thanksgiving, consecration and breaking of the bread, and invitation. Folks over here, like folks in other places, can get bound by the book, and miss the view. One of the things I love most about pastoral ministry is the opportunity to offer bread and cup to others, the sacrament of serving and receiving. In the imposition of ashes, the sign of the cross is placed on the forehead or hand using palm ashes mixed with a small amount of oil. It is special each time I participate. I looked forward to the evening.

I had called the acting superintendent about assisting in the communion serving for the Ash Wednesday service. He was uncomfortable with intinction, having never done it before, but agreed to participate. Later he called back to say he just could not do it. He had spent the morning trying to find out more about it, had called the Alfreton vicar, and thought it had some theological implications that he just could not agree with. He was fine with common cup and encouraged me to do that. Ah, well, do not let the method get in the way of the meaning for the night.

After all the anticipation and thought, the time came. Again the circuit gathered to capacity in Swanwick Chapel to worship together. At the serving of communion, people were able to go to the serving method of their choice. With the beautiful string music, the moving dance by Jacque, and the setting at Swanwick so nice, the ashes were well received. The evening became a beautiful beginning to Lent. It is just a fact that in offering people new and creative opportunities, sometimes there may be hesitation, uncertainty. But it is worth the risk.

My life is in the love of God,
My being in God's eternal love.
There is nothing in life or death
that can separate me from God's love.
So, death, you have no hold over me,
For my life is in the love of God,
My being in God's eternal love.

Creative Source, I give thanks for the beauty and power of dance and music, and for the one who reached deep into the recesses of her soul to bring such embodied life and beauty to the meaning of this Ash Wednesday.

A Walk in the Peaks

THE SOLITUDE OF THE PEAK DISTRICT OFFERED SANCTUARY and sabbath following the busy days of preparation for the changing rhythm of a new season. Lent is a time that by its nature calls for solitude, silent reflection. Being in the countryside after such busy days of work nourishes my own spirit. For this outing I chose to visit Monsal Dale.

Monsal Head overlooks one of the lovely dales of the White Peaks. To arrive there, you travel through the picturesque village of Ashford in the Water, then ascend the hill on a winding narrow road, when the charming Monsal Head Hotel surprises you on your left; pulling into the car park, you face out overlooking beautiful Monsal Dale and viaduct.

Nestled far down in the evergreen dale, just past the horseshoe turn of the Rive Wye, is a small private farm, smoke rising from the chimney of the stone two-story house. A gaggle of geese left over from the Christmas season hover in the corner of a small fenced pasture. To the left and two-thirds way down the hilltop, the old viaduct stretches over the Wye, offering the beginning of this strip of Monsal trail for hikers and bikers, following the path of what was once the Midland Railway route, now a part of the Peak District National Park.

I choose this day to follow the sharp descent of the path on the right, down to the floor of the dale, moving past the farm, past the hissing and honking geese, crossing over the narrow iron hikers' bridge that spans the Wye just above water level. No one else is crossing at this time, so I stand on the bridge, listening to the bubbling song of the Wye, watching the jade green river grass flow and sway just beneath the surface of the crystal-clear water. Slowly moving on from this favorite spot, I take the path to the left, following the curve of the bending water, crossing under the now seemingly tall arches of the viaduct.

Here I decide to continue my walk along the river rather than join the Monsal trail. The meadow is inviting, even on a crisp grey February day, as the path becomes grassy, broad, mere bent green strands bending the direction of the many visitors to this serene setting. The flowing white foamy waters at the weir produce a rush of sound heard in approaching, singing on as I move beyond.

The path takes me into the thick woods as I breathe in the earthy aromas of moist plant life along the water's edge. At a junction I turn right, leaving the Wye and beginning the steep ascent up the limestone hillside. Finally at the crest the trees have cleared, and I see the buildings of Monsal Head far off on the other side. Here I stop and sit to rest, enjoying the magnificent views of the valley, the river, the hills, and sky.

Along this top crest are remnants of an ancient iron fortress, almost erased by the farming that has claimed the fields and all they held. A clay pool in a side pasture collects and holds the water for the herd of cattle that now reside here. A biker slowly pedals past me, carefully picking which ruts of the rugged dirt road he should follow. I am more easily able to find good footing for the rest of my route along the high hill's ridge, as I move back toward the point of the river's bend. The path begins its descent to reconnect with the Monsal trail, where this time I cross over the surface of the viaduct and turn to re-ascend the road to the car park. Arriving tired but refreshed, I cross over and visit the tea room to celebrate my walk with a pot of Earl Grey.

This is the last day of February.

Communion Day

As was their custom, the children were to leave after the second hymn.

This Sunday on their way out, the little children came forward for a blessing at the communion rail. For many it was the first time ever to come to the rail.

They knelt down, held on to the rail, and looked up into my face. I moved from left to right down the row, placing my hand on each dear head, leaning down and speaking quietly to them as they gazed into my eyes. I was the one blessed by those wondrous faces.

As I moved to the end, I placed my hand on the head of the little girl kneeling there and spoke to her as I had spoken to the others.

"Know that you are blessed by God's love this day and every day," I said.

"Oh, y-e-ah-h-h!" She sighed back.

Oh, yeah!

$\mathscr{M}$ARCH: *A Time for Friends*

Lo, the time of winter is past...
                                          Song of Solomon

$\mathscr{M}$arch in Alabama means spring. I hoped there might be some promise of it in England. This felt like a time to just enjoy life here and to look forward to visits from American friends as I shared this English experience with them.

An American in Codnor

ANSWER: "BING CROSBY." Question: "Which American singer had the forenames Harry Lillis?" The first question of American Trivia was followed by twenty-four similar queries, most of which were unfamiliar to this lone American present in the room. Codnor Chapel hosted an American Evening on the first Saturday of March as a fundraiser for their chapel work. Organizers requested a menu from me, so I provided them with a menu of American dishes that they could "fix," as we say in the South: ham, baked beans, cheese grits, congealed salad, with Mississippi Mud and pecan pie for dessert. We translated the recipes into Britainese and tried to locate the ingredients at Sainsbury's. After looking for grits in all the places I knew to look, from Ripley to Derby, with no luck, I called Emily in Alabama and asked her to mail me some grits. She obliged by sending forty dollars shipping worth of grits. With four bags, we had enough for the whole country. But few were eaten in Codnor. People over here think of *grit* as the grainy stuff you spread on the road from the grit boxes when it snows. And not much congealed salad was eaten, either. In kitchen lingo here, *congealed* is the chilled fat from meat, which is not very appealing, it seems. So much for a common language.

In their great enthusiastic, fun-loving spirit, folks came in full Ameregalia. The chapel space, which serves for both worship and life, was now decorated with flags, banners, and balloons. Then they began to arrive: a multitude of cowboys and Indians, including an authentic sheriff of the west, with a few bonnet and high-hat pilgrims along the way, even some famous folks appeared. Red, white, and blue abounded. Thanks to the great musicians and game-planners there, we sang American folk songs, beginning with "O Susannah," then teams formed for trivia and celebrities games. Unfortunately, they appeared to know more about my country than I did.

Our American evening was great fun, full of so much energy, with their joy and enthusiasm for occasions such as this. And their expression of fun, love, and support of my homeland made me feel good to be from the colonies and to be with the motherland.

THE RHYTHM OF MY WEEKS CENTERED AROUND SUNDAYS—the nature of the services, the locations I was to be in, sermon work. As I moved from church to church, I had learned to always be prepared for the new, which never became old. Because Sundays were usually quite full, Mondays became a day at the desk. Working out of my home was a new experience, offering a different kind of rhythm and connection. It was a pattern I continued for the next five years of ministry, working in places where the office was at home. I found that I liked doing so; it was a reminder of my earlier years teaching studio music at home when my sons were young. The rest of the week included visits and meetings. The journal continued to be a place for reflection, responses, and thoughts.

Of Flowers and Blossoms

SOMEONE FROM HOME informed me that the plants they were keeping for me were beginning to bud: the rose bush is full of tiny, tender red leaves, the promise of coming flowers. Two of the pots have sent forth leaves of green. Here a friend brought me branches of forsythia, which have finally burst into yellow bloom. But the weather is still cold and grey. The yellow faces of the multitude of tiny flowers bring sunlight into the house.

I begin to understand why yellow blossoms are needed. There is such illness and poor health over here. It feels that every place I go, someone is ill or is in the hospital. A woman I visited Friday afternoon at Ripley died last night. Another member is in

Derby Hospital; they don't know what's wrong with her. I will take communion to another woman in Belper Hospital. The weather must have a physical effect on people, or even psychological effect; long months of grey dampness must compound health matters and invite Seasonally Affected Depression. I did not anticipate this in England, but it accentuates the importance of fellowship together, of pastoral care teams, of sharing flowers and cups of tea, all ways of offering warmth and sunlight in lives.

A Little Fresh Air Is Good for the Soul, but as for the Body . . .

I FELT BUSY AND PUNY TODAY. This morning has been my Monday schedule, getting on top of the week. In the afternoon, feeling I needed to get out and walk, I laced up my official hiking boots purchased for moments such as this, then loaded up with books for the library, letters to mail, a bill to pay, and a casserole dish to return. I intended to have a little jaunt around town and into the countryside.

The air was thin and cutting, hitting me in the face like a knife, but I briskly completed the town errands, lightening my load stop by stop until I was empty-handed. I then hiked out of town down Pentrich Road past a factory, where on foot I was able to see that they made furniture; you can't notice those things when you are driving by. The narrow sidewalk leads down the hill through Hammersmith village, which flows out of Ripley with no division, although it likely stood alone at one time. I eventually passed under the A38 viaduct and into the countryside.

How open and peaceful it feels. Even with the sound of the traffic from the highway in the distance, the birds can still be heard. I travel up a hill, alongside a pasture where a horse of shiny brown mane watches me and a lovely burled oak tree drapes over the uneven sidewalk, then round the curve to the left, and Pentrich village is at the top of the next little rise. A walk around the block might have been more in keeping with my physical condition, but with a few huffs and puffs and a nudge from the friendly horse along the way, I trek up to the main road of Pentrich.

The village church sits at the top of the rise, nestled among the trees and tombstones. I make a note, "I must come back and visit it sometime." To the right, up the hill, past The White House and The Beam, each stone home has its cottage name sign posted on the stone gate. I walk past the old schoolhouse. On my left I see the village hall, looking a little deserted now, but with a sign announcing fitness classes. What a joke, the village hall and I have some neglect of fitness in common.

ORCHARD COTTAGE. I arrive at my destination and find not only my friends Peter and Elaine home, but also their daughter Sue, who just happens to be driving back into Ripley. "Think I could have a lift?"

Life Reflections

"HOW MANY OF YOU WASHED YOUR FACE THIS MORNING?"

School assemblies are always invigorating; there were two this morning, with younger and older kids. We talked of water, and the ways water can remind us of holy refreshing love. As the last older group rose from the floor and left the assembly with their quiet waves and goodbyes to me, their teacher came over and invited me to spend the whole morning at school. It was a day I could quickly adjust, so I joined them as the one class moved from subject to subject, finally ending back in their modular classroom where we shared continued topics on their mind: water, love and life, stories they wanted to tell. This was a class who had lost one of its own; we had visited on other occasions. Now was a time for lingering, talking, and listening—the way people, even kids, want to share their story, thoughts, and life.

Back home in the afternoon, I alternated between getting a little work done and resting a few minutes. Looking out my bedroom window, I can see the sky and clouds through the treetops. As clouds float by, so my mind floats, in and out of topics the kids chose, topics of life adults want to share, thoughts of my own journey. I remember writing music for life and death lines approximately twelve to thirteen years ago. Now, at my current age and place, the sense of life and death matters seems more acute as I work with the people here. As I move into my fifties, am I more aware of these things?

Congregations too reveal the way they think of life past, present, and future, by the choices and plans they make. Wood Street's church meeting last night revealed some bold decisions made by this congregation. The ladies fellowship decided to move their meeting time from night to afternoon—a major decision that has been hanging over them for several years, and one not without some pain. Out of that will also come the possibility of a monthly mid-age women's group. The church council also approved the three youth confirmands, approved the first lay communion visitor, received a recommendation from one work area to form a worship leadership group, another recommendation to have a church-wide day retreat, and to have a Maundy Thursday service. Hopefully, they will see the gains of these significant decisions.

Life is about the opportunities we are given, the gift of each day, the pleasure of each age, and the ability to reflect, to change when needed, to be grateful for what is. Years later, when I returned to England to work, I again set some words to music, these written by one of the local preachers in that circuit, who had been diagnosed with terminal cancer and was writing poetry about his experience. Everard wrote:

"Life's not like the telly, with channels by the score, so you'd better like this channel, for there aren't any more...." He began and concluded with: "You soon forget the bad days when a good day's at your door." I ended the musical setting of the poem with whistling. Ah, give thanks for a whistling day.

TWO CALLS HAVE COME FROM CHURCHES in the other section, inviting me to be with them for events. I think they, too, miss Vernon's presence as minister in their lives, the Swanwick church, in particular, which is his family's church. They are receiving good help from the neighboring superintendent, but it is natural that they just miss his pastoral presence—as do I, to have someone to talk with, to learn from, to work and plan together. The churches, in hearing and talking about the new ministers—they decide these things very early here—are also aware of my time moving on, as I am. This may be another reason the churches have called me. We have hoped for me to be in all eleven churches of the circuit before I leave. So, everyone starts to feel the endings and beginnings, the coming autumn time of change. The way they plan so far ahead, looking ahead comes sooner and lasts longer. In the wee small hours of the morning, I thought of a closing sermon series: *the ABC and Zed of life together.*

- **A:** *Agendas, any other business, and anniversaries* Balancing the things that seem to take so much of the church's time and energy, with other things which invite us into deeper commitment to being the Body of Christ, to living fully.

- **B:** *Baptism and other beautiful sacraments of life together* Looking at the importance of worship and ritual as shared life, for congregations and individuals.

- **C:** *Contemplating life* A look at daily intentional living, with disciplines, sacred living, etc.

- **Zed:** *Finally, sisters and brothers . . .* think on these things.

Interesting how a time with children can lead us into deeper thought.

The Gift of Healing

ONE EVENING WHEN I STILL WAS NOT FEELING WELL, I turned on the radio as I went to bed, something I had not been doing because even on the classical stations, they play the same music over and over, traditional classical period. I lay there aching, trying to read a little and relax a little and breathe a little, when I heard the strains of Brahms' *Ein deutsches Requiem* coming over the radio. As the melodies I love soared, the beautiful soprano solo of the fifth movement rang forth, and the choral blanket of sound covered me. I switched off the light and lay there, blessed in spirit and body by that great work; it was the first time I had heard it over here. In the hearing soon came sleep.

In the Wee Small Hours of the Morning . . .

IN ANOTHER 5 A.M. WAKE TIME, as ideas again seemed to flow, I began to make a simple list as they came, for later reflection. One thought was to do a sermon on SIN, then in the Matthew Fox book I read later in the morning, the author quotes Heschel: "To the prophets, sin is not an ultimate, irreducible or independent condition but rather a broken relationship between God and man." Fox then writes: "Sin is relational. And the God sin offends is a God of justice. . . ." Simply put, wrong relationship with humanity and nature is wrong relationship with God.

My 5 a.m. list, in no particular order:

- Write lines on chicken soup and Brahms
- Write on pencil sharpeners
- Write "at the end of the day" daily devotional thoughts out of this year
- Write a summary of last night's local preacher meeting and distribute
- Write W-groves church, commending their efforts
- Sermon on SIN, what it is not, what is it . . . ?
- Outline the last four sermons
- Get my music written down
- The end of my jubilee year is almost here
- Mail Doug a birthday gift
- Davis will turn twenty next month
- Call Dan and tell him how proud I am of his new achievements
- Call Carl and see how things are going

- I want to remember the feel of this house, of the streets and roads
- I miss my piano
- I wonder if an inherent "work ethics" mentality can be an obstacle to doing what's in one's heart—creating, writing, responding to life.

Creative thoughts come at this hour like a dream. Floods of thoughts pass through the head like fast-moving clouds, in a short window of time. When this happens, it is helpful to jot them down and have a checklist to later revisit.

The day, including the evening, is uncluttered. Good.

On Sorting

ALTHOUGH I AM AWAY FROM THEM, my mind has been on my boys and where they are in their lives. I so want to make it good and right for the boys in their lives, much like I imagine our parents wanted to sort things out for my brother, sisters, and me. There is an element of that which can be done, but then comes the painful realization that they must sort out life for themselves—at age nineteen or twenty-six or forty or fifty-seven, or whatever age. It can be hard to know when and how to support overtly and when and how to support only by being. Are there handbooks on this sort of thing?

I sat for two and one-half hours Friday with a couple struggling over sorting out her relationship with a former partner, and the matter of the children. I asked if mediation was available. The problem appears to be getting both parties to sit down at the table together. How can there be next steps without that first step? I watched a movie last night about the life of an artist and about the complex relationships of his life. Always interesting: relationships, how important, how hard.

Sunday morning began with car trouble. A steward from Waingroves came and got me for the 9 o'clock communion, then brought me back. We jumpstarted the car, I rode it around for a while as it was popping and chugging, then drove on to Nether Heage for my next service. When I came out of the chapel there, the car started but popped and died out as I left. A member looked at it, but no luck. So the car is at Nether Heage, and someone brought me back to Ripley. I have a ride to Crich at 3 and will come back by the store for stuff for the meeting at my house tonight.

Now to sort out the car. If I had called AA, I would have had to wait out there with the car. So, I can make do until tomorrow, when I will call Marehay garage about it, and hopefully they will just come get the key and go get the car.

I saw some definitions of *sort* in a dictionary: *chiefly Scottish*: to put to rights: put in order *to examine in order to clarify—used with *out* {*sorting* out his problems} *to free of confusion : to clarify, used with *out* {waited until things *sorted* themselves out}.

Right word for the day. We are all called to sort out matters in our lives; some are simple and silly, while others are major factors affecting us and the ones we love. How good it would be to free ourselves of confusion, to clarify, to put things right and in order.

Together in Faith

SUNDAY AFTERNOON in the little hilltop village of Crich, worshippers at Wesley Chapel were joined by villagers from both the Anglican and Baptist churches who had been at the day of prayer service earlier in the week. Teatime following worship was a buzz of energy and conversation. How good to see a community coming together and supporting each other, to have the presence of these new ecumenical friends. May the relationships grow and flourish.

The night's membership class also reflected a welcome togetherness. Participants from Waingroves will attend next Sunday night when the Codnor group has its membership service and communion. Waingroves' membership service is on Easter Sunday, with one person to be confirmed. She has never taken communion, and in a careful and intentional decision, has chosen to wait until her confirmation to have her first communion. Codnor new members will be there to support them; one Codnor couple is in France on Easter Sunday, but told us they will share French bread and wine at the same time.

Beginning our session at 6 a.m., we shared closing communion at 8, then all sat back down and visited for another two hours. That is a sign of community, for sure. When the tendency can be for churches to stay contained to their own work and life, it is so nice to experience common care and life.

Churches Together is the name of the ecumenical movement here, a vision of groups working alongside each other in communities. We had a glimpse of churches sharing life together in these two events.

Do You Know How Hard It Is to Find
A Good Pencil Sharpener?

AND HOW FRUSTRATED YOU CAN BE WITHOUT ONE?

I had a little red plastic one on my desk when I got here. I think it came with the desk set of holders, ruler, sharpener, eraser, great big paper clip, etc. When it came time to sharpen my pencil, I tried. But the pencil went around and around, a little point came on, as I held it all above the wastebasket to catch the shavings. Oops! There went the lead. Try again. Around and around, out go some shavings, oops! there goes the lead. Around and around, out go some shavings, oops! there goes the lead. It's consistent; that's for sure.

So another day I went to town looking for a good little sharpener. Nope, this store doesn't carry them. How about the news store? No. On to my favorite store, Wilkinson's, the have-it-all ten-cent (or would that be ten-p) hardware store, which carries school supplies. I've looked this store over several times, for rubber bands, envelopes, and other odds and ends for a temporary office. Sure enough, a sturdy little silver sharpener, with a shiny blade. When you're watching your money, you want to get the best kind for the lowest price. I passed on the plastic ones (remember, I've tried that brand) and got the sturdy silver type. I even tried a pencil out on it. Worked OK. Home it goes, up the steps, and onto my desk. In the meantime, I try to keep a few pens there, too, but they wander off, into the bedroom, down into the study, into my bag, into the car, who knows where.

The time comes for a pencil sharpening, with the new silver brand. Around and around, around and around, around—oh, it seems the shiny metal blade has slipped a tad. Straighten it. Try again, around and around, around and around, a few shavings, nothing else. I give up. Try the red one again. The phone rings. I need to make some notes about this call. Reach for a pencil. No point. The only writing utensils on my desk are pencils. Some with totally unsharpened ends, left from a set Davis got while he was here. What did he use for a pencil sharpener? Others have broken ends. The silver sharpener finally began to cut the wood, but, would you believe it, oops! The lead broke. This is real consistency! "Would you please hold the phone?"

Another trip to town, I get really serious about this. I visit the one paper supply store. It was closed the other days—some stores close on Wednesday afternoons, and early any day if business is slow, and on Saturdays.

Do you realize that all the tension of being in a foreign country—in a strange home, in a strange office, without your own books, without your own closet full of art supplies and pens and electric pencil sharpeners, and with only some clothes, and no electric hair curlers and no coffee pot, and in cars that drive on the opposite side, and stores that sell things differently, and food that is not at all the same, and a downtown where you're not sure where to go eat and where not to, and family is gone—can be wrapped up in the need for one little pencil sharpener that works?

Luckily this store had one, another shiny little metal one, but this one had a special name on it, meaning it was a good brand. We sharpened two or three pencils to prove it to me.

"I only want one that won't break the leads."

It seems to work. So home I go, to place it on my desk, in place of the other two. Sure enough, it is wonderful. I can sharpen the colored pencils I got, and regular pencils, and pencils with no erasers. The only thing I must do is to make sure it gets back on my desk, after going to the piano, and the couch, and the downstairs study. . . .

Once I thought I had the good one, but it was the old silver one. I went around and around, around and around—three broken leads made me think it had gone bad too. Then later I found the good one on the piano where I had been doing some composition. It is now back in its place.

When I visited a school this week, I saw where one class had made wonderful art pictures out of pencil shavings. With this wonderful new sturdy silver sharpener, guess what my next project might be? There's nothing quite like a good sharpener to make someone happy.

On Change and Challenge

WOOD STREET LADIES GROUP, who formerly had been having eight or three or six women in attendance, made the decision to move to afternoon meetings. They met this afternoon and had eighteen present! They are so excited and are fine about a younger ladies group meeting in the evenings. How good to hear them excited; they have been so discouraged. They were all just bubbling, full of new energy. I heard of it by phone; still feeling bad, I stayed in all day, except to get the car.

My patience ran quite thin with the garage serviceman, the same one who has been condescending to me before. Patrick went with me, and the man directed his eye contact and statements to Patrick, even though I was the one doing the talking, I was the driver. Patrick realized what was happening and bodily turned to face me, and then withdrew from any conversation. The man spoke to Patrick, Patrick turned and spoke to me, I spoke to the man. The man spoke to Patrick, Patrick turned and spoke to me, I spoke to the man. The man. . . . There was a definite bad pattern here.

They had repaired one thing, but not the other I had specifically said to check. The man commented regarding my anxiety about the noise; I told him my anxiety had to do with whether the car was running safely or not. All I wanted to know was had they checked it and was it safe—is that too hard to answer?

Actually, the issue is this particular person's manner of not taking someone, specifically a woman, seriously. Ironically, a British Automobile Association magazine article this month addresses that very issue of servicemen being condescending or ignoring women's car concerns. I think they wrote it about this guy. The manager was not there today but had already heard the sound, stating what it was and telling me to bring it back for repair. I appreciate his polite, professional way. He needs to work with his assistant.

Moving toward Mothering Sunday

THIS HAS BEEN A DEEP AND CHALLENGING DAY. Earlier, before I left the house, I received a phone call from a distressed suicidal older woman; that call led to a conversation with her daughter, which led me to the realization and reminder of the difficulty of relationships. Sunday is Mothering Sunday here, which comes at a different time in the year than in the US. Occurring on the fourth Sunday of Lent and having existed since about the sixteenth century, the day began as a time for villagers to return to the mother church or cathedral. It also became a time for young people working as servants to visit their homes, to see their mothers, bringing gifts of flowers or simnel cakes.* As I put the service together, I am so aware of the diversity of situations I have come into contact with this week: a difficult mother–daughter relationship, a marriage blessing where a mother of a child born before the marriage wants to claim new meaning, a mother who faces the day with the loss of her children. Somehow, having Mothering Sunday occur during Lent seems appropriate.

Colin has invited me to be at his church, Watchorn Church in Alfreton. Using the Lenten reading John 12:1–8 telling of Mary anointing Jesus' feet, I will focus on relationship and healing: the oil, aroma, and feel, the power of touch and memory, images of mother God, but also the incompleteness and hurt of relationships and the promise of healing in God's love. This complex parent–child relationship matter holds struggles for so many people, needing the healing anointing of love.

I had planned to go over to Ruth's after tonight's meeting, but friends had come over to her home. They were having a good visit, so I will go another day. I have learned that her birthday is April 27; she is a Taurus, same as myself. Hearts are aware of this first Mothering Sunday following the accident.

The tragic Lockerbie Scotland primary school event that just occurred is another reminder of the pain many mothers and fathers will feel on this upcoming Sunday. I appreciate this ancient image of church as mother church, a place to come for healing, nurture, and love when the pain of the world is so great—a haven for people who still look to the church for God's presence and grace.

> *Mothering God, be with me as I shape this day of worship together, and be with all who are planning the time of worship for this day, that in the lives of persons who know pain, conflict, loss, a word of healing anointing love be heard. May the church serve to offer your spirit of love. May all mothers in all places be upheld in acts of love and grace.*

PATRICK BROUGHT ME HIS *Methodist Recorder* newspapers, which had more letters about the homosexual advertisement and an editorial on Pat Buchanan's presidential candidacy. At tonight's circuit meeting Patrick informed everyone he was praying for Buchanan to win, because I told him if Buchanan won, I was staying over here. An article about a Sheffield church buying a pub for an inner-city mission reminds me of what some folks in Wood Street Chapel wanted two years ago here in Ripley. They wanted to buy a pub for sale right on market square, but that did not happen. I have been told that a part of the reason for not doing it was a District recommendation not to, based on the fact that it was close to the Anglican church. That was an unfortunate decision, as it would have been just where the church needs to be, in the middle of town life. Whatever the reason for not going that direction, it seems to have shaped their present future, bound by their present location. Hopefully a vision for the right way forward will come for them.

A Celebration of Friends

AFTER A FOUR-HOUR DELAY and an unscheduled but obviously necessary plane re-fueling in Cardiff, Wales, Jim arrived Sunday afternoon just in time to attend Codnor's evening confirmation service.

Jim Cross had first sung with me many years ago as the church choir tenor soloist and member of a talented creative music ensemble. Since those days we had worked together in many settings, both in music and arts and in his field of gifted education; we had become good friends like family. In August the year before I went to England, I had been pianist for him in his fiftieth birthday celebration concert and had composed a song for him, a setting of his favorite poem, Emerson's *Success*. So, it was very special to have him now come to England, to witness and be a part of this unique year, particularly as he was not an appreciator of cold weather and March was still quite brisk. He joyfully arrived, all bundled in warmth, from his head to his foot.

I knew that the Codnor congregation would appreciate his musical presence. In the spontaneous Cross-Mutert fashion we had shared over the years, as we drove to the chapel I invited Jim to join me that evening in a brief musical offering. We parked in front of the church and quickly moved inside to the keyboard for a moment's rehearsal. In the worship service I was using a song I had written years earlier as a theme song for a church, now right for this English confirmation service. At that point, after introducing Jim and the song, I moved over to the little black piano keyboard at the side of the room and we began to sing,

"To be God's people, to claim the promise,
to live the blessing day by day.
We join our hearts and hands as family,
and live the love we are to be...."

How right these words were for this congregation, to join together and uphold each other, to support these adults who had put many months of thought and preparation into this confirmation service occasion. The mood and feeling in the worship room was warm and uplifting, adding to my own joy at having walked these friends through faith matters for the past weeks, with shared conversations, questions, stories, concerns, and now to confirm and welcome them into the membership body of this caring community. Each came forward to stand and state a commitment to the life of this church and to receive the little blue-and-white ticket of membership, a tradition from Wesleyan days. Individuals who had already been an active part of chapel life had chosen to follow this formal path of relationship. Then, as family, we shared the sacrament of bread and cup.

I was glad that Jim, with his own gracious and caring spirit, had become a part of this occasion. His friendship has continued to bless me throughout the years. He again visited England when I returned for more years of ministry, the next time coming in a Christmas visit to sing the tenor solos from Handel's *Messiah*.

After the Codnor service Jim and I drove out to the Excavator pub, which sits at the intersection of the roads to Crich and Pentrich. The sky was still light at that hour, and the golden floodlights pointing up onto the pub with its colorful hanging baskets of cascading flowers caused the pub to shine in a golden glow, matching the inside glow of that which is heaven itself, treacle pudding, the object of our pub visit. There is nothing quite so lovely as warm, syrupy treacle steam pudding cake, smothered in a moat of warm, rich yellow pouring custard. Ah, yes, heaven for the weary traveler. With much to share in our catch-up talking and listening, we lingered over the pudding and cup of tea and chatted until his jet lag called him to the manse.

The next day I maneuvered early-morning traffic and delivered Jim into downtown Nottingham city centre, then I located Kingswood church, not in city centre, for a ministerial meeting with the British Conference president Brian Hoare. Later Jim and I reconnected at the set time with no problem, once I found a car space in the parking deck, then made the walk through the bustling crowd of shoppers and past the regular criers standing in the streets declaring the end of the world and selling their newspapers. I suppose they are in every city.

Nottingham city centre is always impressive, with its historic County Hall where the infamous sheriff of Nottingham was once seated and the large city square now holding bubbling fountains and huge hanging baskets of flowing flowers. Up one cobblestone side street, we located a little French restaurant someone had recommended, then enjoyed the sights of the city and returned to Ripley.

Probationer ministers moving through the process of ordination in England were each scheduled for interviews with the district ordination committee, occurring at a church outside Nottingham. Jim and I had planned to drive down for that interview, then travel on to southern England. We entered the dreaded fight with the M1 morning traffic, destined for Beeston. The meeting, however, was held at Breaston, in the same general proximity. Thankfully I eventually happened to notice the difference in the names and arrive just on time for a 9:30 a.m. interview with the committee. After the group shared a leisurely coffee and chat, our meeting began at 10 o'clockish. After almost a year in this culture, I had not yet learned about these things. When the committee asked me about my experience here, I could have added a word about tea and coffee as agenda items.

Having finished these days of important church events, I was now freer for visiting and travel during Jim's short stay. Making good time down to Kent, we enjoyed an excursion to the white cliffs of Dover and shared a well-known tradition. The English ice-cream vans may be just as important an institution as the venues where they often sit, awaiting customers. We chose the Flake99 cornet, that cone of creamy ice cream offered in many flavors, with a delicious Cadbury chocolate flake standing in it.

Dover castle sits high above the famous cliffs overlooking the channel waters. A first-century keep, a lovely chapel, a massive castle, underground tunnels that may have been the original twilight zone, and a history that dates through the centuries from William of Normandy to World War II, the edifice towers over the ancient town and all who come and go from the busy hub of channel travel. After a good wander around, we returned to the car park to realize that I had left the whole car unlocked, trunk included. I was very fortunate to have a car still there.

Our brief Paris visit via the Chunnel provided a taste of the rich sights, sounds, and foods of that extraordinary city. One highlight was the quiet, moving beauty within Notre Dame Cathedral, in spite of the noise of crowds and the priest on the loudspeaker. As we sat in a secluded-as-possible spot, Jim sang a few lines of music in his beautiful tenor voice, adding his musical imprint to this sacred space.

Ripley manse awaited our return and the arrival of other stateside friends. In the next days Jim would depart and two families from Birmingham, Alabama, active members of my former church there, Canterbury, would pass through Ripley as a part of spring break England visits.

My phone rang. The Faulkners had landed and were on their way to Ripley, Yorkshire. It was good they called. Since I lived in Ripley, Derbyshire, they made a quick adjustment and came my direction instead. I remembered my own map search for the town when I first learned where I would be living, when I had discovered other England Ripleys. They found the manse, also finding dirty dishes and dead flowers, while Jim and I were at town centre buying dishwashing soap and fresh flowers.

I was eager to show the five churches to the visitors, but it would have to be the abbreviated edition, as everyone was starving and jetlag was creeping in. After a quick tour and hearty meal at the Derwent Hotel Pub, four tired travelers were longing for bed. Peter and Elaine Grout had offered their home for my guests while the Grouts themselves were out of town, so Stan, Diane, Jennifer, and Jimmy traveled to the Grout's lovely Orchard Cottage in Pentrich village. Meanwhile, at Nine Clumber Close Jim prepared to travel back to London and the US.

My last guests of March were mother and daughter friends also from Canterbury in Alabama. Cam was keeping some of my plants; this trip was celebrating Kate's high-school graduation. I left early for the Manchester airport, after saying good-byes to Jim.

A Peak District drive is always a pastoral visage to enjoy; however, this day I could not see any of the views for all of the early-morning English fog. Mindful of the early-morning ride in December that became so fateful, I proceeded with care and watchfulness for others on the road at this hour.

Ridiculously obscure signs to the Manchester airport from the Peak direction are a true maze; they lead to nowhere. Absolutely nowhere. I decided that someone intentionally created the crazy maze of back streets to be as confusing as possible. When years later I had conquered the turns and shifting roads to be able to accurately traverse the route, I felt as if I had succeeded in life's journey. Presently I just was glad to eventually arrive and quickly park.

Just as I entered the terminal, the two travel-punchy decompression-happy arrivers exited the customs door.

"How was the trip?"

"Great!"

"Awful!"

It is all a matter of perspective, I suppose. We loaded the car and started out to be on our way. That is, after we got out of the car park metered gate. I have always been picked up here, so I did not remember that I had to pay at the machine before I got to the exit sign. I pulled the car over out of the way, found the card, found the machine, paid for the parking, got back into line, and finally we were off—only to stop after a few minutes of driving, hearing a thunderous clonking from under the car. With the assistance of a most helpful truck driver who looked under the boot, we discovered that the luggage was weighting down the back of the car enough to make it drag. That surely brought back a memory of my arrival some eight months earlier. Kate soon had a suitcase on the backseat with her—a good headrest, I know, I've been there.

Driving across the high hills, past stonewalled pastures, limestone, and gritstone villages of the Peak District, we met the Faulkners at Chatsworth for a visit of the house and gardens, a place I knew these guests would enjoy. Later in Matlock Bath, nestled along the River Derwent, right on the water's edge, The Midland was just serving the last order of the afternoon. From pâté to Yorkshire pudding, toasties to beer, folks sampled an authentic pub meal.

Swanwick chapel was filled when we arrived for the evening confirmation service. I knew this would be an opportunity for my visitors to experience the wonderful enthusiasm of the Methodists in England. The congregational singing was absolutely brilliant and the service very moving. This group of confirmands included Vernon's two daughters. As the confirmands knelt before me, we prayed for God's healing hand upon the hearts of Vernon's dear family, and the joy and upholding of eternal love upon all who had traveled this confirmation journey. In spite of the deep reality of his absence, Vernon's love and presence were felt.

Teatime following the service was in the same schoolroom where I had come so many months ago to substitute for Vernon in opening a meeting. Now the room buzzed with energy, the voices engaged in busy conversation, the tables overflowed with food. It was good to see and feel the energy there, to have my visitors be a part of the conversations and the setting. Jimmy found a fellow boy scout, and the others entered into the talk over tea. Afterward, my visitors and I drove out to the Excavator for a late-evening snack. Finally, at the end of a long day, we parted company—the Bullocks and I to Nine Clumber Close, the Faulkners to Pentrich for a last Derbyshire evening.

Transition morning had come again. After a short shopping trip in Ripley, the Faulkners loaded their rental car and drove into the Welsh horizon to continue their British journey, while we remaining three drove east for Lincoln, a place Cam had thoroughly researched and wanted to visit.

Lincoln Castle within the city is a mighty site, with an original Magna Carta found here. What Cam had not learned, our guide in the Magna Carta room filled in for us, every dot and tittle. In interesting contrast to the majestic castle and the historic document housed there since 1216, the prison within is a stark reminder of humanity not caring for humanity. We humans did and do act inhumanely with great ease. From the prison and prison chapel with its celled stalls, steps lead upward to the keep, a secure inner room in a medieval castle. Up and down the narrow stone steps continue, winding up, out, and over to the corner tower, where the view from the top of the tower offers a magnificent panorama of Lincoln Cathedral and town.

Soon we were ready to discover the grand cathedral itself, even down to the infamous little Lincoln imp residing up in the rafters between two arches in the north side of the choir. Only twelve inches high, it sits with one foot resting on the other knee, half-grinning at all that happens below, somehow reminding us of Kate's younger sister Meg. Years later, I would return to this cathedral in celebration of the John Wesley 300th birthday anniversary and recall, midst the crowds and celebration, the little imp of the rafters. Our present visit ended with an evensong service, complete with the glorious sounds of choir and organ. Filled with sense and sound, we headed out and down. Lincoln Cathedral is on a hill, which is hardly noticeable until you go down it and have to come back up.

With handrails and rest benches along the way, we journeyed back up the hill to discover a cozy little restaurant where we concluded our Lincoln visit with a meal of mussels, chestnuts, and pigeon. Passing a statue of Alfred Lord Tennyson on the way to the car park, Cam spoke of the many layers of history in this fascinating city, grateful for a day well spent.

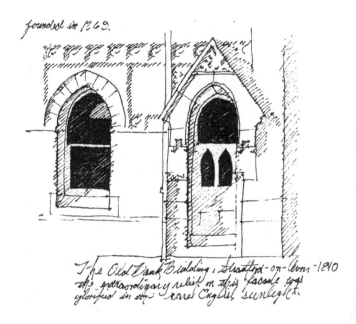

founded in 1269.

The Old Bank Building, Stratford-on-Avon - 1890 the extraordinary relief on this facade was glorified in the rarest English sunlight.

My friends' final day in this area included two places south of Derbyshire: Coventry, whose cathedral is worth all visitors seeing. And from there to Stratford-on-Avon in search of Shakespeare.

Past the tourist push, the riverside town of Stratford-on-Avon offers an entry into the quaint world of Shakespeare. With homes, theatres, church, bookstores, gardens, and riverside walkways, as well as plentiful opportunities for shopping, the town provides a full afternoon of touring. Full of the day's adventures, Cam and Kate eventually arrived at the Derby train station, where I met them following my evening meeting.

Leaving day for Kate and Cam was here. They planned to go to York, stash luggage, and head to Bronte country. We dashed down to Derby for the train, barely making it on time, then the train was thirty-five minutes late. One last time we shared bread and cup, the communion of friends, then they were off on their journey. They too would have to complete their end of the tale.

There are many ways to visit another country. I hoped that this opportunity of visiting a small community in the Midlands—seeing the life of the people and churches, talking with those who live there, staying in English homes, and visiting the places I have come to love—provided meaningful times for all who made the journeys. I had anticipated each of the visits for a long time; how quickly they then passed. But how special to have each of my visitors here throughout the year, allowing the two worlds of my work and life to meet.

AS MARCH CAME TO AN END, I was grateful for the many ways friendship, love, and support were experienced. There is a richness in sharing life with others and in being aware of the joy of relationships. The time of shared laughter, conversation, concern, and care is time well spent. Friendships are a part of the fabric of life that nourishes, enriches, accompanies, and engages. There are those relationships that endure through the changes and transitions of life and those that come to us in the new. In all, the rhythms of life add richness and fullness.

I'D LIKE TO SEE MY GRANDBABY; it won't be too long.

Little blue flowers—I've been told there are tiny blue flowers growing in one of my pots back home, spring is springing all around the world.

$\mathcal{A}$PRIL : *Resurrection Reality*

All in the April evening, April airs were abroad;
I saw the sheep with their lambs,
and thought on the Lamb of God.

Katharine Tynan Hinkson

$\mathcal{T}$here is an Easter anthem, "All in the April Evening," written by an Irish poet and set to music by a Scottish conductor, which draws a pastoral image of lambs and sheep, of nature, of the holy event of Easter. Now here we were, entering April, the lambing season, the time of new birth, observing Easter in the midst of pastures filled with sheep and lambs, preparing for a Holy Week journey and a birthday observance in settings that gave personal shape to the song.

April 1, and Snow Falls!

"IN YOUR EASTER BONNET . . ." sang the CD player sitting on the table in the schoolroom at Wood Street toddler's Easter bonnet parade. The youngsters circled up, then marched and paraded around the schoolroom, their creative hats slipping and sliding on little heads, some proudly bobbing, others shyly tucking chins in. With their colorful signs of the season—flowers and eggs, chicks and bows, bunnies and bonnets—the tiny toddlers were adorable. A good beginning for the first day of April.

This has been a beautiful open-window day, with clear blue skies that seem to go forever, fluffy clouds lazily floating by, and sunny-side-up sunshine—with an intermittent flurry or two of snow. Early afternoon I opened windows and leisurely straightened and fluffed the house. None of the many interpretations of English skies expressed by artists throughout the centuries fully capture the real thing. Such beauty stirs a desire to express it, to recreate it, although it may be impossible to fully capture the moving natural beauty of the sky, a virtual living show of wonder.

A Woman's Story

AS THE AFTERNOON CAME TO A CLOSE, I decided to make two home visits in Ripley. My first call was to see Rene, who had face surgery last Friday, as a follow-up to earlier surgery for a malignant tumor. This visit gave me the opportunity to know more of her story. She talked about Maurice, her deceased brother, who in his life had such a gifted eye for photography. Rene brought out photos of the U.S. capitol, taken when Maurice served in Canada during the war. She invited me to select one of his pictures, so I chose a lovely black-and-white photo of a gypsy caravan, which she then placed in a frame for me. I also chose two little snapshots: one of the peace tower in Ottawa, the other of the skyline of downtown Manhattan at that time. Together we sat and turned the pages of the album, filled with old photos from his assignment in America. What wonderful images of a time past and a country in bygone days. He had such a gift for capturing the moment, the occasion.

Also a photographer, Rene's eye is drawn to different images—bridges, churches, and flowers. Together we browsed through a lovely portfolio of her work, all taken with a simple plain camera. Then our conversation turned more introspective. In her quiet way, this small, fragile, soft-spoken woman returned to the work of her brother, with a reference to a large picture of the Ottawa peace tower hanging in her lounge.

"I want to give you this. Whenever you receive it, you will know my time is up," she simply stated. With her cancer returning, she knew the possibilities and probabilities.

In such a moment as this I am reminded how inevitable life's end is. Rene is now facing her illness and her life in view of that ending. As she served me tea in the quiet of her lounge, we continued our conversation. I learned that Rene had served many years as a communion steward but has never served communion. She has prepared people to come to the table and prepared the table but has never served that special meal. We talked about the possibility of her assisting me some time in the future, if she would like. "Oh, yes, is that possible?" she responded without a hesitation.

"We will talk again about that," I noted to myself.

Rene and her brother have had a wonderful gift of seeing beauty—in nature and flowers, in the curves and shapes and shadows of buildings and bridges, in brightly colored gypsy wagons. Their travels took them to places worth capturing on camera. Or, more true, their innate ability to see beauty enabled them to see and capture the

beautiful all around us. I would love for us to do an exhibit of her church photographs—
How lovely is thy dwelling place—her photos viewed as the soaring sounds of the beautiful
Brahms choral anthem serve as a background for the display. Rene has sung that song
in her heart, in her eye for beauty, in her faith, in her life. And she will continue to see
beauty, as long as she is able.

From Rene's home I drove to see Sara, a woman I had met at a recent community
event. "For a brief ten-minute visit," she had said when she called me to come; once there,
I knew we needed more time. As I entered the front door, the sweet fragrance of freesia
flowers greeted me, then I saw the small vase holding a colorful array of pink, lavender, and
yellow blossoms on the little table in the lounge where we settled on the blue flowered
couch. Sara took time to share with me a little of the couple's history: the loss of a child
several years ago, the difficult physical and emotional journey past that. And now, the
possibility of trying again. She wanted to talk with someone about her fears, her worry.

"I'm sorry to trouble you with such a little thing," she said, "I know I shouldn't
worry."

Oh, my, how can the loss of a dear child and the hopeful but cautious concerns
for creating life be little and not worth sharing. What a precious gift of life story and
journey we who serve as pastors are given to hold and hear, bless and share, even with
someone we hardly know. And how much I as a mother understand her cares and
concerns. I am grateful she trusted enough to share her heart. After our time of tea and
quiet talk, I rose to go, but I knew we would visit again.

As evening came, I joined the women of Codnor Open Door, a gathering of
twenty-plus women from the community who meet weekly at Codnor Chapel. This
night I was to be the speaker for the meeting. My earlier intent had been to talk about
Holy Week, but my thoughts and heart still lingered with the women I had just visited.
As I entered this room created to hold both worship and weekday life, the buzz of
laughter and energetic voices filled the space. How good when the worship space is
grounded in the heart of daily life, daily activities. This group of women comes here
week in, week out to be together, to celebrate the sisterhood of life. I looked around,
feeling very connected with the women sitting there: I had buried a husband for one,
a sister for another, I had confirmed one, had shared communion and laughter. The
way for the night was clear: share story, my story, our story.

When we settled into program time, I offered to answer questions in our conversation. With that invitation, the members began to ask me questions women would ask of a woman. I replied as best I could.

"What is life like in your part of America?"

"In small towns, I think it is similar to Derbyshire. The state I come from is partly rural with farming and agriculture; it also has coal mining and the steel industry, both facing similar challenges as here. I have lived mostly in large cities, where life moves at a faster pace, even in Alabama. But your way of life gives me many gifts: time to appreciate, to share, to discover the beautiful land called the Peak District, to experience the history and story of people and places."

"How did you take the risk of coming over here?" "Was it hard leaving your family?" "What will going back be like?"

"Well, I took the risk because my heart was calling me to. No, I did not want to leave family, but this was a time when I could do so. And I believe they have enjoyed the chance to be in England some. I am not sure what going back will be like. I will have changed in some ways; I will be returning to new work; I don't know yet where I will be going, beyond a little more time in Atlanta."

"What has your experience here been like?"

"Oh, my . . . was it what I expected? So much unexpected has happened, who can say? I have loved being here, with you, with this beautiful countryside of Derbyshire. Perhaps I have fallen in love with it, in spite of the weather and Saturday nights in Ripley." We laughed together, then someone asked a looking-ahead question, "Will you miss us when you are gone?"

I looked around again on this roomful of women, representative of the women and men I have worked with, have served communion, have shared life with. "Oh, my, yes, dear ones, I will miss you."

I spoke of my admiration for what I see in them, in their stories as I know them: their strength, their friendships, their survival ability, and their joy. As I think back over the day's visits, I know for sure that this day is one reason I have made this midlife change, to be with people, to share story and support each other, to laugh and cry, to pray and bless, to hope and face life together. I will go to bed with the questions and conversations lingering in my head and heart.

Later in the evening Dan called. "Hey, Mom, how's it going?" he began. We talked of how things were going there, then he told of receiving one of the Southeastern Conference athlete-scholar graduate scholarships, to whatever graduate school he chooses. If he goes to University of Alabama, it will pay for his year. I regret that I have missed so many of his university activities this year—how proud I am of him. The phone rang again—it was Carl, and we shared parents' joy of the day for Dan.

> *Mothering God, in all that is holy and precious on this day of story and sharing, may each woman I encountered today know peace and love. May those who are facing difficulty or fear not feel alone. May women of all places claim the presence of others. And may Dan and all my family who are so far away know my love.*

The Village

"THERE IS ROOM IN MY CAR FOR ONE MORE PERSON."

With that, we made arrangements for rides, concluded the ladies meeting, climbed the narrow stairway from the basement schoolroom, walked into and through the chapel sanctuary, moved out of the little arched entryway, and drove to the pub for lunch. This was the day the ladies of Nether Heage had decided to have lunch at the Spanker Inn, the attractive local pub in the village on the right of Spanker Lane as it ascends up from the valley. Nether Heage is a wonderful example of a unique, beautiful Derbyshire village, full of history, working to find its future. The flowerboxes and gardens of the many cottages along the little lanes are bubbling over with color like the overflow of a forgotten bubble bath. When in bloom, they bring an aroma of joy and pleasure that brightens the heart.

The Spanker Inn has long been a central part of this village's community life, with a reputation for excellent pub meals. Colorful hanging baskets of red, pink, blue, and white blooms of lobelia, busy lizzies, tumbling petunias, and inviting outdoor picnic tables welcomed us. The friendly pub manager greeted us as we made our way into the rich dark wood interior of the pub, finding our way into the back room. Lunchtime passed so quickly for us—sitting, chatting and laughing, eating and chatting, and more eating. We enjoyed fresh roast beef, yorkshire pudding, roasted potatoes, carrots, peas, and then the wicked joy of steamed treacle pudding with hot pouring custard; the closing benediction was a nice cup of tea. Our ladies were delighted that we had come; their faces were lit

Spanker Inn

with energy and life; their voices were like a lovely mini-symphony of sound echoing on the pub's walls. How I wished that the group had done this sooner. There is great pleasure for the spirit and body in sharing a meal over laughter and conversation.

After lunch, I stayed in the village to visit in the homes of three older homebound persons in Nether Heage. In this year I have realized that in my life I have not been closely associated with many people who have lived to such longevity, nineties and beyond. I never knew grandparents except in the first two years of my life. My own father is now approaching the ages of these three persons; he is eighty-eight and facing the challenges of declining health and mind. Perhaps in some way, being with the older folks here is a way of being connected with him back home. Mother is much younger and in good health and able to stay active. But inevitably if we live, we each will face the reality of our bodies wearing out, our minds and spirits tiring.

Back down in the lower village, in a home directly across from the chapel on Slack Lane, resided Mrs. Alice Goadby, one hundred and one years old, who lived alone—how remarkable that is to me. She sat in the lounge, the lights off, just using the natural light from the windows. Her feet propped on a little stool, hands folded in her lap, she greeted me with a "do come in," and then we talked of her health and of life. I told her of our lunch at the Spanker, and of all who were able to be with us. She graciously offered her apologies, as she tended to nod off in rest and quiet, while I sat there.

After a short visit—no need to stay too long, just to see how she was but not tire her out—I drove back up Slack Lane, veering right on Malthouse Lane with its many cottages lining the street, then right again onto Spanker Lane Hill, stopping at the two-story greystone house across from the pub, home of Mr. and Mrs. Abbott.

Mrs. Abbott welcomed me at the front door, then we moved into the dimly lit lounge, where I found a place on a time-shaped armchair across from the couch where Mr. Abbott lay; ill with pneumonia and cancer at age ninety-three, he was covered with a handmade throw. They both told me of their lives in the village, of how during "The War" (World War II), folks in this village kept children who were evacuees sent to the Midlands from London to be safe from the bombings. "Did you have war threats here?" I asked. "We never did, but we kept the children safe and away from harm. It was hard to see them return home after the war; they were like our own," they reflected. The Abbotts still stay in touch with those children who stayed with them.

Mr. Abbott helped to build the schoolroom under the chapel at Nether Heage, where the ladies' group meets. Mrs. Abbott was a lifelong native of the village. With great joy and pride, she invited me to her kitchen and showed me her fancy new Aga cast-iron kitchen stove, which had replaced the old coal-burning one. "It is so much better, so much easier to cook with, just look at all it does," she shared. I, the non-cook, felt such appreciation for her pride of the new stove, as I stood with her in the small back kitchen with lace curtains on the windows, baskets containing fresh fruit and vegetables, and small collector's pieces sitting on the countertops. Their home is a journal of the story of their lives, holding memory of all they have shared together. Dear gentle Mr. Abbott, weak and ill, lying on the couch, occasionally shared that beautiful smile and rose to share a story of a house, a church, a place, as he was able, while Mrs. Abbott and I sat talking by the fire. I shall hold this memory for a long time.

Ninety-four-year-old Mrs. Spriggs, who recently came home from the hospital, lived back down in the lower village. During our visit, she dozed off a few times, then would stir and apologize. As she talked of being home for the first time in this new year since breaking her leg and the difficulty of trusting again after a fall, her wonderful piercing eyes burned into my memory. Recovering from a fall at this age, isn't she obliged a fall, if she so moves. I soon departed, leaving her to rest.

Amazing. Each one of them. They each live in their longtime village homes, two of them living alone. Memories are still keen, filled with stories of the little chapel and

the village and the families who had lived there so long. I imagine a little rural town in Alabama, a person telling me the history of the buildings, the people, etc. The same stories are there, waiting to be told.

As I left the last home, I drove back up by the chapel and looked over to the windmill, quiet and still, having its own stories of broken sails, of activity and life, then aging health, loved by the community, then forgotten. This late afternoon, I could envision the glow of the little chapel the broken angel overlooked—the windows of cobalt blue, emerald green, ruby red, and sun yellow diamond panes that sparkled with the light of day from the outside and glowed with evening warmth from within in the evening. There they had both stood for a few centuries, the windmill on the hill, the little chapel nestled between the cottages along the lane, seeing and hearing the stories of all who had called this village home, the good times, the difficult times. Nether Heage, like many other villages scattered around the countryside, had a rich past, a changing present, and an uncertain wonder about what lay ahead. For them and for others, life goes on, with gratitude for each day.

> *Under the watchful eye of the broken-winged angel of life's bread, in the warmth of the chapel's glow within and without, in the nowness of sheep quietly grazing in the meadow, may this village and its dwellers be upheld in the blessing of love for this day and the next.*

Windows of Reflection

THE LADIES AT NETHER HEAGE SPOKE of their awareness that I would be with them only three or four more times. As I was responsible for five churches, my time in each church had been and would be limited. That did make the time left seem short. I hoped I would not spend the last four months here in limbo, realizing this was ending and looking to what was ahead.

I knew I needed some time and pre-flection looking ahead to my return, with Tuscaloosa as the home base. That thought felt strange; I had not lived there in seven years. I had not heard from anyone at home about appointments. I still hoped to hear soon from someone about my ordination occurring over here, with the British Conference and the North Alabama Conference working together for this. I so wanted it to happen; this had been such a meaningful year.

I HAD BEEN INVITED TO SERVE ON THE LEADERSHIP TEAM for the thirty-year ministry retreat, a ten-day visit in May at lovely Ammerdown Retreat Centre outside of Bath. One of the strengths of the church here is in its attention to the care for the clergy, as witnessed in various retreats offered to them for times of reflection and renewal. This is something I would carry home with me, this idea of the need for care and nourishment of the soul for all. As I prepared for my retreat responsibility to plan the Sunday framework, I thought of the windows of Coventry Cathedral.

I find Coventry Cathedral to be one of the most moving and magnificent cathedrals in all of England. There is so much nonverbal narrative in the setting itself—the ruins of the old cathedral with walls barely standing and the historic altar built of charred beams all remained after the bombing of World War II. The new cathedral rises out of the old, with the symbolism of peace over war, love over hate evident in every detail. It is a twentieth-century statement, holding to historical truths in the aesthetic language of today's world. Each visit I make, there is more to witness, to ponder, to appreciate in the abilities of the gifted artisans who were called upon to create the cathedral's treasures.

On a recent visit, I was again struck by the beauty and symbolism of the tall side windows that you cannot see until you walk the length of the sanctuary to the front altar, then turn and face back up the chancel. There they are, the beautiful colored stain glass of those side windows, glistening from bottom to top. Is that not a way of looking at life? There is much we miss as we walk into life, but upon reflection, returning, we see the beauty of that which has been all along, a hidden undiscovered beautiful part of our journey. Danish theologian Søren Kierkegaard wrote in his journal, "Life can only be understood backward but it must be lived forward."

With the retreat theme on past, present, and future, I began to create a focus for Sunday: We would center on the seasons, the movement of life, allowing us to acknowledge the different seasons we find ourselves living in, looking back at where we've been as we walk into the light of the future.

This certainly seemed right for those folk who had served so long in ministry, who were being given time away for reflection on past, present, and future. In a sense, turning and reflecting had been a part of my own year here and was surely a reality of Easter. The windows of Coventry, the images of life, not denying the broken, the charred, but rising up in beauty out of the journey into the journey.

An Easter Week to Remember

MY ENGLISH EXPERIENCE OF HOLY WEEK and Easter had arrived, had been filled with activity, and now was past. We moved through the traditional services and events remembering and recalling the holy story, reflecting its meaning in our today's story. It was a balance of reality and possibility.

A COMMUNAL WEDNESDAY MEAL

MIDWEEK OCCASIONS INCLUDED A UNIQUE SHARING. Msgr. Moore invited me to participate in a Seder meal observance the Catholic church held on Wednesday evening. I recognized that this was a significant invitation, a recognition of my ministerial presence, and I was grateful for it. As I stood and read one of the readings prepared for the evening, I knew that this was a right path, a good part of our week's journey, the honoring of the Jewish tradition, the sharing of community, the hope of new bridges of community.

MAUNDY THURSDAY

The time was early evening, the place a room upstairs,
The guests were the disciples,
few in numbers and few in prayers. . . .

THE TIME WAS EARLY EVENING, the place was Wood Street Chapel, the guests were ecumenical, and numbers were good. Because the service was intended to be a Ripley community event held at Wood Street, I had invited other ministers to share leadership. The service was attended by worshippers from several congregations. The monthly Oasis services here had established some groundwork for community worship. On this night liturgy and story drama came from the Iona worship resources I had discovered. After the service ended, I found myself singing our theme text and lovely Scottish tune again and again, its chorus continuing:

Oh, the food comes from the baker, the drink comes from the vine,
the words come from the Maker, I will meet you in bread and wine.

The beginning of high holy drama is in a small upper room with friends, sharing life, showing love.

FRIDAY: A GOOD DAY, INDEED

AS MORNING CAME I LOOKED OUT THE WINDOW and saw white frost covering the ground—on Friday, April 5! After thawing out my totally frozen car, I carefully drove up the icy hill to Crich to start Good Friday with an early-morning service and breakfast. On this frosty morn, the little sanctuary was filled with community gathering from all over the village. In the womb of this little chapel, we shared a simple reading of the gospel for the day and a song, then moved to the kitchen, with the lovely aroma of the warm buns filling the air. Around the cloth-covered tables prepared for our breakfast of soft-boiled eggs and hot cross buns, community friends engaged in warm fellowship and conversation. Such a lovely beginning to the day: the fellowship, the feeling of life and energy, a special breakfast table, a good Friday morning.

"THE MINISTERS WILL LEAD THE WAY, CARRYING THE CROSS."

Ripley's midmorning Walk of Witness through city centre streets began, with members from each participating church following the leaders. I had to walk faster to keep up with the other ministers, a reminder that legs are different lengths. Our downtown walk ended at All Saints, where we gathered to worship. Led by their clergy, the service held a wide range of experiences, most people there greatly appreciating the drama of the service. Maybe I was longing for home. At the point of having the congregation come forward and post notes to the cross I stayed back, along with others who chose not to go up. In that moment I made a mental note to always leave room, space, and OK-ness for those who do not wish to actively participate in a prescribed act of commitment.

Cheryl Love had invited me back up to Crich for lunch after the busy morning, "…to make sure I ate," she said. Cheryl had prepared fresh salmon trout and asparagus and had set the lace cloth–covered dining room table with her delicate English china. We sat around the table sharing this traditional Good Friday meal, chatting about the great sense of energy we felt at the Crich morning breakfast, and then talked of things of Graham's heart: his collections, his joy at reworking mechanisms, his life growing up in Derbyshire. Pushing back from the table, Cheryl and I moved into the lounge, settling on the warm couch in front of the fire blazing in the fireplace. As we spoke of our shared love for music, Cheryl reached to the shelf, picked up an old dark blue book, and gave me a precious gift—a sol-fa edition of the old Methodist Hymnal to carry home. As a musician I had learned the patterns of the old singing schools, so together we chose a hymn and made an effort to sing.

Then Graham, who is so gifted with mechanical things, invited me into his workroom, a magical clock fairyland. With meticulous care he repairs his clocks, bringing renewed life to them. The sounds of ticking create polyphonic rhythms in the room. Ticks and tocks, tick-tick and tick-tock, bongs and boings, all bringing surround sound into the little workroom. The couple has a hundred-plus-year-old large wooden Swiss music box, which, when playing one of its eight tunes, emits a glorious deep mellow resonant ringing that reverberates and lingers in the heart.

As I was leaving their home, Graham offered to give me a brief glimpse inside their caravan—their one-hundred-year-old gypsy caravan, that is! He was in an ongoing process of remodeling it; the inside held festive brightly colored painted tiles and old delicate lace curtains, with sconces on either side of the little fireplace. It is wonderfully enchanting; I could imagine embarking on a magical storybook journey upon entering the little door. What a very special Good Friday lunch visit, a reminder of what time is to be for.

It is good to be here to experience the traditions and rituals of another place, such as the morning's hot cross buns, an English tradition. During the rest of the year, they are just teacakes with raisins or currants, but on Good Friday they have clearly marked crosses on them, marking the sign of Christian faith. I called a friend to find out the history of how that tradition got started.

"Hot cross buns! Hot cross buns! One a penny, two a penny..." she sang, to which I replied, "Now that is a song we know." The familiar nursery rhyme was a reminder that the buns have been around for a long time, even as the church changed from Catholic to Anglican in England. Some say that sharing a hot cross bun with a friend brings good luck for the coming year. Another strong tradition is that of no meat on Good Friday, thus the trout for lunch. The soft-boiled eggs of this morning are also a tradition, although many churches have them on Easter day. They enjoy the eggs in a lovely, dainty way. As the egg rests in an egg holder, you tap and peel a little shell off the top, then use a spoon to dip egg bites out, leaving the shell in a nice egg shape. Surprisingly, they do not dye eggs here, so no peeling of the eggs gathered from an egg hunt. Customs vary.

People were already at Waingroves Chapel for the Waingroves-Codnor ecumenical evening walk when I arrived in late afternoon. Twenty people gathered to begin the journey, then we processed down the descent of the long, narrow Waingroves Road, stopping at little roadside nooks along the way to share witness through a passage read, a song shared, all beautifully planned by Alison. After each stopping point, we continued the walk down and around the curve, past an open field, where we soon intersected with the main Codnor–Heanor Road, turning left and heading up the hill along residences on both sides of the street. The responses of passersby and observers were diverse: As we walked and carried crosses, an excited child called, "I know that story, I know that story!" On the other hand, some passing cars jeered.

Reaching the hilltop, we gathered at the little triangle of green grass around a tall wooden cross. Standing at the foot of the cross, Michael spoke briefly on the familiar Good Friday story, reminding us of the events from the Gospel. As the group moved on around the corner to Codnor Chapel, we discovered just as many people waiting at the chapel as were in our walking group.

In the meditation I shared my own interesting reaction to the day. In the morning's service, when I came to John's gospel words of Jesus to his mother and the beloved disciple, I found myself feeling great emotion while reading it:

Meanwhile, standing near the cross of Jesus were his mother, and his mother's sister, Mary the wife of Cleopas, and Mary Magdalene. When Jesus saw his mother and the disciple whom he loved standing beside her, he said to his mother, 'Woman, here is your son.' Then he said to the disciple, 'Here is your mother.' And from that hour the disciple took her into his own home.

John 19:25b-27, NRSV

A GOD WHO GIVES GOD'S CHILD for all of God's children must surely long for it to be worth something, must long for all of creation to be ultimately seated together in love. A mother's heart knows that. Irish poet James Stephens writes of this in his poem "The Fullness of Time," [2] where he envisions an eternity where "they seated him [Satan] beside One who had been crucified."

American author Madeline L'Engle expresses a similar thought: "I cannot believe that God wants punishment to go on interminably any more than does a loving parent. The entire purpose of loving punishment is to teach, and it lasts only as long as is needed for the lesson. And the lesson is always love." [3]

Though L'Engle speaks of punishment, I am convinced that the intent of the Eternal Story is one of Love, of reconciliation, of presence. Love must prevail. We must be willing for all to be included. If not, we all face a failure. In this well-known, often repeated biblical story, the emphasis is on love, on presence in absence, on understanding suffering and rejection. To those in this world who know brokenness, rejection, humiliation, there was one who knew what that meant, how that felt. To those who want to exclude, to judge, the Judgment of the Holy is ultimate inclusion. These are enigmatic messages on a meaningful day.

In the last ritual of a long day, we shared hot cross buns and tea served by Codnor folks, with people continuing to reflect on the walk and the meaning of the weekend. As

2. James Stephens, Nicholson & Lee, eds., *The Fullness of Time, The Oxford Book of English Mystical Verse* (Oxford: The Clarendon Press, 1917).

3. Christopher W. Morgan and Robert A. Peterson, *Hell Under Fire: Modern Scholarship Reinvents Eternal Punishment* (Grand Rapids: Zondervan, 2004), Madeline L'Engle quote, p. 171.gfvvvv..

I drove home from the event-filled day stretching through four villages, I too reflected on my own journeying.

At certain points of the day I felt very isolated by the masculine nature of the telling of the story. As I struggled with that, I wondered if that too were a part of the enigmatic meaning: Jesus as male comes as vulnerable, loving, passionate; Jesus as female might have been expected to be that way, thus the paradox. But mankind can be so blindly blatant and typically power-moved that historically the meaning was and has continued to be misunderstood. And so "Father," "Son of Man," "Man of Sorrows," and "he" become protective barriers. Perhaps God regrets that decision. But surely, there is no way God could be less parent than the mothering image within, also. If when Jesus earlier denies his mother, how can that be? There is much in this story that is perplexing, even when reconsidered. The limitations of historical traditional religion offer little room to question, to ponder, to wonder.

What it is we are to be worshipping:

A Christ figure?

A God who must be worshipped so strongly that nations bomb each other?

A worship image and language where there is no room for feminine?

A God who does not want us to think or question?

And the forms and language we use in worship often exclude a stranger, a seeker off the street, the very ones we are to be caring for. I can understand why some people, for various reasons, struggle with our church traditions and language.

This Holy Friday is a powerful day, leading to the need for a quiet Saturday Sabbath.

Easter Sunday

Early on the first day of the week,
while it was still dark . . .
From the Gospel of Luke

IN A LITTLE WOODED GROVE ON THE VILLAGE HILLSIDE, we stood around in a semicircle shortly after sunrise. After hearing about the sunrise services and Easter breakfasts that I had known over the years, the Waingroves worship team planned this early Easter service on the hillside, in part for me to not miss this tradition. Twenty brave folks gathered on the hillside at a not-too-early time for a simple service of songs and meditation.

"Christ is risen." "Christ is risen indeed."

In the chill of early morning under a clear blue sky, we greeted each other with words used by Christians throughout the centuries to welcome Easter dawn. Maureen's clear soprano voice floated into the cool morning air, while Alison gracefully signed the words of the song. In her calm melodic voice, Ruth read the Luke passage. The small group was gathered to see in the dawn of the New Day with new hope and promise. A sweet smell of spring woodland encompassed us, and the early-morning birds joined our songs. There are times that "resurrection" may seem unreal, impossible, but here in the early-morning gathering of Easter dawn, how well this small community knew the power of love and faith.

As the service ended, we traveled back to Waingroves Chapel for an Easter breakfast of eggs and buns, then our preparation began for the 11 o'clock service. The stewards and musicians had put great effort into making the service energetic and celebratory. And so it was. From the waving banners of the children in bustling processional, to their delightful dance of Jesus bursting forth from the grave through a little slit in the white sheet as we sang "Sing alleluia to the Lord. . . .", there was great joy and delight. I am sure the young lad who popped up though the sheet as we sang "Jesus is risen from the dead" will never forget his Easter dance. I won't.

With her eye for beauty, Clare had draped the tall wall cross in a simple white cloth and placed a green cross form in the front of the sanctuary so that all could bring fresh flowers forward to decorate. Mark and the music group led us in exuberant singing, with voice and smile and bells and tambourines and wonderful spirits. High energy swirled in the room, while in my heart I gave thanks for the joy of music and the bond of singing together. Just like the early Christian church, this Easter day held a sacred time of reception of new members. Linda came forward to be confirmed and then received her first-ever communion. Maureen transferred her membership, and the membership class friends from Codnor were there to support them both. Then we all shared in the bread and cup of communion. What a special Easter morning.

"Join us for Easter lunch," Patrick and Jacque had invited me. After a busy morning, it was good to sit in the quiet of their lounge, looking out over the garden, and hear the melodies of beautiful music coming from the radio. I know why Jesus enjoyed quiet meals with Mary, Martha, and Lazarus. After the hustle, bustle, and hubbub, the quiet is a gift. Finding some aesthetic energy, we sat in the lounge and listened to the weekend inaugural Radio 4 classics 300 countdown, as exciting as the World Series finals, each of us trying to guess and anticipate what would come next. This national countdown captivated a whole country, a musical treasure chest, and I loved it. Later in the afternoon, after a final cup of tea with them, I visited a few shut-ins for the sharing of Easter communion.

Easter Day ended with an evening service at Wood Street, where the Oasis band had worked to learn some of the songs I had requested, giving them their own flavor, as they led us in a time of singing and sharing. A meeting afterwards, and the day was done.

On Easter Monday, a bank holiday, the Dawsons and I visited beautiful Haddon Hall and finished the day listening to the final top-ten classics countdown.

EASTER MONDAY REFLECTIONS

HOLY WEEK FEELS LIKE A BLUR, with all the thought put into the week and the services, all the expectations, all the services and walks and meals, and now it has ended. Looking back, I reflect:

+ After spending so many years in large churches with the resources to do magnificent things for this festal occasion, I am humbly and gratefully reminded that resurrection joy can come in beauty-held simple faithful expressions of what each community has to share, to create.

+ The journey from Christmas to Easter does not happen immediately. We must follow the path life brings us, with its hills and valleys, and walk through that life into whatever meaning resurrection has for each of us. The churches, the individuals of this circuit and community life hold on to their faith as they approach each step of the journey. Easter meaning does not always come loudly, boldly, jubilantly. It also comes quietly, in its own time and space. This community of faithful believers has journeyed together to this week, day, and place, upholding and supporting one another as fellow pilgrims on the road, knowing and feeling the healing power of the Easter story: a name called, a garden visit, doubting onlookers, shared meals, celebration of Eternal love. I give thanks for this experience.

† The ecumenical slant of the week brought pluses and minuses. It was good to worship together, to see communities coming together for the events of the week. But it can be difficult to enter into ecumenical events, balancing leadership, personalities, uniqueness. There were times to celebrate as groups and leaders came together, walking, worshipping, and sharing, and times where the road of true sharing lies ahead, with work still to be done.

† This Holy Week has perhaps been a reflection of any week, in which the common is holy: people sharing of themselves, in worship, in meals, in conversation. It included the times in homes, with individuals, around the table or sitting in the lounge and sharing good conversation, hearing a child shout out "I know that story!" Easter resurrection came through relationships, simple services, shared food, and shared story.

In this year, this time, this place, as the writer of Luke reminded from the Emmaus road, "They told what had happened on the road, and how he had been made known to them in the breaking of the bread."

RADIO FOUR CLASSICAL TOP-TEN COUNTDOWN OF 1996

THE PUBLIC VOTED, and the top three hundred results were shared over the week. Folks stayed glued to their radios as the countdown progressed. As voted by the public, the top-ten musical countdown follows:

10. Handel, *Hallelujah* from *Messiah*
9. Mozart, *21st Piano Concerto*
8. Beethoven, *5th Piano Concerto*
7. Elgar, *Nimrod* from *Enigma Variations*
6. Elgar, *Cello Concerto*
5. Beethoven, *Ode to Joy* from *9th Symphony*
4. Mozart, *Clarinet Concerto*
3. Beethoven, *6th Symphony*
2. Rachmaninov, *2nd Piano Concerto*

And ... the top choice:

1. Bruch, *1st Violin Concerto*

And April Continues . . .

ON DIRT AND DADS, SNOW AND TIME

WHEN I ARRIVED AT SOMEONE'S HOUSE this week, the retired father and adult daughter were outside loading dirt for her to take to her house. That scene brought back a memory from my last trip home to the US in January. When I went over to Starkville, Daddy and I loaded firewood into the back of my car for me to take back to Tuscaloosa. I thought of many other moments of sharing with him throughout all the years. I had noted today in reading that Terry Waites, in all his writing of his isolation during his captivity, never mentioned hug or touch. It is in a year like this that I realize the strength of love expressed in hugs and touch, the joy of relationship in simple shared activities like loading dirt and logs with dads.

I would absolutely love to dig in the dirt, particularly in the light of this day. I look out my window, and the snow still falls. Now that I am in for the evening, I will light the gas logs, reheat the chicken breast left over from last night, and enjoy a snowy evening. I picked up a recorder book to play a little music, and I want to get some work done on the computer.

My own insight for the day: I love having time—

- time to relish personal things, such as baths, lotion, and caring for self
- time for getting family birthday cards and gifts off
- time in the kitchen—to keep it clean or fix a cup of coffee while working
- time to carefully think about my work, time to read and note illustrations, to reread, in fact to slow down my reading, to do little projects.

So, that's what I'll do tonight, take time to enjoy the evening.

I hear a bird singing in the midst of the snow flurry. I'd invite it in if I could, it's probably singing to keep warm!

Snow!

Who'd have thought it would snow after Easter!

The rules I know just don't fit over here:
"Don't wear white shoes before Easter or after Labor Day."

Well, it's after Easter, time for white shoes and spring clothes.
I'm still in dark green flannel, three layers of shirts, wool coats, and boots!

Snow is unbelievable!

I laughed out loud as I drove down the road this afternoon,
    as I walked thru Chesterfield, covered with snow,
        as I pulled up the drive and moved my car into the garage
           so it wouldn't be frozen in the morning,
        as I pass the daffodils buried in snow.

I think it has snowed every month since November.
I wonder what May and June will be like?

An Adoption

I've been adopted!

Steve and Laura realized that their September-born son Matthew is only a few months older than my recently born grandson Collier, who is miles across the ocean, taking his firsts in his parents' home and love in Virginia. And they know that others in my family are not here.

So, they lovingly adopted me, or let me adopt them
    to hold and cuddle Matthew and know what little Collier must have felt like in each month of growth,
    to share meals and occasions with them,
    to have "family" for England's Mothering Sunday
        and the USA's Mother's Day.

And not only Matthew, but as others were born into our churches, my "family" grew . . . Ben, Josh . . . and other children adopted me . . . and
not only children, but
couples and singles, young and old
    let their adopted family member join them in sharing life,
        for Sunday roasts, for bonfires and special Thanksgivings,
        for Easter meals and birthday celebrations,
           for outings and events.
    Not only am I their pastor,
I am a member of the family!

A Post-Easter Norfolk Journey

WITH A SUNDAY OFF FOLLOWING THE BUSY EASTER WEEK, I decided to venture into Norfolk, which lies to the southeast of the Midlands, easily a day's drive. These lowlands are shaped by characters such as Julian, the gentle mystic of Norwich; Boudicca, the fierce Iceni warrior; and tales of the land and shoreline itself. I drove past wide-open crop-farming fields and huge blooming yellow daffodil fields, then on to charming coastal villages, eventually stopping at a public park nestled into Hunstanton's shoreline. Knowing that a walk on the beach always clears away the cobwebs, I decided on a path along the high sea cliff, then a stroll along the coarse sand shore beneath it, looking from water's edge back up on a wall of white and deep red layers of weather-carved cliff line crafted like the folds of an open paper fan. These rustic colors are picked up in the beautiful buildings of the area, whitewashed cobblestone walls outlined in red clay tiles, uniquely connected with their land.

The A149 coastline road journeyed along through marshes and flatland, eventually passing marine site Blakeney Point, which offered a boat ride to the island of the seals. Although I anticipated a ride in a cruiser or ferry, the dinghy was more like a little open lifeboat. We boarded by moving out over the walkway above the grassy marshes to step into the little coracle, then we rode with the tide out into the sea, around to the north side of the point, to view the colony home. I savored the taste and smell of sea, the spray hitting me in the face, the bumps of the boat.

There, all bundled up together, sprawled on the great grey rocks were the seals, looking out at us looking back at them. Shiny and sleek, stretched and stacked heads upon each other's bodies, they appeared to have much less interest in their subjects than did we in ours. As the fishy smell of their home drifted to our rocking boat, they lifted their round slick heads, turned, and stared at us with curious but unconcerned big brown eyes, then untwisted to get on with their barked conversations. "Ort, ort, ort," their voices sounded across the waters. The boat maneuvered and circled for each of us to have our Kodak moments, before heading back to shore. With rushing tides having shifted, our docking occurred at a pier farther out on the jetty. We were wonderfully and freely controlled by the tides of nature, in a combined rhythm of sea, seal, and captain.

Leaving the seals and boat trip behind, I continued along the coastline, passing Cley by the Sea windmill and driving on to Cromer. I was developing an interest in the windmills, perhaps from my Heage angel. Later I followed the signs down to the city of Norwich and arrived just in time for a Taizé service at Norwich cathedral. I would return another day to visit more of Julian's story.

Taizé is a small French village where an ecumenical religious community has been established, offering worship of prayers and songs that appeal to people from around the world. In Norwich cathedral, the service felt too performance-oriented, but I appreciated participating in it, as a meditative conclusion to a lovely trip.

After the service ended, I drove on toward home, stopping at a hotel along the way. I had planned to stay at Acle, back toward the east in the Broads, to do and see more. But with the nourishment of coastal scenes, the energy of nature's renewal, I was ready to be home the next morning to begin planning for the upcoming week.

I would be baptizing an infant on Sunday. As I thought back to the many opportunities I have had and will have to offer baptism for young babies and children, I was looking forward to the time of baptism for my own grandson Collier. It is such a special and precious occasion to hold a young child, call them by name, let the drops of water trickle down their little heads, and declare them claimed and loved. Sure, many couples over here who bring their children for baptism are not churchgoers. But to have the chance to visit with the parents, encourage them to live in the dwelling of God's love, and to teach their children about that love, what a gift that is. For the wonderful young couples in these churches I have served, their children are blessed to be in such homes of God's love and care. Feeling as if I am a part of their families and they are a part of mine, I am grateful for the way they have embraced me in this year; it has helped fill the gaps of not being with my own family on significant occasions.

THINGS DO NOT FEEL AS RUSHED OVER HERE; people do not live quite as hectic schedules. Therefore, a day filled with many events does not feel as pushed. That different sense may come from no one reason but may be embodied in several factors: this cultural lifestyle, my own intentionality and inner peace on most days, living life in one location instead of darting all over the country—from Ripley to Codnor now feels like a good long trip in comparison to Tuscaloosa to Birmingham to Atlanta. As the new superintendent visited today, I realized how much I enjoy and will miss this house, which at first glance felt foreign and small. How perspective changes through experience.

When I grow up . . .

I received a first yesterday, a picture from little Anneka at Waingroves:
a bunny rabbit, a lady with white hair and green eyes, dressed in a
black robe, and the following message:

"To Kay, I like you and when I grow up I wold like to be a minister too.
love from Anneka XXXX."

The picture is now on my wall above my desk. Just think, if I hadn't
come here this year, she might not have been able to have that image.

On Time and Life

I VISITED A WOMAN WHO TURNED NINETY-FIVE TODAY. She lives alone, has outlived most of her family. She is amazing; she had walked to town four times already today, just to keep her legs moving. As she shared her life story with me, we both became emotional. She thinks her hearing is gone because her husband used to hit her on the side of the head when he had been drinking. She had been thinking back over her life during the day and thanked me for coming, said she felt better. I told her the gift was mine; I too had been lonely today, and she cheered me up. It was a good visit. Her mind is so alert, she just cannot hear. I wonder what she does in church each week.

I borrowed a wonderful book from Monsignor Moore, about the Delany sisters of America. One sister was one hundred and four years old; the other was one hundred and two years old. Wondering if they were still alive, I later learned that Bessie had died in September of 1995 at age one hundred and four; Sadie lived until 1999, dying at age one hundred and nine. The book, *Having Our Say: The Delany Sisters' First 100 Years,* is a powerful story of a successful black family in the US. One of the best jokes from feisty Bessie is this quote:

> "You know what I've been thinking lately? All those people who were mean to me in my life—all those rebby boys—they have turned to dust, and this old gal is still here, along with sister Sadie. We've outlived those old rebby boys! That's one way to beat them! That's justice! They're turning in their graves, while we are getting the last word, in this book. And honey, I surely do love getting the last word." [4]

On a younger note, today was Davis's birthday. I have missed having him here. I spoke with him and then with Carl by phone. What an important transition, moving into the last year of the second decade of life. Davis, the youngest son, is twenty—no more teenagers—Dan is graduating from university and looking at summer job possibilities, and Doug is a parent. The cycle of roots and wings continues.

> *Holy One of all days, blessings of good days be upon those who live into the later decades of life as they are beacons for us all. Watch over our sons, over the one who was born on this day twenty years ago. May he be blessed with watchful protection and held in loving care. May the gift of each day bring blessing to all.*

4. Sarah L. Delany, A. Elizabeth Delany, Amy Hill Hearth, *Having Our Say: The Delany Sisters' First 100 Years* (New York: Dell, 1994).

A Wedding, a Memory

MY FIRST SOLO WEDDING HAS OCCURRED. The ceremony took place at Nether Heage Chapel, a charming setting for a wedding.

What a gift to have the video of the wedding Vernon and I shared last autumn before he died. I watched it before I went to the wedding rehearsal and found it to be a great help. Earlier in the afternoon I had driven out and penciled in the three sets of marriage forms. As Vernon had said, this is important; the certificate calls for the fathers' names and occupations, there are guidelines about the living address, and the bride is called a "spinster" on the form if never married. As I filled them out, the job did not feel quite as overwhelming as did worrying about it. I give thanks that Vernon had trained me well, in his meticulous manner. I could remember and feel our times together, could hear his voice as if only yesterday. To see him on the video was very moving, he was so weak and thin at that point, September 30, and they were still saying it was just a virus.

This wedding was a lovely event; the little chapel was glowing with warmth and beauty. I hope I got everything on the forms filled in correctly. Five years from now, I might be tracked down by the British government if I did not dot an i with the proper blue-black register ink, or the bride might have stumbled over a word in the legal part, or if the wedding went two minutes after 6 p.m.—in England no weddings are allowed before 8 a.m. or after 6 p.m.

Following the church service, the family held a festive sit-down wedding dinner for family and friends at a local club. I sat across the table from a man who went through the entire meal without saying much to me, then announced at the end that he does not like Americans. Fascinating. Thank goodness the Maid of Honor's boyfriend sat next to me and shared with me that they are both in law school, so there was good conversation there; I could speak of Doug and Becky's life at Virginia. After dinner, the party and dancing continued, with more guests coming. I headed home.

SATURDAY MORNING TURNED from disaster to delightful. I had attempted to bake last night what was a disaster of a dish for a Wood Street Chapel cake stall at the town market this morning. Daring to share the failed products, I took them up to the square about nine, had a cup of coffee at one of the Oxford Street shops, came home for something I forgot, walked back up to the market, bought fresh fruit, then visited a used-book stall that I wished I had discovered earlier. The man who has run this stall at the market for thirty-five years can tell you all about each of the authors, from mystery to romance. You buy a paperback at a price, return it, and get half your money back. He has me reading a book by a regional romance history writer, one of three she had written. He is going to save the other two for me, when he comes across them because he says I need to read the whole sequence. He has seen the man who was standing next to me have his children grow up and grandchildren come, and the man still comes and swaps books each week. A story within the stories. And since I have the services prepared, the sermon-polishing time may be short so I can get into the book I purchased.

Monday Reflections

I HAVE LEARNED THAT MY ORDINATION is on track to occur over here. I am in the group with Bishop Woodie White from the USA, as I have to have a bishop ordain me. The British conference has scheduled ordination occurring in several church locations on the same day; I will be at Leyland Methodist Church, where Bishop White is participating. This is so meaningful for me: an African American, he came out of the Alabama area and has gone on to be the Chair of the Council of Bishops. I will be glad when all the parts of this are settled.

We worked through a difficult meeting at Waingroves. They were to vote to approve the tentative rebuilding plan. The architect sent the estimate, which was a cost of £200,000; this was the first time they had seen it. They were thinking £130,000–£150,000, so naturally a strong discussion took place. This was a church of thirty-three members, looking at taking on a £200,000 remodeling project. Hard questions came out of the night's discussion. Their hearts are so into what they need and want for the future, I knew the direction would become clear. The money for remodeling was not as available as that for new building.

Ultimately, they made a decision to sell the old building, purchase new property, and build a beautiful new flexible structure. Some things take time to see the path. In years hence I have returned many times to celebrate life in the lovely new church.

Two phone calls had come, one asking me to do a workshop in another circuit, another to participate in another town's American twin-city celebration worship service. I could tell the diary might get heavy in these last months as I moved toward departure date.

Rhubarb and Radishes

I COOKED RHUBARB for the first time ever this evening.

Earlier I visited a dear lady whose husband's funeral I performed a few months ago. After a cup of tea, we walked through her garden, always a place of healing for people, and another example of the way people care for the beauty of their gardens and find it a haven of peace. Her lovely back garden full of colorful blossoming flowers is outlined with winding walkways.

When we arrived at the rhubarb plants, she offered to cut me some for making crumble. I told her I thought the large green rhubarb leaves would look wonderful in flower arrangements in the church, but I did not know what to do in the kitchen with it. So she told me how to cook it.

I have a cookbook titled *One is Fun* by Delia Smith, the Martha Stewart of England. From a recipe found there, I cooked a rhubarb crumble for one. Hurrah, it worked—and it was good, particularly with warm, creamy pouring custard on top. A successful cook, I am!

But I put some radishes in the freezer in water to fast chill them, then promptly forgot them, and they froze. When I thawed them, I had a wonderful red dye, but soggy radishes.

I am thinking there is a sermon out of *Rhubarb and Radishes*. Perhaps what folks naturally expect is an official, approved, "orthodox" meaning to the text: that means using the rhubarb and radish for what it is expected, in cooking. Isn't that in a sense what folks were expecting from Jesus?

But what comes instead is new meaning, new life, new use in the rhubarb leaves and radish dye—a few minutes of creative words to a few people who have been hungry for it, like the few who will appreciate those big, beautiful green rhubarb leaves when I use them on the altar table!

On Disasters of the Moment

I HELD A DISASTER OF A FUNERAL SERVICE THIS WEEK, a growth experience, shall we say. Funerals are such important times in a family's life, also such emotional times. This funeral was late getting started. One person had asked for a short service; another had wanted the full thing. In the service I looked at the clock wrong and dragged it out forever, then did not realize until driving home that I had been thinking 4 p.m. start time instead of 3:45.

As to names and families, I named some and skipped some, again working around some family directive, but there were various people there, immediate family, not clearly indicated by our conversations. I felt I was caught between two walls, and did an awful job in the middle. I just hoped it came out better than I felt it did.

An evening visit to Waingroves for a program by author Derek Longdon gave me a chance to laugh out loud at someone who was describing regular life situations I related to. It was fun to laugh and to listen to someone else's stories.

THE CODNOR GROUP traveled by coach to the Leeds City Variety Music Hall, which was like an old vaudeville show. The featured singer was Joan Regan, who dated back to earlier days of Music Halls. Geoff Quible, the organizer of the trip, had told me that several years ago while in the shower, the singer had suffered a hemorrhage of the brain, leaving her in a really sad state. She had to relearn to talk, think, and sing. Someone in our group commented how sad it was to have seen her at her prime years ago and to see her now. But I thought how wonderful that she had been able to overcome adversity and to offer what she did to us that day. How moving to see this beautiful woman standing stage centre and elegantly singing.

I CALLED MOTHER TODAY; my brother David has been quite ill. Daddy was checking on him three times a day. Mother caught me up on some other family news. Sounds like bumpy times at home. This is when it is hard to be so far away. Life is about living in the now, being grateful for each day, knowing that distance cannot divide.

Honoring a Life Day

Tell me, what is it you plan to do with your one wild and precious life?
Mary Oliver

BIRTHDAYS COME AND GO, more quickly than we ever imagine. They are occasions to ponder, to remember, to reflect and look forward. This year of being fifty had begun twelve months earlier with a week vacation in the red cliff-surrounded valley of Sedona, Arizona, as I was ending the semester's work and looking toward the coming year. Now I faced the passing of another year, months spent in the unbelievable passage of life in this place. I had kept these days of my calendar clear so that I could take time to honor the closing of the old year, the anticipation of a new year of life. The Peak District holds many beautiful, mystical, secluded spots for such a time; I chose to visit two of them, ancient megalithic circles, for an afternoon pre-birthday reflection.

The circle of nine ladies sits atop remote Stanton Moor. To reach it you must have some idea of where to go: past Matlock, leaving the main A6 road, left up little dusty one-lane roads that divide and split off in several places, each leading up the hill toward the flat plateau on top. Once you are close, you must park the car and head by foot toward the Moor, via whichever path you now face.

Finding my way up a not-so-traveled road to the spot I thought was a moor entry, I parked my car, locked it, climbed the fence gate, walked through a crop pasture, and eventually moved into a new terrain, with the narrow path leading through birch trees and small scrub bushes. The land had opened out so that I could see the hills and dales all around, in a panoramic circle. In the still and quiet, I could hear the song and flutter of birds, the leaves gently stirring in a subtle breeze, could smell the freshness of spring, of gorse and heather, of new growth. There, to my right, in the middle of a small grove of trees, was a round circle of small sky-slanting stones, nine of them, forming what has been named the circle of nine ladies, said to have been here for centuries. What better place to be, for this lady approaching a new year of life. At this moment I was alone, a chance to circle, to touch and feel the cool of the rock, to see the uniqueness of each angled stone, to wonder at the mystery and meaning of the circle, the placement.

This felt like a hidden spot, a thin place nestled among the trees, so that only the seekers would find and visit. No large signs, no tourist office, no gigantic formations, just nine small stones standing in the circle of stillness.

A place for pondering
for emptying
for being still and quiet
for imagining the laughter and singing and dancing
    of voices past
for breathing in deeply and releasing
breathing and listening and feeling
sitting on the moist ground and feeling connected
    to the earth,
    to time, to timelessness
A place for silent, quiet, solitudinal litany
    of thanks
    of love
    of peace
A life's year begun in the presence of the American Southwest,
    in the womb of a Sedona canyon,
now rested for a last day in the circle of nine women
    of story, of memory, of endurance
Quiet peace of nature
No human voice
Birthday blessed by the rustle of leaves, the song of a bird
Breathe in and out, slowly and deeply
Breathe
A smile of joy and gratitude

After a while I continued across the moor. When I returned to the circle, a group of young folks with spiked pink-and-blue hair, tattoos on arms and backs, drums in hand, had arrived, found a place under the trees, and begun their drumming circle. A young family with a child and a dog had also arrived, found their spot, and were bringing current life and activity to the circle's grove. Standing to the side I paused for a while, listening to the rhythms, the patterns, the voices and expressions, and then moved on, carrying the memory of the moment with me.

Back in my car, I journeyed down the road, stopping at a farm on the left. I pulled into its small parking space and began the walk through the cows in the green pasture, through the gate into the next pasture to the stone circle at Arbor Low, again just me and the stones and silent history. This circle is in a working pasture, surrounded by the watchful cows, so that no one desecrates their stoned story. The grey stones here are all now lying flat; they are large and would have been heavy to bring to this spot. Was it a burial place, a place for ritual? The open blue sky above would know the story; the land would have shifted and reshaped and resurfaced; the stones have remained.

Again I sat, breathed in the earthy smell of cow and pasture and old stone, watched the floating clouds drift by, let my mind and spirit feel the presence of past and present. Soon the time came to leave and return to Ripley, to share a meal with a lovely young couple who in their caring ways had honored the markers and events of my year here. Conversation would be good, the home-cooked meal a gift. In departing this silent sacred place I wondered what the markers of time would have been, the indicators of passage, the shared joys and meals, of those who long ago created these ancient signs of presence.

NOTTINGHAM CITY WAS A GOOD BIRTHDAY contrast after the quiet countryside pilgrimage. First, to acknowledge the practical, it offered a chance for a good haircut with a stylist who is a friend of Jacque's. Then I ventured into an under-city caves excursion for insights into Nottingham early life, where whole hidden layers of underground sandstone caverns and tunnel mazes exist, some thought to be from medieval times, some from war years. One entrance is, ironically, through the Broadmarsh Shopping Centre; underneath the busy commercial area, the path leads to old cellars and air-raid shelters, then through recreated earlier cultural scenes.

After that journey through history, I discovered Café Metz, a nice little jazz place in town centre, where I enjoyed a good salad, good music, and good memories of my own layers of history. As I drove out of Nottingham, nature added one more memorable addition to the day; hail came bombarding down and then abruptly halted. My last stop was in Eastwood at the birthplace home of English novelist D. H. Lawrence, whose writings depicted his view of life in the area.

Birthdays are not just to be spent alone, but also to be shared. The people here shared birthday cards and calls, a celebration given by friends from Wood Street, including a lovely cake complete with a musical minister on top, beautiful gifts of Royal Crown Derby china, and sherry for toasting. From home my sister Pam set her clock at

2 a.m. to call me, then I heard from Dan, who shared his summer plans. Flowers came from Carl and Davis, cards from Doug and family, from parents and others. Not just this day but throughout this year I have deeply appreciated flowers, letters, cards, and news from family and friends at home.

At the end of the day, I was so tired that I cut out the light at 10 o'clock, too exhausted to write much, though thoughts still circled within. Fifty-one was seeming much older than fifty. Borrowing a word from author Scott Peck, that fact is "overdetermined," having a multiplicity of reasons. The fact is, I AM older, my body is feeling it, in part because of this long grey winter. Fifty had been a benchmark, a freeing for moving to a new decade, a new plateau. At fifty-one, the plateau is there for the long run, or so the plan is. This date marks officially the beginning of another year, the close of a real jubilee year.

We who are able travel this life road with the gifts of opportunity and health, with space to reflect upon the past, to be grateful for the chance to celebrate the now, to look to the future, to claim a jubilee year, perhaps any year. In his last book, *To Bless the Space between Us*, John O'Donohue writes, "On certain birthdays the shape of our unfolding life comes into clearer view.... When we look back, we can identify the key thresholds where the vital happenings of our lives occurred." [5]

April comes to an end, and the markers of time move on.

5. John O'Donohue, *To Bless the Space Between Us* (New York: Doubleday, 2008), p. 214.

In The Newsletter: Dream!

As I think of the quickly approaching Sunday School anniversary and its presentation of *Joseph and the Amazing Technicolor Coat*, I realize that there is direct connection to another Sunday gathering that occurred here recently: the gathering of persons in a church retreat, to share fellowship and talk about who we are as "the people called Methodists" in the town of Ripley. As the afternoon progressed, people offered wonderful ideas of who we would like to be. We talked of community action, prayer, Bible study, and creative sharings. And we committed to hold ourselves accountable to action on these dreams.

As some of you may be aware, I just celebrated a birthday this week—an occasion fully in the midlife years! As I hit the age of seeing what has and has not occurred by this time in my life, I face choices: I can take life and the givens as they are, and live in the dead reality of that fact, with all its strengths and losses. Or, I can claim a future, whatever it holds, based on the foundation of my past, but being open to the dreams and possibilities of a new day, in new shapes and textures and colors, coming out of past and present.

Dream! Dare to dream

- How can this sanctuary take on the aura of enthusiasm and life, which we want for this congregation?
- How can we develop a network of caring and concern for each other?
- How can those persons outside the church find a place of welcome and nourishment for facing tough living?
- How can we take the beauty and meaning of the stories of our older congregation, coming not just from one church but also from many church histories, and weave them into the life stories of our young, the babies we baptize each week?
- How can the artists and creative persons within our community find places of expression in our acts of worship?
- How can we—WE, each of us, just who we are—be and see the face of Christ in the market town of Ripley?
- How can we awaken ourselves to new possibilities?

I encourage you to come to the Sunday School anniversary with much enthusiasm and support for the performers—it will be a wonderful production, of that I am sure! But more than that, come with an openness to being awakened to the dreams which lie asleep in your own being: dreams for this congregation, dreams for yourself. Be reawakened to the possibilities and meanings of life at any age and time—whether the life of this church or your own life. Be open to dream!

Blessings of dreaming,

Kay 29/4/96

May: The Path

Bless to me, O God, the earth beneath my foot
Bless to me, O God, the path whereon I go.

from Carmina Gadelica

May came in its full glory, the earth alive with color and beauty. The month brought opportunity for journeying to places with people young and old, with those who have been on their faith journey for a long time and with those just beginning. Following where the life path led, I again realized that inevitably it leads home.

Dovedale

NESTLED BETWEEN TWO LARGE HILL RANGES, the river flows along, catching the grey riverbed rocks at just the right angles to sing its pebbled way through the little dale. Worn footpaths along the river follow the bends of the streaming waters. Flat stepping stones stretch across a span of shallow, calm waters, offering walkers a way to carefully step across the river's width.

Dovedale, a favorite spot for walkers, can sometimes be overrun with the human forms of pastoral presence. The ice-cream wagon stands at the entrance, ready to refresh beginning or returning hikers with the fruity tastes of the cool treats. This day the dale was not so crowded; it offered space for each body of walkers to find their own way and enjoy their own favorite spot along the river.

The ride here is through pleasant rolling hills marked by the familiar greystone walls and sheep lazily grazing on the hillsides. The road meanders down the last hills lined with streams of downward scree. The Dovedale sign points to the entry of the dale, announced by birds talking and greeting from the shrub-lined riverside.

This is a place to clear the head, to breathe in the fresh aroma of spring greens and flowering yellows, to stroll quietly along the river, then move up the riverside path along the dale's life-giving artery. Along the way are spots to pause and stretch—a warm rock, a grassy meadow. There is a sense of moving into sanctuary, moving away from clutter, being one with the earth. This is a place to journey in solitude, on a good-weather day if you are lucky, a time to walk with a friend and let shared conversation float in the air or claim the silent comfort of friendship.

Voices float into the air nearby but at a distance. Bubbling waters sing their song, meadow larks reply, and grazing sheep offer gentle rhythmic background. Fleecy clouds float overhead in the crystal-blue sky. The water is cool and fresh to the touch. I am grateful for the little dale and all it offers to me, for the time close to nature, for the peace and serenity.

After a winding walk along the river's edge, I come to a bend that serves as my marker of time's restraint. Retracing my steps, I try to capture nature's details in my mind—the varied shades and shapes of green, the patterned to-wits of birds, the sweet aroma of small blue-buttoned flowers. With careful steps back across the stones, I return to the gravel parking area, reticent to leave, but glad for the visit. The water's song lingers in my head. Refreshed, renewed, immersed in the beauty, I start the engine, carefully lick the dripping cream running down the cone in my hand, and begin the journey home.

The Story of Rene's Journey Continues . . .

"Do you have time to come for a cup of tea?"

Rene had called, inviting me to visit with her this afternoon. As we have done before, we both sat on the couch in her quiet cozy lounge, sharing a warm cup of tea. My eyes moved again to the beautiful pictures hanging on her walls, images of gypsy caravans and church steeples, roses and bridges. I recalled the picture of the U.S. capitol building that she had given me earlier, and I remembered my delight in having her show and talk about her albums.

Today she arose and went to the dining room, returning with a frame in her hand. Sitting back down on the soft brown couch, she handed me the picture her brother had taken of the Peace monument in Ottawa, Canada. In that moment I recalled her words of an earlier day: "When you receive the Peace picture, you will know."

Rene chose to give the photo to me this day. She had received a visit from the doctor on Friday—the cancer had spread. We sat and talked of life and death. She voiced feelings and fears with me, as she faces the reality of her own death and tries to get things in order. She moves into this moment in her life as I imagine she has faced all the challenges of her life: with dignity, with faith, with honesty, with grace. I am thankful that I have been blessed by her life and friendship, her heart and soul of beauty.

A Day on the Path of Life

THE CHILDREN AT THE JUNIOR SCHOOL this morning were, as always, filled with energy and enthusiasm, wanting to know about life in the US. "Have you been to Disney World, to Graceland, to New York City?" "Do you have tornados and snakes?" "Are your houses big?" I wonder what our American children would want to ask of a British visitor. I leave these settings invigorated by their curiosity and energies.

A SEVENTY-EIGHT-YEAR-OLD LADY in Codnor has been waiting two years to see the doctor for eyes and bone problems. She has now seen the doctor but has not gotten the cataract surgery, nor does she know the cause of and treatment for her backbone and bone problem, although she has lost four inches of height. She does not get out at all. The warmth of this home in the midst of such health concerns brings warmth into my spirit and soul. As our visit ended, an added gift: they gave me rhubarb.

Do you want to be made well? . . .
Stand up, take your mat and walk.
from John 5

SMALL HOUSE GROUPS ARE THE LIFELINE FOR CHURCHES HERE, meeting biweekly for study, prayer, and fellowship. When Swanwick's house group invited me to join them for a May session at the Cracknell's parsonage, the leader had suggested two topics: something uplifting, encouraging or something healing, with people still grieving over Vernon. His death highlights the challenge of the health-care situation here. There is such a sense of despair for many, with this health system. Problems that could and should be avoided are instead multiplied because of the lack of immediate attention. It is obviously draining for ministers to maintain the energy needed for pastoral care for such ongoing situations with a sense of nonresolution for many.

The Gospel of John story about the man at the well offered direction for our conversation about Vernon, about all of us moving to the new: new situations, new circumstances, new challenges. People spoke quietly of their own journeys, their life challenges, the challenge for the church community, then together we sang the hymn "Hear Good News." I remember when I wrote the music for this text, I chose to go with a quiet introspective affirmative setting versus a blatant blaring announcement full force. Pain sometimes needs news of God's love and grace as a quiet reaffirming truth.

Thoughts on a Book and Baptism

IN A RECENT BOOKSTORE VISIT, I had discovered the book of liturgies and prayers for homosexuals[6] for which Bishop Desmond Tutu had written the introduction. The first ordained Anglican priest to speak out on this issue, Tutu wrote:

> We reject them [homosexuals], treat them as pariahs, and push them outside our church communities, and thereby we negate the consequences of their baptism and ours. We make them doubt that they are the children of God, and this must be nearly the ultimate blasphemy. We blame them for something that is becoming increasingly clear they can do little about.

One of the authors begins the book by sharing a moment from her past:

> On a crisp Dakota Sunday morning, tightly wrapped against the November cold, I was carried off to the town's Methodist church to be the delight of the baptizing family of God. Cheery smiles and wiggling fingers greeted my arrival on this important day. The hymns in the morning light sounded for me the story of God's love, of the Savior's compassion. I was in the House of Unconditional Love, the Church, bundled in joy and expectation.

6. Marilyn B. Alexander and James Preston, *We Were Baptized Too: Claiming God's Grace for Lesbians and Gays* (Louisville: Westminster John Knox Press, 1996).

What a lonely, isolated journey it must be for people who feel estranged from and by the church, from questioning the meaning of their baptism to claiming their place of service in the community of faith. I have appreciated the position of the British Methodist Conference, where there has been no statement for ordination concerning one's sexual orientation. Ironically, here I was, in a home denomination with ordination exclusion clauses regarding that. Hopefully my voice and heart could offer healing in wounded places.

I had finally talked with Ken about my ordination; things have been worked out. So, thanks to the work and efforts of many folks on both sides of the ocean, including the Board of Ordained Ministry at home, the ordination would happen over here. This decision excludes friends and family members at home, but after all that has happened in the year, the people in my first place as pastoral minister would be able to support me in the official act of ordination. Tonight we talked about how our lives will never be the same. That applies to me and this ordination process, as well.

Whether facing death or accepting change, from young children with inquisitive minds to an author willing to challenge our ways, in moving to new unknowns or struggling with the hurts and conditions of life, in decisions of future, of balance, of compromise, and challenge, we as human beings should not have to journey alone. For each human whose journey I have encountered in these days, may the Celtic blessing be known:

"Bless to me, O God, the path whereon I go."

To bed, with the quiet sounds of the hymn in my head:

Hear good news of saving grace, God's mercy is forever.
All may claim the priceless gift, and know their lives set free.
Believe God's word of wondrous love, revealed upon the cross of Christ;
Receive by faith his saving work, and move beyond your fears.
Give thanks for blessings given you, praise God for life created new;
With gratitude declare the fact, "I am a child of grace!"
Walk each day the way of Christ, that all the world may know his love;
The Spirit calls and strengthens you to share good news of life.
We journey now by faith, together walk the way.
As children of the Savior's grace, we move to God's new day.

"DO YOU REMEMBER YOUR BAPTISM?"

With two baptisms scheduled for the morning and a lectionary reading of Ezekiel's words, "I will sprinkle clean water upon you," the day was an invitation for all of us to remember the waters of baptism as we had experienced it. At Crich's worship this night, in response to the question I asked, people began to share their baptism stories, from infant baptisms to recent faith baptisms, from sprinkling to immersion. One woman told of being baptized in this chapel: "I don't remember it. I was an infant, of course, but my parents brought me here to their chapel." Others had traveled a long faith journey, through other denominations and traditions, and now here remembered those roots. I recalled my own story of baptism, as a young child receiving immersion on an Easter Sunday evening in my Mississippi hometown church. Stories continued over tea. How precious those times of sharing are, when worship holds living stories that become meaning for worship.

Tonight's service at Crich marked three times we have left together. The nature of the circuit plan and the need to spread ministers around causes each visit to be so precious, so important, so valued. I appreciate the smallness of these congregations and the importance of the church in their lives, the commitment the faithful few have to it.

In the afternoon a member whose wife has been in Derby Hospital called with news that they will send her home; there is nothing left for them to do. That makes two people this week who have heard such news. A third person has asked me to stop by for a visit; I think it may be a similar situation. This kind of living puts things in a very different perspective. In my music work I did not see the pastoral care needs of the congregations except in a limited way. Then my AIDS internship at the university clinic introduced me to Fred and other care-team clients, who taught us all so much about living until death. Fred had such a beautiful outlook on life. Dreaming takes on a different meaning for folks facing such situations as these. It is easy to want to DO SOMETHING, a feeling coming out of a fix-it culture and my own fix-it syndrome. The health systems here do not always try to do something to prolong a physical life. There are two sides to that issue, such a hard one to consider. Which is the better right?

In light of these reminders of our ending, the warm waters of our beginning baptism are a reminder of belonging. Together we sang:

Come to the water, sign of God's blessing.
Always remember and live as a child of God.

Of Dreams and Life

I HAVE LESS THAN THREE MONTHS LEFT of this experience; with my schedule and people coming and going, the time will fly by. What a year it has been. Collier will soon be a year old, and I am a year older. Life moves on for everyone. I am aware that as I wrote recent dream words for the newsletter, many people feel past their dreams. Perhaps that is why I so appreciate the visits with Rene and other older people who are able to talk of their feelings and their lives.

On bank holiday, I fixed lunch for the Dawsons. What fun—they stayed until late afternoon. In the evening I had a baptism appointment and then a youth-service planning meeting that ended late. I woke up at 3 a.m., called Dan at 5, which would have been 11 p.m. his time. The energy of having so many things on my mind bumped my adrenalin flow. Sleep can sometimes be elusive.

At the End of a Long Day . . .

THE AFTERNOON CIRCUIT LADIES' NETWORK SERVICE was not covered for me to leave when I finished what I thought were my responsibilities, so I decided to let go of any stress and just stay to see it through. Later, at the youth-council meeting we discussed the plans for the youth service in June, deciding to use the theme "Dare to Be a Dreamer," then I left them deciding on activities for the Saturday of the youth weekend.

In the late hours of the long evening light, I drove up to Crich to visit with the man whose wife died this week. Watching for me, he invited me in and made hot cocoa for us. We sat in his lounge sipping the warm drinks as he shared with me the situation, another of these hospital tales: at age seventy-five, she was in good health, but went in to have a leg ligament replaced. Something went wrong; she hung on for five weeks, with twenty-seven pints of blood, but died yesterday. He feels lost without her. Ironically, the leg healed, but she died.

From meetings that are an important part of the women's lives to care and planning for the young people of the community, the church serves such a major role in community life over here, doing it with deep commitment. For those who do not have a community to care for them, how difficult it must be to face illness and death alone. I end another day, knowing it was busy and full, but also knowing that these caring communities of faith are doing what they can to be God's love in their world.

Ammerdown Revisited

THE AMMERDOWN TEN-DAY MINISTERS' RETREAT is now over. It was good, these two weeks of May working with this group of clergy. To be in a relaxed retreat setting with those who have been in ministry thirty years—only men were in the group—was enlightening. There were those who were worn and discouraged, those who felt fulfilled, and most felt tired.

The British Methodist Conference seems committed to providing retreat and renewal settings for the ministers here. A regular schedule of retreat times at various benchmark years of service is a part of the general church's program. Don't we all need that? How much better we could function if we received renewal, working in any field. I have experienced such good retreat settings in England, including the offering of quiet days, days apart, small gatherings. Though I was a part of the leadership team in this retreat, I listened and learned from the many gathered there, hearing stories of struggle, visualizing enthusiastic windows of enriching ministry, making new friends and colleagues. The minister who would be coming to the Ripley circuit was among the participants. On one free afternoon, we were able to travel together to visit Glastonbury Tor, with time to walk up the labyrinthine hill, as we chatted about the place I would soon leave and he would soon enter.

Ammerdown Retreat Centre and the surrounding land are beautiful and peaceful. The centre itself is a place initiating multi-faith dialogue and experience. Their stated purpose:

> The Ammerdown Centre is an open Christian community dedicated to peace,
> reconciliation, and renewal while providing a programme of opportunities for
> study, mutual learning, and the chance to hear and absorb new ideas and insights.

Our extended times there were opportunities to enjoy the historic setting, peaceful grounds, and plentiful resources. In the book corner, I discovered the voices of two who have given their lives to interfaith work. *When East Meets West,* by Father Bede Griffith, tells his experience of living and working in India. Would we not appreciate God's world better if we understood and appreciated all the children of God's world better? *Awareness* is the writing of Anthony de Mello, director of an institute of pastoral counseling in Poona, India, and a member of the Jesuit province of Bombay, bringing together eastern and western spirituality.

Tranquil walking paths at Ammerdown move through picturesque pastoral settings. Monday's twelve-mile hike through the countryside for the ministers became a highlight of the week—something hard to imagine happening in the US. On another day, I took my own private walk through the green pastures, meandering up the path to the top of the hill, then lying on my back on a large grey flat rock, and gazing up through the trees to the clear blue sky. Sacred time with nature is beneficial for the interior dwelling.

Tranquility quickly became a blur. I arrived home at Nine Clumber Close to the news that the house next door was broken into the previous night, with much being taken. I am gone all week, yet they are home and get robbed! I did not sleep well the first night back. The only good thing is, there wasn't much to steal in my house.

Later in the month, I attended an intern retreat with the other Americans. At the same time a yoga/meditation retreat was going on. Talk about two different sound levels: noisy Americans and silent meditators. It was an interesting contrast. Hearing about appointments there, it seemed strange that I had not officially heard a word about my appointment. In some way, this year had held so much that it could be sufficiently meaningful for my ministry experience. Perhaps Jehovah's Witnesses and Mormons have a wise idea, to want a year or two of service and ministry from all people. It has been good to live in the now of this year and to be so content with it.

Ammerdown was a gift of place and time. Both of these recent trips provided space to see the beauty of the setting, the wildflowers, the quiet, the coo of birds and murmur of breezes, to feel the sanctity of the place, to discover new writers with words that touch my heart, and to be with colleagues on the path. I am grateful for the time there.

BACK AT RIPLEY I received a call that one of the people I had been visiting in Derby, who had come home right as I left last week, had died. I had planned to see her later in the day. Now I went on out to see the husband. In moments like this, guilty feelings easily creep in about what I have not gotten done. Just when I become too idyllic about life here, a jolting reminder of the health-care situation comes to the forefront. No wonder ministers here face stress and health problems. Another minister of many years' experience offered this word: "It is hard to avoid the guilt, especially when you want to 'be there' at the right time and are not. All the 'I can't be everywhere' and even 'There was no way for me to know' doesn't eliminate it. It goes with the territory."

Apples and Adventures

AT THE CORNER OF DERBY ROAD AND HEATH ROAD, I regularly walked past the large two-story red-brick family home hidden behind the Manvers petrol garage, a family business spanning several generations. In my time here, the day-to-day work of the business had passed on from the hands of Olive Manvers Paradise and Reg Paradise, a delightful, energetic, and life-living older couple, whose rich stories and learning offered great joy to my visits with them.

Olive is a woman of remarkable inner strength, knowledge, and ability, not unlike many older Southern women. Not until I met and learned from Olive did I discover that apples have sides, and that an apple connoisseur knows the kinds of apple by the number of sides it has. An apple tree grown from a seed that came from the US when the country was only a colony, perhaps from the orchards of George Washington himself, still grows in Olive's garden.

My visits to the warm, hospitable Paradise home were adventures in themselves. I would ease past the garage work, walk up to the house side door on the right, and knock or ring the bell, to be met with a warm welcome from Olive and Reg, their eyes sparkling with life and joy. We moved through an entry hall, filled with stacks of magazines and books, pictures and memorabilia, into the lounge where we sat and talked, in the company of an original Steiff bear and other intriguing collections. Over the months Olive had shared with me not only apples but also magazines and journals describing Derbyshire life and places.

In his earlier years Reg ran a taxi service and had driven many well-known and many little-known people through the Derbyshire countryside, with delightful tales to tell from those experiences. He knew the roads and lanes with great familiarity. So, from his wealth of expertise and knowledge came an invitation from them to treat me to an outing in our beloved Derbyshire countryside.

Reg drove us in his black taxi car to Matlock, on the edge of the Peak District, for lunch at a Matlock garden shop. It is delightful how, beyond the plants and plant accessories one would expect, the garden shops all offer excellent meals and teas. A visit to a garden shop is in itself a real treat, an outing. But our day was only beginning. Following the meal, we drove into the back roads of the Lower Peaks, with Reg flying up and down the hills, talking, pointing out the hills and dales, naming points of interest, even the little-known crests and peaks, without missing a beat of talking or driving. Our adventures continued throughout the afternoon as he carried us to places I had not yet seen and probably could not ever find again, places with mythical names like Robin Hood's Stride. What pride and joy he showed, in the sharing of story after story and place after place.

The clock ticked away. I needed to be back in time for an evening service at Nether Heage. But as we headed into Matlock on our way home, the Sunday afternoon drivers' congestion clogged up main routes through the popular riverside town nestled between crests and ridges.

"Never mind," our valiant chauffeur responded to the situation, as he took a quick left turn and started up a small side road. "I know a back way!" And onto that back way we went, flying up and down one laners, turning this way and that way, out of town, through the moors, over and around, up and down, until . . . he did it! We were back home in time for me to pull up into Nether Heage village to the front of the chapel, catch my breath, and walk in to calmly lead an evening worship service.

Ah, Reg and Olive, I thank you for your joy of life, for your spirit of sharing, for your love of creation. May I learn from you.

Creator God, who made heaven and earth, apples and peaks and dales, I give thanks for your children who live with such joy and care for your creation. Watch over and protect them, that they might continue to spread their joy of life to others.

An Occasion to Remember

In the evening I went very unwillingly to a society in Aldersgate Street, where one was reading Luther's preface to the Epistle to the Romans. About a quarter before nine, while he was describing the change which God works in the heart through faith in Christ, I felt my heart strangely warmed.

—From John Wesley's Journals

I THINK I KNEW what John Wesley's heart must have felt like on that night two centuries ago when he wrote those words. Our present night's circuit Wesley celebration at Crich was such a special evening, a Wesley Aldersgate celebration night commemorating a significant faith incident in the life of the founder of Methodism, in this little chapel where John Wesley had preached. We had planned this event for weeks. Patrick, Cheryl, and others shared their great dramatic talents, including a monologue about Susanna and a funny improvised scene about Wesley's Georgia fiasco experience of love forlorn. Naturally we sang Charles Wesley hymns; they all know and sing Wesley hymns in four-part harmony. And, of course, there was a sermon; this is a Wesley service. I actually climbed the many steps up and preached from the high pulpit, the Wesley pulpit with its gated door and candle-burning sconces. This will be another occasion to remember and cherish.

> From the gathering of believers some two centuries ago
> in a little place on Aldersgate, London,
> to a gathering in the last decade of the twentieth century
> in a village chapel still witnessing to the words of grace
> which John Wesley spoke,
> then learned to trust and know
> by the warming of his heart,
> the fires of faith still burn.

"WOULD YOU LIKE TO GO WITH US?" I was invited by the Waingroves primary school year-six class, a group I have visited with several times, to join them on a trip to London for a visit to the Houses of Parliament. What a treat! I am grateful to Jennifer, their teacher, for the invitation. Many of these boys and girls had never been to London, so the day became a special occasion. I had seen the outside of the long stately buildings that line the bank of the Thames River, these buildings which glow gold in the evening light, with the familiar Big Ben rising over the river. I now had the opportunity to see what lay behind those thick wooden doors. As we entered the historic sites, our tour escort explained to us the unique settings of each of the bodies, the House of Commons and the House of Lords. Images of the many televised debates from these chambers came floating back into my head as we walked through the halls, and I could picture the decisions of history that had been made within these walls. As the coach traveled back through the streets of London on our return ride, from both sides of the aisle the boys and girls would shout, "Look!" and "See that!" With postcards, good memories, and even a pen with a picture of the parliament building on it, we settled in for the ride home to Waingroves. It was an occasion to remember.

DISTRICT CHAIRMAN GEOFFREY CLARK has agreed to participate in the ordination service with me in the role Vernon would have taken. I am so grateful for that, for Geoff has been such a support and model for ministry for me in this year, even as he has faced his own cancer battle, with treatment and concerns of his own. I know that Alabama folks who have been a part of my ministry journey will be with me in spirit. Having my ordination here completes in a special way this wonderful and meaningful threshold year of ministry. It will be an occasion to remember.

I feel emotionally drained, with a funeral today and Rene's situation. The emotions of the retreat, the reality of leaving (two Americans head back this next week), Nora's death the week before, the loss of Gwen and doing her service—all this has added up. I felt a bit fragile as the family and casket arrived, but got through it. The husband reminds me of Daddy, with his gentle way and frail build. Regretful that programming and activities prevented me from seeing these people in their last coherent days, I would like to clear the diary of events and spend the last two months just visiting with folk. It is that simple sharing that I love. Most of us, in our busy lives of activity and doing, treasure the quiet moments of sharing. Sometimes we just forget which occasions we want to remember.

The Thorn Tree is one of the centres of the community life of Waingroves village; Malc and Anne, who are also a vital part of village community life, took me there for a meal. The Waingroves folks have held on to their identity through the chapel, which is the only church in the village, the pub, the community centre, the primary school, the Friends and Neighbors singers. From my first clown-outdoor service to the spring flower festival I opened, I have experienced a village life to remember.

It is 10 p.m., and I have just come in from mowing my lawn. Outside the last vestiges of light begin to fade.

Barometric Pressure

NEWS FROM HOME about a person with terminal cancer reminds me that this vicious disease knows no national borders, nor does the surprising coming of death. I have felt so bitter about how many lives cancer claims. I am sure that this news is hard on many of his friends at home. It stirs up memories of conversations with him in my visits to the church where he worked. Life does not stay the same.

Patrick came by this evening with the delightful news that the circuit wants to give me a stole created by ecclesiastical textile artist Juliet Hemingray. I have admired her pieces of beauty; now I am to select one for myself. Choosing is in itself a lovely gift for creative thought. What color stole? What images: light or creation, color, or sheep? Her superb work brings out beauty and creativity within the simple shape of stole. And there is such great diversity within her many designs, some elegantly stitched in multiple fabrics and threads, some freely painted in sweeping signs of cross and candle. My, what a great gift, I shall treasure it.

The time of family being here for ordination will be busy. Mother and Ann will be here, and Carl is thinking of bringing Dan as a graduation gift. I regret not being at home for the many honors Dan has received and for his graduation. I wish I had flown home for it. This is the difficulty of the balance of life.

The sun has been shining all day—a record!

Sunday Memories

GARDEN PARTIES ARE A LOVELY SUMMERTIME PART OF LIFE HERE. Sunday lunch with Codnor folks was planned at a home where they had worked diligently in their colorful, large garden, getting it ready. Unfortunately it rained, and we had to be inside. Such wonderful people in that group, who have become good friends this year—I shall miss them.

Our six-week journey of youth confirmation came to its ending and new beginning with the evening confirmation service at Wood Street. Having planned it themselves, the kids' modern slant on the Bible reading brought laughter. We sang the songs they had selected, and in a beautiful sharing, each of the families came for communion, youth kneeling alongside parents. I have so enjoyed working with these youth in this confirmation study. On one occasion, they each stood in Wesley's invisible footprints in the high pulpit at Crich to see what the preaching life felt like. As we stood in Wood Street to have pictures following the service, I gave thanks for having them in my year's life. Having William in the class after having the Dawsons as close friends this year is very special. I will not forget Davis and William sitting in the balcony at Wood Street worship during the months Davis was here. They would sneak out their electronic games up where no one could see. Now chapel life makes room for these new young members.

After the evening service, I called Nottingham City Hospital, checking on Rene. Having expected her to die at any time, her family cousins asked me to come down; once there, I was able to sit with her for a while, as they took a break. How much we want her to release and let go, yet she lingers. As I sat, thinking of her whole being consumed with cancer, I again found myself hating the disease for what it does. And in the speed of the disease, she never served communion, nor did we have a photography exhibit.

Her wishes are to be cremated, ashes to be scattered at the Carsington reservoir, where she had spent some memorable time. When she told me she wanted *Jesu, Joy of Man's Desiring* played for her service, I promised her we would have it.

With a full-fledged head cold, complete with sneezes and sniffles, I had no business being in a hospital, but figured on this wing it did not matter. That is a crass joke for glossing over the matter of being with people waiting to die. Four people in a single open ward, each struggling with life, and the other three having to listen to Rene's heaving breaths. However, this hospital is a caring environment, better and more comfortable than some of the others I have visited. And Karen, one of the members of Wood Street Oasis group, is a nurse there who has done so much caring for Rene. What a difference that makes, to have someone who knows and cares for a person close by.

At the End of the Month

IT IS MEMORIAL DAY IN AMERICA, as we celebrate Bank Holiday here. With a beautiful azure blue sky dotted by floating sheep clouds offering a real holiday gift, I spent the morning casually cleaning my bedroom and windows. There is a wonderful heady sense about opening up a window with no screens with an outward thrust, being up in the trees, hearing the doves coo as I clean. Of course, there was also the passing thought that if I lean out too far, I fall two stories down. From the bedroom window I looked down on little blooming bedding plants I set out, already adding lovely color to the back fence.

In preparation for the arrival of my American friends, the Ritchie family, on Friday, my homing plan was to take a room or two a day to clean and fluff, and to also fluff the garden. Although the grass was wet outside, I went to the garden in the afternoon for a close encounter with my ever-hovering Flymo. With balanced floating machine, I mowed the entire side lawn, creating a pea soup green mess. The next day I paid for it all, and not with money: my hands and elbow ached from the workout. What a pasture that little patch was!

"I love days of tree time," my fingers typed. What I meant to type was "I love free time," but the tree time today was fun too. It reminds me of the afternoon at Ammerdown lying on the grey stone under the towering oak tree at the top of the hill in the pasture, looking up into the tree limbs, into the sky, dozing and gazing, and being.

Wendy and Paul Rose's baby boy was born this morning, down at Nottingham City Hospital. I guessed that Rene lingered on, because there had been no phone call. As evening came I drove down to Nottingham and saw the new little fellow and proud parents. Such a doll with a head of thick dark hair, he looks like he has been here forever. Then I quietly eased into Rene's ward and sat beside her bed for a while. She held onto life, even though they were not feeding her, having taken all tubes off last Saturday morning. A baby born and a person on the edge of death—the cycle of life.

BACK AT HOME I called Doug and Becky, catching up on news from them as their lives continue in Virginia. I tried to get the rest of the family but missed them all. Later, Carl left a phone message saying Dan was coming with him in June, as a graduation gift. I look back on the Christmas visits and am thankful that all the family could come and be together then. Now how good it will be to soon have family come for the closing weeks. I talked with Davis this afternoon; he starts summer school next Tuesday.

NO MESSAGE CONCERNING RENE; she must be still holding on. I plan to do some pastoral visiting tomorrow and Thursday afternoons.

A Candler catalogue came in the morning mail, helping me look forward to returning home, see courses and schedule, even faculty names for a final semester's work. My British Conference badge and information also came, and with that arrival I felt a surge of energy and excitement about the event.

When I came home, I worked in the yard until 10 p.m. Amazing, that summer light. Later I discovered another Iona song whose Scottish folk tune plays in my head: *Let your restless hearts be still. . . .* And the people sing *Kyrie eleison . . .*

Rene has died. *Kyrie eleison.* May her soul rest in peace.

The phone rang. Another death. May has ended.

$\mathcal{J}$UNE : *Travelling Mercies*

May the grace of the Lord Jesus Christ, the love of God,
and the fellowship of the Holy Spirit be with you all.

2 Corinthians 13:14

$\mathcal{R}$e-transition in the year of transition had already begun. At the end of the month family would arrive, when we would travel to Blackpool for my ordination at the British Methodist Conference. Until then, June held last visits to places, last opportunities with churches and groups, precious moments with friends, and time for reflecting on the year. I knew that these encounters and events were coracles of meaning, holding bits of the narrative of relationship, of life's joys and challenges, of work and personal, of things simple and matters deep.

Warwick Window into the Past

ALABAMA FRIENDS—Gilbert, Lynn, Erin, and Glynnis Ritchie— arrived in time for a real treat. Warwick Castle holds a medieval festival on certain days during the summer. This day was one of those times, so

Warwick Castle window

we drove down for a splendid trip into the past. One of the largest and best medieval castles in England, Warwick comes alive during the days of the festivals. Jousting, fighting, demonstrations of bow-and-arrow skills, flags flying, horses prancing, wandering musicians and court jesters, dungeons and torture chambers—we tasted the full colorful flavor of medieval chivalry, from the day's entry to exit. This is an event not to be missed for the brave and bold of heart. And the Ritchies certainly enjoyed it, Gilbert himself is part of a medieval music group. We could have stayed there in the time capsule, simultaneously celebrating the splendor and repelled by the horrors of medieval life, but the beds at Ripley Manor at the end of the day were quite twentieth-century welcome sites after such an exciting day.

Of Midges and Well Dressings

BECAUSE I HAD ENJOYED mystic Stanton Moor so much on my birthday, I decided to take the Ritchies up to see the secluded, ancient Nine Ladies stone circle set in the tree arbor. The difference in the two visits had to do not with location nor with who was there, but with the presence of tiny little insects known as midges. They did not seem to be present in April, but now they were in full swarm—everywhere. You walked into them, and they flew into you. They flew into you, and you walked into them. The mood and setting of the moor was not quite the same. Somehow, swatting interferes with a pleasant stroll through ancient grounds. Well, maybe my guests got a taste of a druid venture and a Bronte-ish moor.

Leaving the midges behind at the moor and finding our way back across the field to the car, we then descended the narrow country road and drove up the A6 to the lovely little riverside village of Ashford-in-the-Water for the well dressings. This uniquely Derbyshire custom mixes folklore and Christianity in villages throughout the county. Each spring the ancient spring wells offering water for the life of the village are decorated and blessed. The actual construction of the well dressing is not dissimilar to the U.S.'s Rose Bowl parade float materials mixed with the construction of a local high-school football homecoming float. After months of planning and design by a community committee in each village, materials are gathered, the clay-lined life-size wooden frame is built, and the picture comes to life with flower petals, seed, bark, and other natural materials pressed into the wet clay. The frames are set in place on the sites, as the wells in the town are "dressed" and ready to be blessed.

At the appointed time, a crucifer leads the local priests, bands, and townfolk in a joyful procession to each well site for a service of blessing, and then the dressings are on display for locals and tourists during the next week as long as the materials last. Morris Dancers may even be seen dancing and twirling at some of the village gatherings, and the mythical Green Man, symbol of nature and spring, occasionally appears. Each village adds its own touch, theme, and events. In my later years of English ministry, I was able to be one of the ministers who are a part of the ceremony, the processionals, and blessing, as the well-dressing practice spread to other towns.

This little village was well known for its spring weekend festival; large crowds attend the event. We parked in the grass car park already filled with visitors. Unlike the moor, down here the air was crisp and clear. Walking through narrow village lanes, we found the first of five beautifully decorated wells. They were scattered among the flower-draped, cottage-lined streets, with themes ranging from a seventieth birthday greeting for the Queen, to the pied piper, River Dance, and The Lamb of God. Each was exquisitely and colorfully crafted with many tiny bits of nature, seeds, petals, moss, and bark. The village itself is nestled at the edge of the River Derwent and has an original stonewall sheep wash along its shore, where sheep were once herded from one side of the river to the other to be washed.

Across the way, the lovely village church was also holding its annual flower festival. We walked up the uneven stone sidewalk past the deep blue-green yew trees and weathered gravestones, pushed open the heavy wooden door of the greystone Norman church, and entered an aromatic collage of colorful fresh floral interpretations in every corner of the sanctuary. Even in the rafters, we discovered floral wreaths on the ancient maiden garlands floating above us, reflecting an old English custom of when a garland was carried before a young girl's coffin in a funeral procession, then afterward displayed in the church in a privilege given only to virgins. From one colorful arrangement to the next, we toured the church interior, then rejoined the crowds in the streets wandering from one site to another.

There, in the back pasture behind the two wells located on the curve of the road leading up to Monsal Head, was a flock of deep brown sheep huddled along the fence. Amazing, I had never seen brown sheep before. I just assumed brown wool was dyed brown.

Finally, at home after a long day, Gilbert prepared a delicious dinner of chicken milano. I wondered if he could stay as a resident "chef." Later, as I lay under the comfort of my cozy duvet, thoughts quickly sank into slumber, and the house and mind were quiet.

A Yorkshire Visit into the Past

AS THE RITCHIES VENTURED through the multilayered history of the ancient and interesting city of York, they discovered that one day is not enough to intake all, moving through layers of Viking–Anglo-Saxon stories. But it is better than not being there at all, and having Yorkshire pudding (which is not a pudding at all but a brown, puffed popover-like pastry served with roast, vegetables, and gravy) in York itself is a fitting ingredient of their visit.

Up the road a short distance lay a place I had hoped to visit before I left, the ruins of Fountains Abbey, an enchanting setting in a magnificent peaceful dale. So, while my friends had their taste of York, I took this time to discover a haunting, beautiful spot of monastic story. It is a gift to walk in and among the standing walls of sanctuary and cloisters, with latticed empty window frames opening up to the heavens. In the morning light, birds fluttered in and out of the open-air sacred space, chirping praise to a creator and creation that outlasts all our human edifices. In the stillness, I could feel the presence of timeless quiet. A voice heard on the wind, a chant lingering in the open rafters, a floating movement around the corner of the open hallway, a walk down a mossy path, feeling as if I do not walk alone.

I wonder of the stories and lives of those who called this place and others like it home, who lived and breathed and served in these spaces, who were driven out and destroyed by the power and force of other humans driven by other passions. It is a strength of human beings that we have developed these human attributes of thinking and feeling. Is it also a curse of destructiveness that we do not yet, even today, understand our compulsion to conquer, to control, to homogenize? The lovely solitary walking path winding through the simple gardens and green woods and along the gentle water offers the gift to contemplate, to be at one with nature, to listen for the sounds of long-gone chants, to wonder at that life gone by.

My solitary visit brought peace, quiet, and reflection time. I appreciate the needed space and silence that a setting like this offers. It is one of the treasures of this country, the reminders of the communal life, the choice to live together apart, as a living of one's faith. How good that such sites are still here, untouched by modernity edging closer and closer to their borders.

Having the afternoon, I chose the road across the Yorkshire moors, including a straight-up-the-cliff entry to them, which was a much longer drive than appeared on the map. Finally, the city of Scarborough perched on the sea's edge. The familiar song floating in my inner hearing, no fair this visit, I merely had time to drive into the seaside city, down and up hills, to find a site near the castle overlooking the bay. Small brown signs lead to the burial grave of Anne Bronte of the Haworth parsonage writing family. In her novel *Agnes Grey*, this lesser known of the sisters described the beauty of the Scarborough shoreline she loved:

> *When my foot was on the sands and my face towards the broad, bright bay, no language can describe the effect of the deep, clear azure of the sky and ocean ... there was just enough heat to enhance the value of the breeze, and just enough wind to keep the whole sea in motion, to make the waves come bounding to the shore, foaming and sparkling.*
>
> *My footsteps were the first to press the firm, unbroken sands; nothing before had trampled them since last night's flowing tide had obliterated the deepest marks of yesterday, and left it fair and even, except where the subsiding water had left behind it the traces of dimpled pools, and little running streams. ...*

Dying of an illness at age twenty-nine, Anne was buried in St. Mary's graveyard here, overlooking that shoreline, her dreams of a boarding school unfulfilled, her stories to be untold. Another thread of connection was woven into the tapestry fabric, reaching from the two-story parsonage in the somber little village of Haworth halfway across the country in West Yorkshire, where roots of creativity were so richly planted in this young family, a place Davis and I had visited in October with Glenis, then again in November with Ann and Bobby. Here, in what probably felt far away from that home, one young Bronte sibling was laid to rest, with words on the page left to speak her eulogy and history to reunite her with home. More than a century later, the waters continue to sweep into the cliff's edge and wash away the footprints in the sand.

With voices from the past murmuring in my head, I turned the car back toward York, to pick up people of the present, as two young and two adult Ritchies awaited me. We returned home, each carrying visions of places and persons gone by.

In reading de Mello's *Awareness,*[7] I had come across this quote:

> The great Karl Rahner wrote: "I must confess to you in all honesty that for me God is and has always been absolute mystery. I do not understand what God is; no one can. We have intimations, inklings; we make faltering, inadequate attempts to put mystery into words. But there is no word for it, no sentence for it. . . . The task of the theologian is to explain everything thru God, and to explain God as unexplainable."

De Mello continues: "Unexplainable mystery. One does not know, one cannot say. One says, 'Ah, ah. . . .'"

The visits to Yorkshire, the drive across the moors, the visit at a young woman's grave stirred questions of history and story, meaning and choices. Our world's story is shaped by the drive to know, to express, to conquer, and contain. But to those who walked the ground at the abbey, to a young writer who left home never to return, there is a place to at times say of the mystery of life, "Ah, ah. . . ."

The Ritchies were soon on their way to other places; the time with them had been so good. And as a bonus, Gilbert cooked three straight nights. Thank you once again, friends of mine, for taking time to be with me in ministry, in my life here, in this lovely land. Traveling mercies. . . .

Retreat and Risk

I HAD ONE LAST RETREAT TO LEAD, this one a creative-arts event down at a picturesque retreat centre in Reading. I had been invited by one of the ministers on the May retreat design team to come down to his circuit to lead a morning of creative music. After completing my part of the day, I stayed to join them in the afternoon watercolors session. Ah, how easy it is for me to encourage others to express themselves creatively through music, my medium. "Don't worry about right or wrong, just sing, just play. . . ." But how challenging and risky it is to place wet paint on the canvas, to try a

7. Anthony de Mello, *Awareness* (Image, 1990).

new language, a new format of expression, where the rules are so different. Watercolor lives in its own inverted world. Work around the space, begin with the background, the outside, be patient and wait until the first is dried, then let the focus come alive.

The pale little landscape I created in that afternoon still occasionally finds its way back into view on my shelves: the slightly out of proportion little cottage with funny odd shape clouds floating through a bluewash sky is there to remind me of that afternoon's joy of expression.

Isn't that true of most of us? In our own comfort zone, we wonder why others may be hesitant. When we try the new, we find our own hesitancies. The inclusion of creative arts in retreats, such as they do here, is something needed in all places, as a part of renewal of spirit and expression. Retreat settings here include arts centres. These encounters would provide ideas for my work upon my return, and my later work in spiritual renewal. All people need these outlets. Another idea would go home with me.

On Ordination and Local Preachers

I HEARD FROM FRIENDS about the North Alabama Conference ordination service and realized that the Alabama ordination occurring at that time might have been mine. My own was not too far away, now. I was realizing that this ceremony not only marked my future but also honored my year's work and life here. In a sense, this year was enough for the moment.

As I thought of the work to get to this place for me, in this year I had also come to appreciate the strong program of Local Preachers that help keep the church alive here in England. In my last chance to meet with the circuit's Local Preachers, I glanced around the room at each one present and told them they had taught me all I know about local preachers, as we laughed at all that meant. In that meeting Paul from Wood Street had his interview to continue in training as an LP. In the same way that I have worked at my ordination process, the local preacher process in England is quite thorough and intensive. A person must be committed to see it through, and there are checkpoints all along the way. But it offers a direction for those who want to live out some form of ministry leadership but are not led to go the full ordained route.

My good friend Jacque was also pursuing this path. I had recently attended the worship service she led at the newly renovated Pye Hill Chapel. The small congregation included a young child whose activity filled the very resonant church room first with pattering sound and then sweet snorings; she was completely at home at church. And Jacque led a beautiful service as she worked to fulfill her local preacher requirements. It has been good to walk alongside them in our journeys.

Rene's Rest

RENE'S FUNERAL HAD FINALLY ARRIVED. Her death seemed so long ago. As I sat in her home with Ike, her partner of six years, Ike's daughter Vinette, and Rene's best friend Alice, we shared a sherry, toasting Rene's life. I looked around the dim room that now felt so different, remembering our visits, our talks. Ike and his daughter gave me an envelope of little photos Rene had set aside for me, more of Ottawa and the U.S. capitol during war times, taken by her brother, Maurice. Rene had so much hidden within her, treasures of beauty, of life. I wished for some way to express that for her. The photos tell of her love of life, of experience, of nature and creativity. Her desire was to have her ashes scattered at the reservoir she loved to visit. Thankfully, Patrick was later able to fulfill that wish.

The Case of the Missing Wallet

A LONG AND FRUSTRATING DAY ENDED. I rearranged my schedule where there had been some conflicts so I could drive up to Chesterfield Public Library to pick up the piece of music Rene wanted the organist to play as her coffin was carried out. Having only a short time in Chesterfield, I got the music from the library, then stopped for a quick salad at a Pizza Hut, of all places. Somehow, unbelievably, my wallet with money and credit cards disappeared. It did not reappear. I had taken it out of my purse and set it on the table to pay the bill. I remember that a large family group walked by my table and left the restaurant at that same time.

I immediately went to the police station, walking there quickly because my parking meter ticket was expiring. The on-duty policeman said I needed to buy a new ticket, forty pence! I didn't have *any* money—how was I going to buy a 40p parking ticket? He told me there was a free lot down the street where there might be a space. I knew that this was market day, and there was no space anywhere, but there certainly were quick hands around. As I did not have time to leisurely stroll around looking for a free place, I went on home. The officer did not offer me 40p or help with the issue. If I had time, I would have gone to see the head of the department, who I knew through the Chesterfield memorial service for the Hogarths, to borrow 40p, but at that point I really just wanted to cry. I think what angered me was the sense that I might have been pegged "American tourist, easy hit," which I was, an easy hit. In retrospect, my frustration and anger at myself probably shaped how I saw the policeman's response to the situation.

The world looks different in the evening light. The folks at a meeting tonight graciously loaned me £20 for the weekend, and a dinnertime visit in Derby helped me let go of the stress of the day. Minister Geoff Pratt had tried some of the worship experiences we shared at Ammerdown, and had invited me down to visit his church and to talk more about worship possibilities in the light of his setting. Before dinner we enjoyed a leisurely stroll in their back garden as Geoffrey showed me their gooseberry bushes, the fruits of which we enjoyed in the evening's desert. I would have enjoyed their friendship earlier in the year; I had missed the social, relaxed, collegial visiting of this type.

A thunderstorm passed through in the night, a rare sight and sound for here, a good omen for washing away tiredness and frustration. In the next morning, sunshine and clothes on the line.

Days later, after receiving a message that my wallet was found, I drove to Chesterfield to retrieve it. Absolutely nothing was missing—all credit cards were there, all cash. Interestingly, it was found in another area of downtown. I thanked the police, then called the man who returned it, to thank him, but he was not in. Who knows what occurred.

Blessing and Calling

OFFERING BLESSING TO LIFE IS A WONDROUS GIFT of opportunity. For me growing up, "Bless you" was a figure of speech said at sneezing, and "Bless their hearts" was a Southern phrase often said just before the criticism was leveled about someone. I suppose if you bless their heart, then it is OK to say the next sentence. Alabama minister and friend Joe Elmore, for whom the phrase "blessed to be a blessing" was a descriptor of his gentle and gracious approach to living life, had planted in so many people the idea of living life with blessing. Now I found that one of my greatest joys of ministry was in being in the place and situation to offer blessing upon others.

The afternoon for a couple's renewal of vows and blessing of marriage service to which we had all looked forward had finally come. This pair, who gave so much of their energy to the chapel, now invited friends who had walked alongside them in their lives to come to their home and share in the special occasion. Their back garden was lovely, with cascading flowers in full bloom, a white canopy tent shading the friends and family from the crystal-clear blue sky and warm June sun. The time for vows came: Gill and Bob moved to stand on the patio facing me, with their daughter Chantele not far away. After I led a renewal of vows for them, each spoke words of love and commitment to the other in a simple but very moving ceremony. I placed my hand on top of their joined hands and blessed that which they had just done, and the years past and to come. The toasts flowed freely, then the table of food called, as the gracious spirit of the couple and their lovely daughter touched all.

Bless you, dear ones, you, your daughter and your home, that the love which has been present from the beginning, continue to shine upon and within you, now and in the years to come.

As evening came, I drove up to Crich village in the realization that it was perhaps my last service there at the little Wesley Chapel. I felt that this year had moved so quickly; all that I had hoped to accomplish had not been done. But what good life we had shared together. And now, what a wonderful attendance from the whole Crich community: Maurice, whose wife I had recently buried, was there, as were Derek and Katy from the Anglican church, and so many others. Mary and Joe and their faithful little pooch Mitch were sitting on their usual pews on my left. After the service they gave me one of Mary's paintings, a framed watercolor of a woman in a lovely flowered hat. I placed the gift on my office wall.

As the service ended, we shared the benediction traditionally said by all in the congregations here, the familiar blessing of Second Corinthians 13:14 offered to each other. We drank our last tea in the little china cups in this small chapel, then we all moved slowly to the front door and stood together in the evening daylight in the little walled outside entry space, as cameras snapped pictures of the congregation, doggy Mitch included. I thought back to the first time I visited that entry, when Glenis and Geoff Quible were showing me my churches, and I saw the board waiting for the name of the new minister. With the click of the camera, again came the realization: I am down to last visits at the chapels. So each occasion became precious. And the photograph became my concrete holding of the stories and memories of this place. The side garden still rambled out of control, the chapel still lacked for new energy and new life coming forth from the community, but oh, how special was this place, these people, this time.

The sermon I had used was an effort at tying together this upcoming significant moment of ordination in my own life with the significant meaning of calling for all followers of the faith, the calling of those I had grown to love in this year as they lived out their commitment to their faith and as I left them for a new minister to come and be with them. It is one I would, with adjustments, use at each of the other churches, as a small effort to honor their role in my own journey, to encourage these small bodies of Christ to value their own place, their own role, as ministers came and went, as circumstances changed, as they tried to follow the calling of their faith in these challenging times and places. Their lives had been touched by so many, they had seen hope and setback, had weathered the storms of culture and crisis. As I in my own life had asked the question of how to best live out my commitment to follow my faith—in the lay role or in the pastoral role—I now hoped to affirm the calling, the opportunity for all to be a witness to a new way of living, a way of saving grace and love.

CALLED TO SERVE   SERMON, JUNE 1996

For as in one body we have many members,
and not all the members have the same function,
so we, who are many, are one body in Christ,
and individually we are members one of another.

from Romans 12

TWO SUNDAYS FROM NOW, I will be seated in the sanctuary of Leyland Methodist Church, waiting for my name to be called as one of the ordinands at the ordination service of the 1996 British Methodist Conference. I imagine I will be feeling a deep bucketful of emotions—that is part of who I am, those emotions that show on my face and creep into my voice. Upon hearing my name, Kay Quinn Murphree Mutert, I will rise and take the vows of service; in another moment, I will move to the communion rail, then kneel and receive the laying on of hands from those gathered round me—an American United Methodist bishop, a British Methodist presider, a dear district chairman. With me in spirit will be Alabama ministers who have been a part of my life. And I will feel one more set of hands quietly placed on with all the others, the hands of a departed colleague. For me it has been a lifelong journey to arrive at that day and that place. But it is not the end or beginning, it is a moment in a lifelong call to know and live God's love and creative spirit, a life story I have shared with you over these months. So now, as I invite you to share in that moment of my ordination, may I also invite you to reflect upon your own story.

Only a few weeks ago, I placed my hands on the heads of some of you and called you by name, as you came forward to express your own calling, to recognize full membership in the life of your church. I will have an opportunity to do that yet again, before I leave England. And together, we have taken vows of support and commitment. Many times this year, I have gently held precious babies, have blessed them with the cool waters of the font, as you have spoken out of love for them your own words of responsibility and faithful living. I have offered you bread and cup, a sign of God's wonderful grace for you and for me, as you have knelt at the communion rail. And I have sent you forth Sunday after Sunday to go from this place to live in God's love. You, too, are called to serve!

So, what does it mean to be called to serve? For me there are many things that are not clear, those details that can get in the way, get us bogged down: what am I going to be doing when I return to America, what exactly will the situation be, what kind of church, who … where … how …? No, much is not clear about the years ahead, but of this part of my calling, I am clear: I am called to remind you that YOU are called; that whereas others may or may not be declaring the sacredness of the ordained, I want to proclaim to you the sacredness of your life, your gifts, your potential, your place in the living of God's love in this world. All the ministers in the world do not matter if the living of ordinary day life is not deemed holy. Hear the reading from the epistle of Romans, which I will hear on the day of my ordination:

> *Let your gift come alive! Help ignite the spark of God's love in those around you!*
> *Romans 12*

As I spoke with someone recently about finding a person to fulfill a particular church responsibility, to develop a new area of ministry, I suggested the name of someone I have observed to have wonderful gifts to share. "Oh", said my friend, "I had thought of that person as just one of my friends. Now that you say that, yes, I think that's a brilliant suggestion!" Seeing with new eyes the people around you. Is that a part of your calling? Look around you! There are wonderfully blessed persons sitting all around you! You are in the presence of the holy! These people gathered here are made by God! (With parents' help, of course!)

Look around you! Now you see: "Oh, he's a wonderful parent!" "She has the gift of patience!" (I could use that!) "That person could help start a new Bible study!" "I can always talk to that person about anything—perhaps they might consider pastoral care." We as a church want to be active in the community life, in hearing the voices of the people in the marketplace—"Look, she is so good at helping others just where they want help and support." "Now, who here could help us start a new youth Bible study?" "I didn't know he could act!" "Have you heard her sing!" See with new eyes!

Are we really willing to celebrate the gifts of others? Can we recognize that when we are an arm of the body, we need a leg, not a stronger arm? Celebrate the call and gifts of others! In the epistle reading, Paul is reminding the Christians in Rome to love each other, care for each other; the Christian message is in relationships! Is your call to step aside so that others may flower? What a difficult calling, but a needed one; and in responding to that call, other avenues will appear for you: a time of contemplation, a time for self, a voice of encouragement to others, an occasion for inner growth to rediscover new gifts?

And what are your gifts? What is your now calling? Is it to teach, to lead, to give in generosity, to be compassionate, in cheerfulness? As I reflect upon this time of ordination for me, I acknowledge that I have had a very full and eventful life. There have been times when my teaching was my focus, periods when the care of my children was a precious gift for me, years when my work was with individuals and other times working with large groups. Life comes in a varied rhythmic pattern, changing as the years pass. Our calling is to live in love, in God's love, in the knowledge given by Jesus, who gave fullest love to this world. How we find ourselves able to live out that love will change within our lifetime. Find your place, and live it to the fullest, now! Don't wait until you "have time," or don't say "it's too late." The beauty of this God of love is that we each are called, all of our lives. It does not mean giving up who we are, it means being who we are, in the fullness of God's love and grace!

In the Hebrew scripture reading, you heard the call of the prophet Isaiah: "Then I heard the voice of the Lord saying, 'Whom shall I send, and who will go for us?' And I said, 'Here am I, send me!'" As I celebrate my call in the holy act of ordination on June 23, 1996, may we also celebrate the call of God for each one of you present this day, a call to be God's people in a world needing God's love and grace, a call to choose to love, a call to serve, a call to life!

Conversations of Caring

WITH TWO LADIES' FUNERALS this week, it seemed appropriate to share together about this subject at the ladies' group gathering. In his book *Our Greatest Gift*,[8] Henri Nouwen offers reflections on dying and caring. We had a good conversation about his thoughts and about the losses that are felt, particularly in the lives of older people, as friends die and health declines. It is too easy to avoid talking about this matter of end of life, of dying, of living in the knowledge of our deaths. And yet, time and conversations are precious gifts, not to be wasted.

I had taken communion to someone at Ripley Hospital and found the place to be so understaffed. While I was there, the elderly woman I was visiting had to wait ten minutes for a nurse to help her to the toilet. Other women had dark bruises on their faces where they had fallen, trying to walk to and from bed, toilet, sitting room. Dignity of living is a tenuous gift, so quickly and easily taken away, something not easy to talk about.

"I'VE NEEDED THIS CHANCE TO TALK, to share, to question," one of the men in an evening membership class shared. In this particular class, there are only the two men, but one just had surgery, so his wife came with him. Besides enjoying our classes, I have found it very helpful to be with these men in a pastoral role; it has helped me be cognizant to hear all voices. Naturally, I am tuned to the experiences of a woman, so I appreciate this personal time of faith conversations with the men here and in the other group.

It is interesting how places and spaces affect people differently. As we talked tonight about churches, Brian offered Liverpool Cathedral as an example of a cold space—no chairs or pews. I understood what he meant, but when I had seen that space on a day visit with the Grouts, I thought: what a wonderful open space for using the arts! Dance, instruments, drama, I can see the place alive with the creative spirit. What a great gift diversity of insights can be, that we each see life, place, setting, experience differently.

In our final evening membership class, we talked about the significance of the sacrament of baptism and communion, then in the quiet of the manse lounge, where we had met weekly, we shared sacrament itself, a closing blessing to our weeks of study and sharing.

8. Henri Nouwen, *Our Greatest Gift* (HarperOne, 1995).

DUNCAN CALLED FROM ALABAMA, on his birthday. I had planned to call *him* to wish him happy birthday. How much I am strengthened by the thoughts and love of people in my life such as Duncan, who is a real icon in the story of the North Alabama Conference, coming from his witness during the difficult years of racial integration. Duncan, in his retirement, has continued caring for the transient off the street, sees that the Soup Kitchen exists, offers the blessing of presence to the hospice program. As we talked about ordination the next Sunday, I told him I would know that his thought and support would be present with me. I had heard about Manchester and the bomb explosion there, and shared with him that I hoped Mother did not hear about it; she and Ann were flying into Manchester. It is absolutely crazy and unpredictable, what happens in this world. But it is good to know a birthday consistently comes around, year after year. Birthday blessings to a dear friend.

I DROVE TO WAINGROVES for a meeting with Ruth and Maureen, to talk about a worship service they are leading in July. Sitting in the lounge, we talked about it for quite some time, but then just visited and caught up. Ruth was gone for two weeks; coming back to an empty house must have been difficult. We also chatted about tension felt in their church and another one over building decisions. An earlier appointment was about hurt and miscommunication for someone there. How sad that so much energy goes into concern over buildings: people wanting to move into the future, people wanting to remodel, people wanting to keep the old buildings as they've always been. It's never a simple situation, it is more than that, it is the story of proud past and possibility of future, but this can truly drain energy. Perhaps it is a part of the birthing pains of new creation, new possibilities, which need to be housed. Maybe we could learn something from Jesus, who didn't deal with building temples of the stone type. The women's theme for the worship service was friendship. Now there is something worth building on.

FATHER'S DAY IN ENGLAND was not yet a well-advertised occasion. If they celebrate it here, it is no big deal, hardly mentioned, but give Hallmark time. During my years in England, Carl spent some significant Father's weekend golf trips with the boys. How much they love their dad, how significant and special the memory of those times together would eventually be. Years later the trips would stand out in their minds as unique occasions. To end this special day, I talked with Carl, hearing all about their time together; then I called Daddy and had a good conversation with him. Finally, I faxed Doug—it was my first son's first Father's Day.

I WALK DOWN THE STREETS HERE, passing people working so diligently in their gardens, and I love having conversation with them. I would truly miss walking and talking along the way to people over their hedges. The irises are in bloom, and the roses are getting ready for their first big burst of color and aroma in the next week— I couldn't wait for that display. I do love seeing how much care and effort they—both men and women—put into their flowers and gardens.

I am grateful Mother and Daddy planted that seed in me through their love for working together in the yard in Mississippi, back in my growing-up years and even now, still in the same flowerbeds. Mother's beautiful roses bloom outside the bedroom window, and Daddy's daylilies along the front drive brighten the heart of all who pass by. As I walk by and talk with the people on these streets, perhaps I am remembering days long gone on Greensboro Street, conversations on the sidewalk, when neighbors greeted and talked, and gardeners saw their flowers as companions in the conversation.

Continuing Conversations and Goodbyes

PATRICK AND I WENT TO DERBY Thursday to meet with the textile artist Juliet Hemingray and talk about stole design. What a wonderful gift the circuit wanted to give me, one of her exquisite ministry stoles, which would take several weeks to make. I almost called someone in Alabama to send me a design, then I knew that no, this stole needed to come from the present lines and curves of my life.

Folks here may understand the quick passage of time better than I do, as the goodbyes and congratulations had begun. The trip with Patrick to Hemingray's studio was a joy. I selected an appliquéd design of a white background, with multiple rainbow colors rising up diagonally on each end, flowers and creation on one side, and peace dove and flames on the other. At the bottom of the stole will appear the monogrammed Greek letters A (*alpha*–beginning) and Ω (*omega*–end)—good symbols for remembering the beginning of my pastoral ministry here, the beauty of Derbyshire, and the year ending.

As I arrived home a beautiful bouquet of flowers was being delivered, an early ordination/parting gift from a dear young couple of Wood Street. I had placed my ordination service seating reservation that morning, and in the afternoon made arrangements for some of the time while family would be here, a few days in Ireland. A phone message was waiting from a homebound person in the other section who wanted to see me before I left. Meeting work responsibilities in those next weeks, having visitors and traveling, my ordination, saying goodbyes, thinking about what lay ahead, packing up . . . it was all a little overwhelming.

The day's morning was quiet, here at the house. I like and need those mornings. Later in the day folks from the Belper circuit came to the manse to visit about an American coming to them the next year; they wanted to use my furniture. Funny, it *had* become *my* furniture in this time of living here. I would miss this home and all it had held for us in this year.

The buzz of words in an evening wedding rehearsal at Wood Street soon turned to melodic sounds as we then held a choir rehearsal for my circuit celebration. Everyone was enjoying these opportunities to be together and sing and make music. They have such a heart and gift for music, I love that, and the joy of conducting was still there for me. Our upcoming circuit event would be quite memorable, complete with a sing-a-long of Handel's "Hallelujah," kettle drums, trumpet, and all.

A Weekend Revisited

SATURDAY MORNING I WALKED through the little alley uptown into Ripley, where the hustle and bustle of a market day filled the streets with the energetic movement of a busy ant hill. Joining other weekend shoppers for a cup of coffee in a little pastry shop, I then did some shopping of my own, locating needed items for Sunday's circuit youth service. The church here uses the term "youth" to mean youth and children, which has seemed somewhat mislabeled. The theme of the service, "Dare to be a Dreamer," had been floating in our heads for several weeks.

In a burst of afternoon energy, I washed windows, worked in the garden, and flymowed the back yard. The rose bush that was almost dead when I moved in now had some wonderful large buds (white, it looked), which should bloom this week, if the few little flies on it did not get too hungry. I was pulling for the buds to make it; they had become a sign of survival and new life.

I had not planned to help with the Saturday youth event because I was working with Sunday's service. But when Saturday plans fell through, I invited the older youth over for pizza and to get stars ready for Sunday. Six came, ages thirteen to nineteen, and with great enthusiasm and midst much conversation and energy and eating, they created a bucketful of bright multicolored stars. This event was a first, so I hoped it all went well. They were doing various parts in the service, and the music led by Oasis was all upbeat contemporary. I wonder how the British Methodist church or any church expects to have a future unless they work at nurturing the young people.

I had called Doug to see if he could help me with a resource for the sermon; he did have the Martin Luther King "I have a dream" speech and faxed it to me. My, what a powerful expression of a dream! I planned on taking a course at Candler in the fall entitled "The Theology of Martin Luther King," which I thought would allow me to go back and revisit some of my youth and young adult days again, with a better understanding of what was going on in the country, in my state of Mississippi, in my hometown then. Much of that era at the local level was a blur to me as a child and teen. For now, I wanted these young people in this Midlands community to realize that they too could dream, that their dreams were valid.

More than one hundred fifty folks came to the youth service at the park; it was a great success. We had not planned for that many, but it was not a problem, in fact, a great joy. The weather was brilliant, and all who participated did a brilliant job as well. The youth vision statement was well written, and lots of star dreams were pinned onto the rainbow. It all came together in a beautiful way, with Oasis providing great creative leadership to the morning. There needed to be more services like this!

After a nice lunch with Constance at her bungalow, I arrived home in time to enjoy a beautiful sunshiny afternoon, good either for being in the garden or taking a nap, or both. At the end of the day, I drove up to Swanwick for their evening worship, leading worship this last time in their chapel. The Cracknells were at the service; I was so glad to see them. At worship's end one of the church members, who is also a local preacher, had a word to say about my time here and the upcoming ordination, sending blessings with me. I used the same sermon I had been using, but on this night it had even more meaning, with Anne and the girls there and memories of Vernon so alive in our heads in his family's home church.

After the service the Cracknells invited me over to their Swanwick home for a short visit; over tea, they gave me three dear gifts—a cross-stitch "Day of ordination," a cross-stitch Beatrix Potter figure, and a beautiful communion napkin crocheted with a butterfly, all three items handmade, each gift very special, to become meaningful reminders of them and of our year together. While at Swanwick I learned that Julian, the circuit steward from Swanwick and Jenny's father, planned to be at ordination. Then at home a phone call came from dear Ken Cresswell at Wood Street, asking for four tickets. The occasion continued to be held in ever-increasing circles of love and support.

On the way home I joined the Waingroves group at the local hospital for hymns and prayers, a peaceful blessing of closing to the day.

A-ah . . .

What a wonderful morning—I have washed sheets, hung them out to dry in the sunshine, put the pictures from the Ritchie trip into the photo album, worked at the desk, and worked in the front yard, doing some edging and trimming. Oh, how good it has felt! Family arrives tomorrow afternoon and Friday afternoon. One of the things to make my morning so nice was the arrival in the post of a package of pictures from Doug and Becky, one of Collier for me to carry at the ordination, so they will be with me; also enclosed were a beautiful note from Becky and a deeply meaningful one from Doug. *Ah, the love of family. . . .*

At the afternoon Waingroves school concert in memory of Andrew, the first song was the Beatles' "With a Little Help from My Friends." In the invitation to the concert, titled "A Concert for Andrew," the signature said: "This is for Andrew, from your friends." The children, teachers, all of us shared tears as the familiar song filled the room. Following the concert, the class invited me back to their classroom, these students who had become my friends, where they presented me with a booklet of prayers the students had written. Oh, my, what a good gift. *Ah, the love of friends. . . .*

I then visited two women, each in her fifties, who are ill. Both have elderly in-laws for whom they do much of the care-giving, and each has traditional home roles—one was ironing her husband's stack of shirts as I arrived. But both women also work part-time, and each has young-adult children who still look to the women for help and care—one with a new grandbaby; the other with sons who have returned home to live (she is doing the wash, the meals). Ironically, I was just checking on them, but both are exhausted from doing for others. I know men also feel the pressures of life, and there are very established traditional roles, but there must be some self-care. This matter of care-giving for both ends of the age spectrum, plus in-law care, is a very real issue. *Ah, the need for self-love and care....*

The phone rang tonight. It was the vicar of Ripley, setting a time for the three ministers to get together before I go, but also telling me that Sylvia, the dear housekeeper for the Catholic priest Monsignor Moore, has been diagnosed with pancreatic cancer. *A-agh, cancer, I am beginning to hate that word.*

On to the occasion of my ordination.

A-a-ah, it is here.

Remembering Ordination

Be still, for the presence of the Lord ...
From the hymn by David Evans

THE WEEK HAS FINALLY ARRIVED. So much preparation, so many arrangements, conversations across the ocean, considerations, and now it is here. And the time is to be shared with those family and friends who could come and with the love and thoughts of those who cannot be here. Mother, Ann, Carl, Dan, I thank you for sharing this with me. Doug and Becky, thank you for letting this event matter enough to send the picture of Collier, to send your notes of love. Davis, thank you for sharing the first half of this year with me and for your love and thoughts at this time. Daddy, I wish you were here. Vernon, you have helped shape my understanding of ministry. Your spirit is present.

AFTERNOON

THIS IS NOT MY FIRST VISIT TO BLACKPOOL; Davis and I had been before. But this time is such a different occasion. As we were driving over, we listened on the car radio to England playing Spain in the European Cup football match. Carl almost ran off the road, in the excitement of the game. England got off a shot, it was up, going, oh! It hit the goal post and bounced away! We—England—lost! That shot made it onto the stole, which was presented to me by the children and church of Wood Street upon my departure from England. I may be the only minister ever to have a losing soccer goal on my stole.

Emotion floats in the air, on the beach, all around. We are staying at the Aloha, a small hotel facing the north beachfront, where Davis and I stayed last autumn. The beachside drive of Blackpool is fascinating. It feels something like a time warp into how our American beaches may have looked fifty years ago: a long strip of beach road, with hotel after hotel on one side and beach on the other. Periodically, there are long piers reaching like fingers out into the ocean, with amusements, restaurants, and souvenir shops sprinkled along the walk. Singles, couples, and families stroll up and down the distance. Before the conference begins, we join them. Blackpool is known for its festive lights decorating the beachside drive, as well as its Needle sky-high ride and the bright colors and glitter of its entertainment venues. What a site for the Methodist Conference!

At the hotel I iron the black suit and white turtleneck top I had decided to wear for this occasion. When we are all ready, we load the car and head downtown, where we park and find our way to the centre. Inside the large convention centre we walk through the many displays of the church and supporting organizations, and through what feels to be a maze of rooms and people. In time, we find the majestic ballroom.

It is now time for me to leave the family and join the conference activities, become a member of the ordination group. I knew the family would be fine, but I know this was a strange new place for them to be, too. All the nerves of emotions are working inside me. I feel both the little child, nervous and anxious in a new and strange environment, and the adult woman, conscious of all this means in my life.

I walk up the long hall and enter the room where according to my pre-conference instructions the ordinands are to gather. Finding my place at the end chair on the second row, I am between deacons and those uniting with Methodist Church. I am aware of the uniqueness of my own situation, with the two conferences across the ocean having worked for this day to be possible. Ken and Ann lead us through the instructions. I recognize friends I have come to know this year who are here to also be ordained, and I begin to feel more comfortable and very excited.

The time comes.

We walk from the gathering room down the hallway into the great ballroom and up onto the stage. The chandeliers glow; the sea of faces ebb and flow. The rhythm of time pulsates with energy. The official conference opening begins, with Methodist representatives from various countries around the world processing up to bring greetings to the president and vice-president of conference. I note Bishop Woodie White of the United Methodist Church, who brings greetings from the United States. He is the bishop who will participate in my ordination.

As we move through the proceedings, the different groupings of people on the stage stand as they are called up and action is taken on each group. Then the time comes for me, a group of one. Before I know it, there is the reading of the resolution for me, then I stand. Alone. And the entire representation gives a standing order of approval. I could not have anticipated the deep emotions of that moment as I look out into the crowd and see them—friends and strangers, all colleagues in ministry, standing for that vote. After all the months, all the work, all the worry, I am approved for ordination. It is official. What a moment.

Following the official actions, conference Vice-President Jan Sutch Pickard rises for her address—it is memorable for both its honesty and its story. She shares words of her own life story, which includes a divorce from one of the conference ministers present. Her presentation ends with the beautiful Iona song "A Touching Place," led and sung unaccompanied by Fiona, a Scottish musician with a beautiful rich voice. But oh, how the audience of British ministers joins in on these songs. Again, the beauty of Iona music touches me, this time a song I had used at the thirty-year retreat. Looking out into the audience I see faces I know, people from that retreat and from the year. There, about eight rows back, right in front of me, are Geoffrey and the delegates from Nottingham/Derby district. And there is family, in the balcony, with glows of love on their faces. It is an occasion to cherish for a lifetime.

After the session is over, people come and speak with me. I feel so much a part of this body of faith, so warmed by its fellowship. In the lobby, Bishop Woodie White and I get to meet and talk. I am glad for that occasion, so that when the service of ordination comes, we will not be strangers. I am sorry Bishop Fannin was unable to be here, after his support and work in having this occur, but I am grateful for the significance of Bishop White's involvement. Now I wait for the next step, the ordination itself.

EVENING

THE MINISTERS TO BE ORDAINED have been assigned to various local churches. I am a part of the group at Leyland Methodist Church. Driving from Blackpool, we have a missed turn, and then we find it, a modern church, with cross on the brick front wall. The marquee outside the church welcomes us.

We peel out of the car and see that Judi, my colleague and friend from the Alfreton circuit, is already there to greet us! Friendly guides direct us into the church hall for tea. Geoffrey waits there for us and welcomes us to this occasion. We share around the low table, sitting and chatting. Geoffrey is so good at giving attention to each of the family members: Mother, Ann, Carl, Dan. Patrick helps everyone with food and drinks. John Vincent, the evening's presider, comes and speaks, as does Leslie Griffith, the preacher for the service.

Then the ordinands and assisting ministers are called to the back room. Sitting in a circle, we introduce ourselves to each other, with Don Pickard (Is this Jan's former husband, to whom she referred in the afternoon address? The answer, yes.) leading us through this orientation. One of the leaders talks and enlivens the place, perhaps a part of his personality. I find myself in a more serious, reflective mood. It is strange that the assisting ministers, Geoffrey, in particular, do not have a copy of the service with my vows in it. I've heard of paper conservation, but...? He tries to locate one but can't. Ah, well, perhaps one will appear.

First we move to the sanctuary, to see where and how we will be. As I look up to the balcony, I see that my dear friends from my circuit are already in place—Brian and Pat, Ken and Constance, Averill. The sanctuary is an interesting space, built on an angle into the corner, with a high chancel platform. A video will show this, as well as the service itself. We walk through the choreography of the service. Then returning via the basement halls to our for-the-occasion "vestry," we sit and wait.

Time to go. Again we stand and prepare to move. The walk begins down the concrete back steps of this building, into the basement area, where we gather in a circle and have prayer—the presiding force all in their robes and regalia. Up the hallway we move. For some reason, I remember standing in the hallway—hush, people who are talking and making humor; this is sacred time for me, thoughtful time, silent time, a period of remembering the saints who have accompanied me to this moment.

Geoffrey stands with me. The wait seems so long. Someone is still instructing the congregation, I think.

Finally, we enter the filled sanctuary and the service begins. Action will be permanently recorded on the video; feelings stir within. I have thoughts of Vernon, of people back home, of what this means. I look around and see family and friends gathered behind, up to the side in the balcony; and there is another Geoffrey—the Pratts have come!

The service moves through its rhythms, each person on stage leading at the right time. All of us respond when directed with the vows and promises, then comes the time for each ordinand to move up onto the chancel. I am last to go. I have decided to take the picture of Collier standing, taking the first few steps, a new phase in his life, never to go back to before-walking. Is that not like what I have done in this year? I carry the picture up with me and kneel as hands are placed on my head. Bishop White, Geoffrey, are there others? I seem to feel so. Oh, my, all of life is there. . . .

We receive the gift of our Bibles and then the service moves to Holy Communion. Now the music speaks to me in a beautiful enveloping manner. The first hymn sung in communion is "Be Still for the Presence of the Lord." Vernon, you are with me, for that hymn will always connect me with you.

And then we sing many hymns and choruses as each ordinand's group goes to stand for communion. We have been instructed as to who could sit in this designated area and come forward for communion with us, each ordinand being allotted so many tickets. As my time comes, I invite my family, Carl, Dan, Mother, Ann, and friends Patrick and Judi to come and stand in a circle for us to share communion together. One by one, I move around the circle and offer each loved one standing there the gift of blessed bread as they offer me the gift of smile, of tears, of love. In our particular circle serving time the congregation is singing the tune of a J. S. Bach chorale—in my heart, another sign of the "presence" of my friends, this time, my dear music friend, Mr. Bach. And then, the final hymn of communion is Brian Wren's "I Come with Joy." Brian, with whom I have collaborated on some hymns, whose work I use so often, another friend present. No, it's not the familiar tune for me, but at least I know the presence of these much-used-by-me words to end this sacred time.

The service over, we go back to the hall to gather again for tea. Dody and camera capture some images for posterity on film. And the video will remind me of things that slip my memory. I know I am surrounded by the love of Carl, Dan, Ann and Mother, and the dear friends who came to support me here, as well as my family members and friends who could not be physically present. It is difficult to move through the high of the moments, to let go of the occasion, but after a while, we depart to the car and to other matters.

Ponder this day, Kay.

> *Be still for the presence of the Lord, the Holy One is here.*
> *Come bow before Him now with reverence and fear.*
> *In Him no sin is found, we stand on holy ground;*
> *Be still, for the presence of the Lord, the Holy One is here.*
>
> *Be still, for the power of the Lord is moving in this place;*
> *He comes to cleanse and heal, to minister His grace.*
> *No work too hard for Him, in faith receive from Him;*
> *Be still, for the power of the Lord is moving in this place.*

David J. Evans
Kingsway's Thankyou Music, 1986

$\mathscr{J}$ULY : *A Time for Goodbyes*

Your way through life will not remain the same ...
But God has a firm hold on you through everything.

Rule for a new brother

Old-Family Hellos and New-Friend Goodbyes

IN THE EVENING HOURS, as ordination ended, we five family members traveled from Blackpool across northern Wales to the ferry crossing for Ireland. This four-day journey to track family roots and feel ancient family culture seemed a right pilgrimage. Both of my parents' ancestries are Irish: on Mother's side, the Quinns of Cork; on Daddy's, the Murphrees of Wexford. My brother David had researched our family history, giving us some facts of where our family might have begun, so the trip was shaped around those places.

> We traveled through the Irish countryside,
> in a tale of give and take,
> golf and heritage,
> quaint inns and elegant resorts,
> Murphy's Stout and Irish jigs,
> cemeteries and seasides,
> lost purses and passports and found relatives,
> fields of peat bogs, emerald green hills, and magnificent sea views,
> narrow dirt roads, beehive huts and greystone walls....

How much better I understand my roots, my nature, my heart's stirrings, by visiting this land of my family. If only everyone could visit their family homeland to walk on the ground and feel the presence of folk who shaped their history. Perhaps we would view ourselves and others with more understanding. The trip was a meaningful conclusion to the year's reflections on my enthusiastic response to the Celtic stories and music, the history and heritage experienced.

In the final weeks came final visitors from home. Carl's sister Carol and her friend Kelly flew in for a grand adventure through the Midlands and other great sites of England. Robin Hood's hangouts in Nottingham and Sherwood Forest had a couple of new merry folk from Florida. While they were still here, my close friend Emily came over from Alabama to spend the last two weeks with me and help me pack for home. In her beautiful gentle manner, she met and befriended the members of my churches and, in such a brief time, shared in the goodbyes with me. We drank tea in Mrs. Bamford's delightful Nether Heage cottage, visited with the Grouts, the Pells, and in other friends' homes, breaking bread and telling stories of the year. And in the closing visits, Ruth and Emily were able to meet and create a lovely bond of friendship in a brief space of time. Each visit was special; each place a marker of memory.

Sweet Peas

"DO COME IN," Mrs. Bamford greeted us at the front door of her whitewash Nether Heage cottage. The sweet fragrance of red roses wafted over to where we stood, waiting at the low-framed doorway to enter this storybook home. Gently bending our heads, we entered the little two-story cottage, which had been on this spot for over a century. Everything there was made to proportion, just right for this tiny English lady. To see her, one wondered how she could even reach the pedals of the boxed pipe organ she commanded each Sunday at the little chapel nestled across the street on Slack Lane.

We sat on the cushioned couch in her living room, which was crowned by low-hanging wood beams and whitewash walls. Her collection of elegant china plates hung on the wall, pieces of memory and place. She moved to serve tea in delicate china cups, offering to Emily and then to myself a chalice of warm welcome tea, drink for the soul.

"Do come see my sweet peas," she invited. I knew that there might be the possibility of an aromatic gift to carry home from her fragrant garden.

Moving through the kitchen out the wee back door, we walked up the slight rise to the spot where her sweet peas rose, twisting and curling up the tied strings of trellis made for them. The sweet aroma greeted us, as she spoke of her love for sweet peas.

A distant memory stirred in my head. Though I have little knowledge of my grandmother who died when I was only two, there is a memory of a passing aroma of thick, rich sweetness from Mama Quinn's garden. The same twisting, turning vines, tendrils curling around carefully twisted twine, the long-necked blossoms mixing to offer a palette of pastels: pale pink, rich rose, delicate lavender. There, too, in that garden of memory was the sweet aroma of the window of time, blossoms on the vine, sharing fragrance and beauty.

The ground slanted up farther into a rise, framed by narrow strips of garden and backyard. Other rows reflected the toil of her hands, a mix of vegetables chosen for supplying the kitchen produce. But over them all, the sweet peas flowered.

This was the last visit I would be having in this unique home, so matched to its dweller. Emily, too, with her love for the beauty of gardening, her heart of care for gracious presence, would cherish the moments we shared there. When we left, we carried a bouquet of sweet peas.

Years later, when I returned to visit, the roses were gone in the front yard, and Mrs. Bamford was gone as well. The house had been fully reworked, inside and out, to serve the needs of a younger family, with a new life story rising on the little plot of land. The village has now become a site for city workers to escape and live and for retirees seeking a place close to the Peaks. Things have changed, but I am sure there lingers the faint sounds of an organ, the gentle tinkle of a cup and saucer, the soft scent of sweet peas floating in the air.

At the Year's End

As the circuit had gathered in Wood Street to greet me those many months ago, now they gathered on the evening of the circuit farewell celebration. As Patrick had welcomed me into the circuit, now he compèred this goodbye evening with his great wit and humor. With participants wee and tall, young and old, from all the corners of the circuit, the night included joyful music-making, dancing, drama, laughter, and tears, and concluded with great surprise in the presentation of my stole … my stole … my stole … my stole. This dear circuit presented me not only with the beautiful Hemingray stole I had selected, but also with three exquisite hand-painted seasonal stoles I had admired while at the designer's studio.

I would have these gifts to cherish for the rest of my ministry life, draping me week after week in the worship and sacramental settings of my future. As we had shared arts and beauty all year, so this evening they gifted me with visual images and memories to remember them by. My tears flowed as I tried to find the words to say what this year had meant, what these communities had meant in my life, in this unique unpredictable year of ministry, which had gone by so quickly.

The many other gifts given to me became precious keepsakes as well—the book of prayers written by Waingroves schoolchildren, treasures of Derby china and Denby pottery, the communion cushion made with a cross-stitch by each member of Codnor chapel and given to me at a barbeque picnic farewell, a hand-stitched map of Derbyshire, and other beautifully crafted gifts. These treasures offered from the heart of so many were overwhelming. And I would definitely be the only minister who had a stole with the image of the Blackpool tower and the football goal missed by the English team in the Eurocup playoffs, thanks to the young artists of Wood Street.

As there had been the mixing of work and travel all year, so there was time for one last adventure with my friend from home, a great trip to southern England via sites of magnificence. Of course, we had already visited Chatsworth—I mean the *other* great places. In a quick circular tour, we discovered Blenheim Palace, Salisbury and Chichester cathedrals, seaside Brighton, and then we finally drove up to Ashford for an early-morning one-day Eurostar Chunnel trip to Paris. I had already purchased the tickets. Arriving late night at the hotel, we double-checked our travel documents and discovered a disaster. I had left my passport in Ripley! No amount of phone calling, fretting, what-if-ing, or fussing was able to solve the matter, and Paris became a hope for the future.

Emily and I traveled back to Ripley for the last final goodbyes and the endless packing of a year's story. In the results of all I had collected, decisions had to be made as to what to leave and what to take. I left behind treasures that had seen me through the year and took those items that would see me into the return home with memory and meaning. Once items were packed, Em and I journeyed across the Peaks to the Manchester Airport baggage office to send two heavy-laden boxes Alabama-bound.

Then the time came.

A few days later, with more stuff but definitely less stress, with much sadness at ending this year's journey and many questions about the upcoming journey at home, with the awareness that the year would be in my reflections for years to come, and people in my heart for a lifetime, the year moved to a close.

I had been given the gift of this year as a chance to live out the new calling of my heart, a setting for a major threshold in my life. And now I had been given the treasures, the challenges, the deep enriching experiences of this year as an affirmation of my heart. Together, we had moved through the rhythms of daily life, facing all that each day brought, these communities who opened their lives, homes, and faith journeys to me. As I had tried to share some part of my world with them, so they offered their countryside, their history and traditions, their world with me. And for the gift, I was grateful.

EARLY ON THAT GREY AUGUST MORNING, Jacque and Patrick drove us through the green Derbyshire hills and dales, past the greystone walls and grazing sheep, through the villages and towns where I now felt akin, toward Manchester and the beginning point of a year ago. In the airport international terminal, we shared the sacrament of one last cup of coffee, then moved to the line for departures.

Standing at the entry to security, I spoke the difficult goodbyes to these two friends who represented all that I had grown to love so deeply during this jubilee year. Turning away, Emily and I passed through security, and I moved toward back-into-the-world-of-before-but-yet-changed as we stepped on the plane and began the long journey home.

> *Holy One of all time and place, I give thanks for the blessing of this year, for all who touched my life, all who supported me in this venture, all who loved and cared for me in the journeying, for all who blessed my life with love. May the continued journey hold love and blessing for all.*

Of Days and Years

Your life unfolds
in a continuous succession
of experiences and expectations.
No two days are the same,
no year leaves you unaltered.

Every day has enough trouble of its own.
When you go to sleep,
bury all that has happened in the mercy of God.
It will be safe there.
Stand back from what has happened
and be grateful for it all.

When the day begins
be sure that you yourself can be
as new and pure as the new light.
It is like a resurrection.
The first hour is the most important of the day.
Don't yield to laziness,
but greet with joy
the new opportunities God offers you.

Even in the complicated world of today
try to keep close to a natural rhythm of life.
Meals taken together
should be moments of rest in your day.
See your encounters with others as high peaks in your life,
and upbuilding.

The evenings are particularly suited
for talking and companionship,
joy and relaxation.
But here too the more you give
the more you will receive.
Be careful
not to prolong your evening indefinitely.
In the long run it will produce nothing good.

If you are visiting friends,
don't keep them away from their rest
but know how to end your visit at a decent hour.

Your way through life
will not remain the same.
There are years of happiness and years of suffering.
There are years of abundance,
and years of poverty,
years of hope, and of disappointment,
of building up, and of breaking down.
But God has a firm hold on you through everything.

There are years of strength
and years of weakness,
years of certainty, years of doubt.
It is all part of life,
and it is worth the effort
to live it to the end
and not give up before it is accomplished.

You need never stop growing.
A new future is always possible.
Even on the other side of death
a new existence waits for you
in the fullness of that glory
which God has prepared for you
from the beginning.

Taken from *Rule for a new brother* by H. van der Looy, published and copyright
© 1973, reprint 1982 by Darton Longman and Todd Ltd, London, and used
by permission of the publishers

℘OSTLUDE : *A Personal Note*

𝒯his journal has taken some fourteen years to compose and arrange, to bring to its calling. In that time so much has happened to people mentioned in the book and in my life. The road I walked with friends in England became my own road as Carl and I faced the years to come. Doug and Becky added two beautiful daughters, Quinn and Campbell, to their family. We celebrated the marriage of Dan to Melissa and Davis to Lori. But in these years also came our own challenges with life and death: first the deaths of my father and my brother, then came my own breast cancer diagnosis and surgery. Soon after, in 2003, we experienced the sudden, abruptly brief, and difficult lymphoma cancer–related death of our Doug. Thus the year's family adventures became precious memories and the year's experiences a deeper connector to our story. We have known the birth of grandchildren Claire Douglas, Marlea, Amelia, and Stone, and Becky's remarriage to Ed. Collier is now a teenager and has returned to England to see it for himself.

Young Jennifer has since died from her cancer reoccurring, as have Geoff Clark and others. Mr. Pells and others who blessed me with their stories have also died, as time moves on. Fred Grace recently died; I shall not forget his crushing handshake, even in my most recent visit to his church. Others live on in good health and joy. Many trips back have allowed me to stay connected with the people of the Ripley circuit and the British Methodist Church. My English memories have been enhanced by two later years of ministry in the Ashfield circuit with equally rich and compelling stories and experiences. Infants I baptized in the Ripley circuit are now young lads who recently welcomed Collier to England. Anneka is a student in Cliff College, Derbyshire, studying religion.

Patrick now sings with the national Gilbert and Sullivan performance ensemble, Jacque continues as a local preacher, and young William is now a police officer with the Derbyshire County Police; perhaps Davis was indeed a good influence. Glenis and Geoff Quible are retired and thoroughly enjoying grandchildren, as are the Grouts and other friends. Vernon's family has relocated and moved on in their lives, but not without missing their gentle and beloved husband and father. Others live their lives fourteen years older and wiser.

Ruth continues to be a dear *anam cara* friend, blessed with a beautiful new marriage to Dave Beresford; I was privileged to perform their marriage ceremony ten years after the great losses in her life. Others who loved and supported me throughout my year continue to be a part of my life, with visits on both sides of the ocean and ongoing friendships.

The chapels of this story continue in their faith journeys, now with only one circuit minister but added lay staff and continued challenges of ongoing life. Waingroves built a lovely new building on new property up the street in their village. Wood Street, known now as Ripley Methodist Church, has just completed its new building on its original site. Codnor is active and alive in the life of its community. Crich and Nether Heage are still in existence, serving the needs of the faithful. New life and energy are evident throughout the circuit, but change awaits them as new circuit boundaries have been redrawn in ongoing restructuring work. I am fortunate to be able to return on occasion and visit with them.

Regretfully, some of the abbeys and retreat centres that held such peaceful experiences for me have closed, and the British Conference no longer offers ministry retreats at the various stages of ministry years. Perhaps other resources have filled those needs. My time there planted in me a lifelong commitment to encouraging individuals to seek out the quiet places, the Sabbath and jubilee times for their lives.

Derbyshire and the Peak District National Park continue to draw visitors to the beautiful hills and dales and breathtaking walking trails. But in its discovery, roads are more congested, solitude harder to find, and fewer sheep roam the pastures. Still, each visit to England, as I enter the area of greystone drywalls, green fields, and nesting lambs, I feel a sense of home.

My ministry and work have taken me many places in this time since, including rich and meaningful years of local ministry in Alabama and the establishment of my own ministry work, called *DaySpring*. My thanks to the Trussville Tuesday Women's Group and other dear friends for a circle of friendship and care, and for letting me share this journal with them in our journey together.

I am ever thankful for the love and support of my family during that year: Carl, Doug and Becky, Dan, and Davis, and to the family members added since then, Melissa, Lori, Ed, and my dear grandchildren, all of whom are joy and love. Finally, I am grateful to my parents, L. C. and Dody Murphree, in whose home my love of the Eternal was birthed.

I find myself at another threshold, a move into another segment of life. This one, too, calls for insight and vision, of a new genre. I still know the challenge of holding balance, of finding and claiming the quiet, the reflective, of not taking on too much. Yet out of my own journey, I hope to help others find that better way of living. I have learned that as life changes, so we must change yet hold to the things that sustain and uphold us. I am ever grateful for the lessons learned in my year in Derbyshire. At the end of the day, for all who are a part of this story then and now, I give thanks.

To all who read, may you be open to the transitions of life,
>   the seasons of change
>   however the journey goes.

May you not be afraid to risk,
>   to be vulnerable,
>   to listen to your own heart.

May you know and experience sabbath and jubilee occasions.
May friendship and love abound,
May eternal love
>   uphold and sustain you.

Blessings of journey,
Kay Mutert
2010

Acknowledgments

I AM GRATEFUL TO ALL WHO MADE THIS EXPERIENCE POSSIBLE, particularly the faculty at Candler and the leadership team of the British Methodist Church, who selected and invited me, and the leadership of the North Alabama Conference of the United Methodist Church, who worked with me. I would have no story without the dear and gracious members of my churches in the Ripley circuit and the people of the communities in which I worked, all of whom shared the deep love of their land and history, their stories, home, faith, and lives with me. I have attempted to share the essence and heart of life there while honoring the privacy of people and congregations, to describe the traditions and beauty of Derbyshire and English life and land in a way that gives some glimpse to the reader. If I have erroneously described any event, I hope those same dear and gracious people will accept my intentions.

I thank Glenis, Ruth, Patrick, and Jacque for recalling facts and stories in my recent visits to England; and to Glenis and Carol Devoe for proofing the manuscript and encouraging me. To Judy, my lifelong friend, initial editor, and encourager on this project, who died before its completion, my love and gratitude for your ever-present spirit. To the many friends who encouraged me through this project over the years; to the Trussville Tuesday Women's Group and other dear friends, for a circle of friendship and care and for letting me share this journal with you in our journey together; to Jim, who has read, re-read, listened, and encouraged, I thank you all. I am grateful to Marge and Bob McCarthy for the time in your beautiful Santa Fe home, where I was able to work on this book. To my friends at Menasha Ridge Press, many thanks to Susan Haynes and Bob Sehlinger for your advice, and to Holly Cross for your wonderful editing help.

To my dear loving family, Carl, my sons and their families, I thank you. And to Doug, this book is for you.

My gratitude to the following for permission to use their work in this book:

Sketches by my nephew, artist Stephen Smith, from his England journal, November 1995.

Church drawings by C. J. Moore, husband of Sister Pat Moore, former deaconess in Ripley circuit.

Song texts by Joe Elmore and Kay Mutert, with my gratitude for the creative years of collaboration and friendship.

Biblical quotes from the New Revised Standard Version. Other quotes and texts are acknowledged in the body of the book.

A portion of the sales of this book will go toward charities for lymphoma research and Candler School of Theology scholarship funds.

About the Author

THE REV. DR. KAY MUTERT is a minister and musician who shares her love for music and her story with others. Through her work *DaySpring,* she brings her pastoral and life stories, her own compositions, experiences of leading others in music, and her work with Iona and Taizé worship resources into each unique setting and audience. She is a master teacher with Veriditas Labyrinth Organization (www .veriditas.org), offering facilitator training and workshops.

She loves digging in the dirt, listening to the birds, and gentle walking, whether on the golf course with family or on a quiet path of nature with friends.

For information on her work, or to contact Kay, visit www.kaymutert.com or write Kay at:

DaySpring
P.O. Box 20036
Tuscaloosa, AL 35402

The stoles

GLOSSARY

Boot Trunk of a car

Centre I have chosen to use the English spelling rather than the American spelling when using this word as a noun in the book.

Ensuite facility Bathroom/toilet connected to the bedroom

Lounge Living room

Manual gearbox Stick shift or manual transmission

Pasty A pastry case, shaped in a half moon, filled with beef, onion, or various ingredients

Pâté A finely ground mixture of meats, liver, or other ingredients, used as a spread on bread or crackers

On holiday On vacation

Queue up Get in line, wait your turn

Rasher A thin slice of fried or broiled bacon

Roundabout A circular road intersection. All traffic goes in the same direction, left. Enter and exit at the driver's own risk.

Simnel cake A fruit cake made during the Lenten season, often created for Mothering Sunday, the fourth Sunday of Lent

Toasties Toasted sandwiches

Trash bin Garbage can

Wellies Wellington boots, high-topped gardening boots made of green rubber

INDEX OF PLACES

Heage windmill through the window of Nether Heage Chapel

MUSIC INDEX

*Music by Kay Mutert